Group Rights

The concept of group rights has become crucially important in the growing number of multicultural states around the world. But nowhere, so far, have the theoretical, analytical, and philosophical issues been so directly addressed as in Canada, where the historical experience of the founding peoples has made group rights both politically topical and philosophically important. This collection introduces a uniquely Canadian perspective on a prominent set of issues in contemporary political philosophy.

Some argue that the Canadian constitution and ordinary laws protect both universal individual rights and rights accorded to individuals as members of specific communities. Others find that the conflict between community and individual rights remains and gives rise to a number of questions. For instance, is it acceptable to accord rights to some people on the basis of their cultural membership, rather than to all people universally? Are the rights of Aboriginal peoples different from the rights of English or French Canadians? Do immigrants, once accepted for citizenship, have special rights? What are the rights of refugees and those claiming refugee status?

By giving the debate a theoretical and philosophical focus, distanced from the give and take of current political discussions, these essays make fundamental distinctions between kinds of group rights and the arguments one may offer for them.

(Toronto Studies in Philosophy)

JUDITH BAKER is Professor in the Department of Philosophy, Glendon College, York University.

Group Rights

EDITED BY
JUDITH BAKER

UNIVERSITY OF TORONTO PRESS
Toronto Buffalo London

© University of Toronto Press 1994

Toronto Buffalo London
Printed in Canada

ISBN 0-8020-2975-2 (cloth)
ISBN 0-8020-6945-2 (paper)

Printed on acid-free paper

Toronto Studies in Philosophy

Canadian Cataloguing in Publication Data

Main entry under title:

Group rights

(Toronto studies in philosophy)
Includes papers presented at a conference held at
Glendon College, York University in Feb. 1992.
Includes bibliographical references and index.
ISBN 0-8020-2975-2 (bound) ISBN 0-8020-6945-2 (pbk.)

1. Minorities – Legal status, laws, etc. – Canada –
Congresses. 2. Minorities – Legal status, laws,
etc. – Philosophy – Congresses. 3. Civil rights –
Canada – Congresses. 4. Human rights – Philosophy –
Congresses. I. Baker, Judith. II. Series.

JC571.G77 1994   323.1'71   C94-930722-X

This book has been published with assistance from the
Canada Council and the Ontario Arts Council
under their block grant programs.

Contents

GROUP RIGHTS

Introduction

JUDITH BAKER

In February 1992, Glendon College at York University in Toronto hosted a conference on group rights. It was, with the exception of one participant, a local conference in which philosophers, political theorists, and law professors from Toronto's institutions of higher education took part. All but one of the papers in this volume are those of its participants and discussants. They include very general justifications for group rights, as well as sceptical doubts, a sketch of a theory of federalism, and case studies. There is both theoretical and detailed examination, with respect to specific rights, of possible conflicts between individual and group rights. Language rights, the rights of women, Aboriginal rights, and refugees' rights are discussed.

The essays as a whole demonstrate the unusual contribution of Canadian thinkers to two issues that could not be more important for the world today – group rights and the federal unity of culturally diverse communities. Few philosophers have looked at the nature of either of these. Rarely have philosophers joined with political and legal theorists. Perhaps more important, the papers are not utopian. A decade ago, at a conference on Liberalism organized by the Guelph-McMaster doctoral program in philosophy, John Dunn, the political theorist from Cambridge University, diagnosed North American moral thought as what 'may illuminate the nature of the good but contribute little to the assessment of what men have good reason in practice to do.' The essays of this volume, on the contrary, demonstrate a willingness to test conceptions of justice in terms of their power to illuminate and resolve contemporary disputes.

Will Kymlicka situates his discussion of group rights within the Canadian debate; the entire body of his published work provides a standard of reference, as is evidenced here by the remarks of several other contributors. He looks at the views of Canadian political leaders and critics to questions of fairness and unity within Canada. He notes that the relationship between individual and community rights is one of the underlying themes in constitutional debates and that respect for the rights of its constituent communities is a fundamental characteristic of Canada. But acceptance of community rights is not unique to this country, and his essay seeks to show that strategy mistaken which regards community rights as distinctively Canadian.

He begins chapter 1, 'Individual and Community Rights,' with a discussion of community rights in the Canadian constitution and a distinction between two characterizations of such rights and the issues to which they give rise. The first regards the rights of communities as independent of the individuals who compose the community. On this view, the rights of the individual members may conflict with, as well as live alongside of, the group's rights. The second sees them as 'rights owed to people as members of a particular community, rather than universal rights owed to all people as human beings' – but ones that may well be individual rights. Kymlicka dubs the second sort 'special rights' and offers an analysis of contemporary conflicts to argue that they are the more important for the constitutional debates in Canada.

He claims that arguments that would show the interests of communities to be independent of their members would explain why members are obliged to maintain cultural practices but would not explain special rights – why some rights are unequally distributed among groups. Whether or not he is overly optimistic in supposing little support for the first kind of right, even in minority communities in Canada, Kymlicka is helpfully clear: he distinguishes the debate over special community rights – about according to one group rights and privileges that other groups do not enjoy – from disputes involving the relative priority of individual and community.

The fundamental issue for Kymlicka is thus 'whether it is acceptable to accord rights to some people on the basis of their cultural membership, rather than to all people universally.' As opposed to rights that may be accorded to groups but whose justification is rectification of oppression – provision of a 'level playing field' for their members – the rights that would protect cultural membership seem to Kymlicka to be permanent. He presents two basic arguments for special community rights: equality and historical agreement.

Despite a tangle of questions that such arguments provoke, Kymlicka concludes that a person might accept that the arguments show community rights to be fair yet refuse to recognize them on grounds of what federalism requires. Both former Prime Minister Pierre Trudeau and Newfoundland's premier, Clyde Wells, have argued that special status is inconsistent with what they see as federalism, which requires equal rights and status for all citizens and provinces. Critics such as Wells are 'prisoners of their own a priori definitions of federalism, or a priori assumptions about the possible basis of unity'; a survey of other countries shows that special status is workable and indeed can help keep a country together.

Melissa Williams's contribution (chapter 2) takes Kymlicka's work as its focus: its central question, however, is both general and fundamental to any inquiry into the validity of group rights. What is the basis of the authority of liberal justice when it regulates a culturally plural political community?

Williams is sympathetic to Kymlicka's defence of the rights of cultural minorities: she agrees with him that prevailing conceptions of liberal justice are implicitly committed to protection of those groups. She endorses his argument: the interest that an individual has in his or her own good is central to liberalism; the need to be able to reflect on, criticize, and revise one's own ends requires the freedom to do so. Cultural membership can then be seen as a primary good for a citizen, enabling the individual to articulate and so choose the kind of life that for her or him is a good one. Given the commitment to equality, protection of the individual's culture is required if individuals are to be respected equally in their capacity as agents promoting their own good. But, Williams argues, this insight ought to lead Kymlicka and other liberals to abandon what she calls the 'juridical' model of justice. Rather than regarding rights and justice as defined prior to politics, she thinks that the content of justice is to be determined, at least in part, by processes that are both political and democratic.

There are a number of sources for the dispute between Williams and Kymlicka. Most importantly, and at greatest length, Williams attributes them to the foundation of liberal conceptions of justice, to the question whether agreement among those who are to be governed by a conception of justice 'is a constitutive element of the validity of that conception.' While Kymlicka answers 'no,' she answers 'yes.' One of the virtues of Williams's essay is the overview that it presents; it looks at the many articles and books by Kymlicka in an attempt to present his reasons for refusing to make agreement constitutive of justice. Another is the dialogue between Kymlicka and her. His responses to an earlier draft of her essay feature most prominently in two places: first, a long note (no. 61) in which Kymlicka defends as necessary the role of agreement in political authority-cum-legitimacy while denying that agreement is required for the moral truth that undergirds the conception of liberal justice. His defence rests on a distinction between 'epistemological' and 'political' authority that Williams argues is untenable. Whatever conclusion the reader reaches regarding this dispute, the issues have been enriched. Uncoerced 'consent' is not monolithic; we may question the stability and validity of a federal unity according to the bases of the parties' consent, and we need also question what bases are such as to make their agreement 'moral' in content or basis.

The second presentation of their dialogue comes in the body of the text and concerns what is perhaps Williams's most distinctive contribution. Her defence of the public culture of justice is motivated by a strong sense of the distinctiveness of groups and of the partiality of theories that hurts those most disadvantaged, marginalized, and 'different.' Because, she claims, the perspectives from which anyone theorizes are social and partial, epistemological humility requires that marginalized groups regularly participate in the definition and determination of rights, of what equality demands. It may be, as she admits, that she has exaggerated the difference between the definition and the interpretation or implementation of justice, and hence the differences between her position and that of Kymlicka. But she has clearly provoked what must be a thorough examination of the political process and the ways in which disadvantaged groups may be given their voice in it.

Sherene Razack, of all the contributors, occupies the most ambiguous of relations to the language of rights. Her essay, chapter 3, begins with a story about the constricting features of rights discourse but then explores the ways to acknowledge publicly the realities of women's oppression and to argue the legitimacy of their group-based claims for justice. She insists on the difficulties and limitations of a rights-based conception of justice but does not argue that they are insurmountable. Her position is perhaps that of one who cautiously accepts a return to liberalism and the strategic use of collective and individual rights language, with an eye turned always to the 'social construction of meanings' within it. She thus reminds us that rights need not be viewed as providing an ultimate language in order to provide an important critical tool.

Razack describes her essay as one about seeing and perceiving. She emphasizes that partiality of theories of justice by appealing to what has been unseen. Like Melissa Williams, she focuses on what rights theorists have regarded as unproblematic – that the perspective of those looking to apply 'equal concern' is critical to the very recognition of differences. She argues that dominant groups often do not see those who are very different from them as oppressed. She emphasizes the ways in which self-interest blocks the reality of others but also recognizes that the oppression in question may be too unseemly to stomach. Here are some examples. We may be blinded to the extent of violence against women or the plight of domestic workers, who do not enjoy the same employment rights as other workers. The white majority in Nova Scotia may lack essential information about blacks. And a male judge who considers an incident of sexual harassment is required to make an enormous conceptual leap to move to the feminist position that what happens between individual men and women on the job depends on their respective socialization and status as members of unequal social groups. The language of Razack's essay sometimes gives the impression that a simple analysis in terms of self-interest of dominant groups will explain all failures to see, a view never the less corrected by her examples.

But Razack claims that the language of individual rights is itself one of the obstacles to perception: the emphasis on choice, on individual autonomy, may mask the very real societal constraints on individual choice. She discusses the example of Nancy B., paralysed from the neck down and living on a respirator, whose care dominated the news for a few days. Razack argues that few commentators noticed the societal constraints under which Nancy B. made her choice. The able-bodied did not think her desire to die was a result of social as well as physical conditions. Many of us did not ask whether she would have wanted to live, had she the kind of attendant care that would have enabled her to have a better life.

Razack's essay is personal: it presents us with the summary of one feminist's path. She started out teaching the story of individual rights to activists, then rejected the framework of rights. She turned academically to a critique of liberalism from a communitarian standpoint, then recognized its limitations: communities have been oppressive places for women; and the conception of a community of women would universalize women's experience and thus leave unexamined the realities of women of colour, lesbians, and women with disabilities. Enriched by the work of feminists in the law and the views on social construction of Michel Foucault, Razack returned to what she terms a strategic use of the language of collective and individual rights. But she insists that discussion of rights be grounded in a social story of oppression, that one emphasize descriptions of the realities of oppressed groups that will 'bring the relations of domination and submission to the surface.'

Kymlicka argues in chapter 1 that the acceptability of arguments for community rights rests not only on issues of fairness but also on an adequate conception of federalism. The general idea behind his assertion is more fully articulated by Wayne Norman in chapter 4, 'Towards a Philosophy of Federalism.' Norman claims that showing a group to be entitled to a special right is only half of what justification of group rights requires: collective rights are characterized 'by forms of control over or representation in political institutions.' Hence justification will require demonstrating that fair political institutions can be designed through which the right may be exercised. But philosophers have so far regarded programs of federation as pragmatic both in origin and for purposes of evaluation. The task of his essay is to provide a theory, or rather the sketch of a normative theory, of federation.

His argument is that the only viable basis for a stable social union in a multi-national, liberal democratic society must be some moral or quasi-moral bond between the federating polities. Here he joins Melissa Williams in rejecting both a modus vivendi agreement, which would not ensure stability, and a basis in the form of some particular comprehensive moral doctrine, whose acceptance in a pluralistic society would require state coercion incompatible with liberal democracy. Norman thus adapts, or seeks to provide, an analogue to the overlapping-consensus theory of justice proposed by John Rawls.

An explicit test of his theory, according to Norman, is met by its ability to illuminate actual debate, as illustrated in this essay by an analysis of competing principles put forward in Canadian constitutional discussions: from historical figures such as Henri Bourassa and J.P. Tardivel to Pierre Trudeau and Clyde Wells. The pluralism of Canadian society is seen to include not only languages and cultures but also conceptions of citizenship and identity. So the commitment to equality of provinces and a single conception of citizenship is viewed as a comprehensive type of normative federal principle, while the official rationales of various commissions illustrate forms of overlapping-consensus accommodations.

In the latter part of the chapter, Norman sketches the content of this overlapping domain. His chosen strategy is indirect: rather than asking what principles would forge solidarity or promote nation-building, he looks for those principles that would prevent or lessen the impact of potential federation-busters. Réaume in this volume (chapter 6) looks at independent grounds for the justice of language-policy. Norman, while recognizing these, examines the role of a language policy along with the control of nationalism in preserving federation.

Chapters 5–8 look closely at the rights of special kinds of groups: internal minorities, language groups, immigrants, and refugees. These essays, although addressing quite specific and historical issues, are at least as theoretical as their predecessors. This is because the authors address some of the most pressing concerns of those either sceptical about the validity of such rights or fearful about the consequences of recognizing them.

Leslie Green argues in chapter 5 for the rights of a group that many will not have considered – the internal minority. We have seen some of the arguments for protecting minorities against the majority, as well as the difficulties in preserving a federal unity, in the context of a culturally plural society. But the problem is more complex; minority groups are rarely homogeneous. Even when a cultural community is not geographically dispersed, it often contains other minorities or groups that are weaker than its own majority. How then to ensure that in protecting minority groups from majority oppression we do not make it more likely that those minorities oppress their own, internal minorities? Green stresses that this issue is urgent for modern liberalism, which not only values personal autonomy but, as he sees it, is prone to 'a naive collectivism of the middle range.' His conclusion is a sober one: liberals will not be able to defend every culture, since minority rights are more dense than initially appeared and conflicts are inevitable. The conflicts may indeed be tragic, if it turns out that respecting the rights of their internal minorities will undermine some cultures.

Green begins with an examination of the nature of rights, which he thinks are interests sufficiently important to ground duties, on the part of others, to respect or promote those interests. His analysis of those group rights that Kymlicka calls 'special rights' rests on the claim that in addition to the interests of an individual in individuated goods such as personal liberty or exclusive property, there are urgent interests that lie in collective, rather than individuated goods. Green's thesis thus happily accommodates Kymlicka's argument for the rights of cultural minorities based on the interest and value of cultural membership. The individual pursuit of the good life requires not only that we be able to choose that life for ourselves but also that we be able to set forth the choices and conceptions available to us. However, cultural membership provides the necessary and unchosen context in which we frame our options. The vulnerability of some minority cultures argues for the attribution to them of special rights.

Green also considers the (collective) interest in national self-determi-

nation and reviews the kinds of rights that are at issue. He claims that
what looks like a simple move to according similar rights to a minority's
sub-cultures presents us with controversial examples, such as English-
speaking Quebecers and Aboriginal women. Dispute brings argument
with it, and Green looks at two of the more important objections raised
against attributing similar rights to internal minorities. The first involves
the claim that the sub-group is free to leave the (minority) group; the
second alleges that internal minorities do not need to be protected from
their relevant majority because, as a minority itself, that group itself is
weak.

When membership in a group is (even partly) ascriptive, the issues
regarding means and permission to exit are more complicated. Green
considers the case of a British Columbian, David Thomas, who claimed
that his individual rights had been violated by a particular minority group,
the Lyackson Indian Band. Thomas did not live with the Band but was
considered an Indian within the meaning of the Indian Act and recognized by the Aboriginal nation as one of its own, although he did not see
himself as subject to its traditions. Membership in ascriptive or partly
ascriptive groups is, however, only a complicating factor in the difficulties
of exiting; these are well illustrated by the historical example of Mormon
women, whose rights J.S. Mill thought violated by the practice of polygamy.

Green concludes that the argument from exit is weak, insofar as the
real prospects of exit differ significantly both in meaning and in cost
from those in a voluntary association. He distinguishes absolute and
comparative judgments of power in his reply to the second objection –
that minority groups are weak and, hence, that their internal minorities
do not need to be protected against them. Green concludes that neither
the absolute weakness of a minority group nor its relative weakness vis-à-
vis the majority proves that it is also weak vis-à-vis its own internal minorities. Green insists that questions about power and strategy are both factual and complex.

Denise Réaume's contribution, chapter 6, attempts to answer two kinds
of scepticism. The first part asks 'What Is a Group Right?' and addresses
sceptical concerns of a philosophical sort – that there is neither need,
nor conceptual room, for collective or group rights. Réaume uses two
conceptual tools to argue for their validity: she applies the notion of
participatory goods and exploits the implications of the relationship of a
right and a correlative duty as articulated in her analysis of a right. She
applies her analysis of group rights in the second half of the essay to a
detailed examination of three kinds of conflict. Réaume attempts to

answer sceptical practical concerns: that group rights, once recognized, will dominate individual rights in any conflict. She argues that the conception of a group right that she has presented both illuminates the conflicts and allows us to see new ways in which the conflicts might be resolved.

Réaume shares with Leslie Green the notion of a right as an interest-grounded duty and the belief that recognizing collective interests and goods is essential to the attribution of group rights. Although an obvious consequence of such a view is that an agent, in order to claim a right to the protection of an interest, must have the interest in question, Réaume denies that once collective interests are recognized one can easily read off, from a consideration of those who are interested, who the right holder to the good is. Réaume examines three views of collective rights and argues at some length for her own – that groups are the rights bearers to collective interests. Her argument, summarized, is: a collective interest is one that is public not only in being communally enjoyable and nonexcludable but those value lies in its public production or consumption. It is a participatory (or in Green's terminology, 'shared') good. This distinctiveness, when factored into the definition of a right, has implications for who can hold each kind of right, for no other candidate bearer of rights can sufficiently ground the correlative duty. An individual's interest in participatory goods cannot be sufficient reason to impose duties on others, precisely because it is for the sake of all who participate in its enjoyment that the good is provided. We cannot, therefore, say that it is for one person's sake alone that the duty is imposed.

Réaume questions the assumptions that group rights as such will always override individual ones and that a larger group's rights will override those of the minority group. One would maintain these two theses only by improperly adopting an aggregative approach out of keeping with the nature of rights. But she recognizes that the fears of totalitarian implications can be allayed only by providing substantive accounts of the rights that groups are supposed to have. She begins to fulfil this demand with regard to the right to linguistic security.

In order to assess the interests of duty bearers, those who will be called on to protect the right in question as well as those of the group claiming the right, Réaume examines three instances of language conflicts in Canada. The third involves use of a minority language in the courts and is particularly interesting for the two strong claims made by Réaume. She comments on two decisions made by the Supreme Court of Canada, which ruled against both plaintiffs, settling on much narrower conception of the right to 'use' French or English, limiting it to the right to make sounds with no guarantee that one will be understood.

According to Réaume, the court saw only individuals on both sides of this conflict – the litigant and the court officials – and sought to avoid an interpretation of the right to use French and English that would impinge on the right of judges and court officials to use their own language. Réaume argues that an account of conflicting group rights would allow the court to see the issue as one of the design of the court system rather than of the burdens that can justifiably be imposed on individual officials, and so provide for linguistic rights.

Joseph Carens, in 'The Rights of Immigrants' (chapter 7), is occupied by questions about the exclusion and admission of immigrants. Do immigrants have the right to free movement across state borders? Carens begins with some disclaimers: immigrants as such do not form a group united by culture, country of origin, interests, or even by a single motivation for immigration. They do not form a group in the sense discussed elsewhere. But the people already in a country, the citizenry, is institutionally characterized as a group, and Carens asks whether any political community has the right to keep people out because it has some group characteristics that the outsiders do not possess or because the outsiders have some that the community doesn't want.

This central question – the moral status of criteria of exclusion – is addressed in two halves of the essay, using two different theoretical perspectives. Carens calls these the frameworks of idealistic and realistic moral theory. The difference is not the more familiar one between legally constituted criteria and moral standards. Ideal moral theory refers to what is right and wrong regardless of the likelihood that people observe the standards, while realistic moral theory admits only moral principles that might actually guide action. The ideal, or the just-world framework of analysis, asks: if the world were just, what would be a community's moral rights to limit the entry of immigrants? What rights would an individual have to travel freely and settle wherever s/he chooses?

The just world is characterized by liberal commitments to the moral equality of persons and the value of human freedom. There is thus a strong presumption of freedom of movement. Carens presents arguments that explicitly connect it with such traditionally liberal values as equal opportunity and freedom to pursue one's own projects. He argues that the same reasons that make restriction of movement within the state unjustifiable apply to movement across borders. Moreover, given the inequalities among states, he argues that to be born a citizen of an affluent country such as Canada is like being born into the nobility. Restricting entry to such affluent countries therefore gives to birthright privileges a decisive role in determining one's life chances.

The limitations of this approach are, however, manifest. In ignoring problems of historical contingency and injustice, one ignores those features that are the most troubling: our responsibilities towards refugees, determining how many, and which ones to take in, the weight to be given to the responses of other countries. There are questions of priorities, tradeoffs, and strategies for change.

Such issues make Carens turn to the perspective of realistic moral theory. It starts from conventional moral understandings but does not necessarily stop there. Critical revision within a realistic approach is limited by the requirement that the changes that it urges must be feasible. Carens uses two kinds of arguments. One starts from universalistic, albeit not ahistorical moral principles that set minimum standards for all social institutions. They formulate standards for all people and for what we typically call human rights and duties. The second argument appeals to the shared norms and values of a community, to those ideals that one recognizes need not be universally shared. So the Canadian community, or any like it, is arguably committed to common law traditions regarding the rule of law. Carens observes that arguments that are based on such non-universal commitments reflect moral ideals and are more than prudential.

Carens notes that even the second approach leaves unsettled some of the thorniest current problems. These include the definition of refugees in the face of rising numbers of non-political refugees. How is one to assess the costs of refugee determination procedures and resettling versus the costs of helping individuals in their country of origin? Form a moral perspective, we seem to reach easy agreement only on the principle of non-refoulement and on the rights of family members to reunification with their families; conventional moral understanding just as securely assigns to states the right to limit immigration. Carens recognizes that one will often recommend actions that are deeply problematic from the point of view of moral principles. One persistent theme in his essay is, however, his commitment to the admission of refugees. It overrides appeals to cost-analysis or to possibly greater benefits to individuals that would result from helping them in their home country. It also outweighs an appeal to a history of collective tradition, which in countries such as Japan supports closure. Although one may appeal to universalistic anti-discrimination norms in addressing those countries that agree to the entry of immigrants, it is not clear that any arguments within realistic moral theory are sufficient to ground the basic rights of refugees or the freedom of movement within a state.

Howard Adelman's essay (chapter 8) presents a case study of a specific group, or rather four different groups of Palestinian refugees, claiming the right of return to their land. Adelman, like contributor Jim Graff, is an activist in the cause of refugees. But he argues as a philosopher that the right to return is a foundational and human right. Adelman takes issue with the traditional view, the same one held by Jim Graff, that human rights are both universal and individual. He argues that there is a triad of human rights which are group rights, which arise out of particular historical conditions and apply to restricted groups. The most fundamental of the three is the right of a people to self-determination; its two corollaries are the right of a citizen to return to the state of which s/he is a member and the right of asylum – the right to live in a state and on a territory that provides protection.

Adelman argues that although only some peoples are acknowledged to have the right to self-determination, every people has the right to self-determination as an ideal. How this is to be realized, and what duties are mandated for the multicultural state, are not articulated in this essay: Adelman says specifically only that this right is best protected by preservation of a people's language and culture. He discusses the right to asylum only at the level of political conventions that define a refugee entitled to asylum, which brings home the need for a complementary essay, one that would connect contemporary political recognition of these fundamental rights with the moral ideal.

Much of Adelman's argument is, however, informed by a conception of what is required in order for individuals' interests to be protected as rights. He argues that the three fundamental collective human rights are not derivable from individual rights, nor from a vision of what it is to be an autonomous individual. In an appeal to a communitarian rather than a liberal ideal, Adelman interprets the right to asylum, for example, not as an attempt to guarantee the dignity of a human as independent of his or her citizenship but as an attempt to enable the individual to be a citizen somewhere so that the basic condition required for the protection of human rights can be provided – namely, membership in a state.

What theoretical basis for considering a right to be a group, rather than an individual, right could Adelman use? One might press into play the distinction proposed by Réaume, whose analysis in chapter 6 rests on a distinction between private goods, which can be enjoyed alone, and public goods, which are enjoyable only with others. For an individual refugee's good or interest is seen by Adelman to depend on the good of citizenship; and this cannot be privately enjoyed. But this account of a group must be forward-looking in the case of refugees. For the refugee represents a breakdown of basic membership rights, of the normal mutual bond of trust and protection between an individual and the government of one's home country, and there is no reason to suppose that refugees as such constitute the kind of group or sub-group whose actual common interest grounds group rights. It is the group-to-come, to which the refugee aspires, whose good cannot be privately enjoyed.

Adelman joins with other contributors in considering whether there is a conflict between individual and group rights. He is concerned to show that nothing in his conception of a group right leads to the assertion that a group right takes precedence over the individual rights of its members. He argues for a stronger relationship than no inherent conflict: he claims that the three rights discussed in his essay are preconditions of there being any individual rights at all. The basis for his argument lies in the political vision that there are no human rights without states that are responsible to and for their citizens: rights demand duty bearers, and these are always the governing states.

Jim Graff presents a voice of opposition in chapter 9. Although all of the contributors agree that the moral rights of collectivities must ultimately be justified by appeal to the well-being of individuals, Graff believes that this position leads to rejection of a right to self-determination as attributed to a collectivity. He argues that the ideal of the equal worth of all individuals is incompatible with the claim that each people has a right to self-determination, whether one interprets 'a people' as referring to a citizen body or as meaning some ethnoculturally defined collectivity. He argues that we should favour instead the equal rights of individuals to certain freedoms and to certain socially providable elements of well-being. This stance, it turns out, will support, in his eyes, the right of only some 'peoples' to a sovereign state.

Graff argues that the conception of each people as having a right to self-determination has moral legitimacy only within the framework of a morally justifiable world political order of sovereign states. That is an ideal world in which there are no victims. The inequalities of our world show this to be an illusion. In our world, for the foreseeable future, there will be irresolvable conflict and victimization where different communities overlap inextricably within the same territory, no matter how bounded. Woodrow Wilson's doctrine of self-determination for all loses legitimacy. But some peoples may require self-determination. Graff argues that struggles over territory and power, repression, state terror, and the varied forms of violence in the existing world make statehood the only political option for some 'peoples' if the individuals who comprise them are to enjoy their equal, individual rights. Graff's examples include the cases of contested rights between Palestinians and Israelis, the countries of the former Yugoslavia, as well as Quebecers in Canada. Other contributors argue from the value of cultural membership to collective rights. Graff shows the ugly side of cultural identifications – what some may wish to classify as the abuses of a useful conceptual tool. He passionately evokes the 'ghettoized world' as a 'morally repugnant vision because it is racist in character.'

In this volume, the terminology of group, or collective rights differs among contributors. The reader should note each author's usage.

1

Individual and Community Rights

WILL KYMLICKA

Community Rights in the Canadian Constitution

The relationship between individual and community rights is one of the underlying themes in contemporary constitutional debates in Canada. According to the federal government's constitutional proposal of September 1991, one of Canada's fundamental characteristics is that it respects the rights not only of its 'citizens' but also of its 'constituent communities': 'In the Canadian experience, it has not been enough to protect only universal individual rights. Here, the Constitution and ordinary laws protect other rights accorded to individuals as members of certain communities. This accommodation of both types of rights makes our constitution unique and reflects the Canadian value of equality that accommodates difference. The fact that community rights exist alongside individual rights goes to the very heart of what Canada is all about.'[1] These 'community rights' include minority-language rights (section 23 of the Charter of Rights and Freedoms), Aboriginal rights (sections 25 and 35), and the affirmation of multiculturalism (section 27). Ottawa's proposal would have added a new community right to this list: recognition of Quebec as a 'distinct society' by virtue of its status as 'the only society with a majority French language and culture in Canada and in North America.'[2] According to the federal proposal, Quebec's 'right to be different' was implicitly recognized by the British North America (now Constitution) Act in 1867. However, the right of that province's French-speaking people to preserve and promote their language and culture was now to be made explicit so that the constitution could 'be modernized to reflect today's reality while respecting the original bargain of Confederation.'[3]

Community rights in Canada share two essential features. They involve the political recognition of ethnicity or nationality, and they are defended (in part) by appealing to the importance of cultural identity or membership. Of course, the various community rights also differ in many ways. In the case of the Québécois and of the Aboriginal peoples, a community is seeking constitutional recognition of its existence, as well as the rights and powers necessary to ensure its continuation. Multiculturalism policy enables immigrant ethnic groups to maintain some aspects of their cultural heritage without fear of state disapproval or discrimination. But all community rights involve political affirmation of cultural identity and measures to protect or promote that identity.

Hence community rights form a specific subset of the broader category of 'collective rights,' which includes the rights of trade unions and corporations, the right to bring class-action suits, and the right of all citizens to clean air. These rights have little in common with each other, and it is important not to lump the idea of community rights with the myriad other issues involved in 'collective rights.'

Acceptance of community rights is often said to be unique to Canada. This statement is quite misleading. Such rights exist in many other federal systems in Europe, Asia, and Africa.[4] Even the US constitution, which is often seen as a paradigm of individualism, allows for community rights. For example, American Indian peoples are viewed as 'domestic dependent nations,' Puerto Rico has a special status as a 'commonwealth,' and there are a number of 'protectorates,' such as American Samoa. Each of these cultural communities has special status within the American federation. Many of the objections to community rights lose their force once the experience of other countries is considered (see the section of this chapter below on arguments for community rights).

Two Conceptions of Community Rights

While the idea of community rights is pervasive in the Canadian debate, it is not always clearly defined. In particular, many discussions alternate between two characterizations of these rights. On one view, communities have rights independent of, and perhaps conflicting with, the rights of the individuals who compose them. On this view, the rights of communities exist alongside those of individuals. The other view sees community rights as owed to people as members of a particular community, rather than as being universal and owed to all people as human beings. According to this view, community rights may themselves be individual rights, but they are not accorded to all people, only to those who belong to a certain community.[5]

So we have two versions of community rights. They can be the rights of communities (as opposed to individuals), or they can be community-specific (as opposed to being universal). I believe that the latter form is the most important for Canada's constitutional debates. Unfortunately, most of the literature on community rights deals with the former, and this has led to some confusion in the public debate. It is crucial, therefore, to distinguish the two forms clearly.

Both kinds of community rights can be seen as protecting the stability of cultural communities. However, they respond to different sources of instability. The first kind is intended to protect the community from destabilizing internal dissent, and the second, from external pressures (such as economic or political decisions of the larger society).

These two types of rights raise different issues. The first involves intra-group relations – the right of a group against its own members. This type raises the danger of individual oppression. Individual freedom may be restricted in the name of group solidarity. Critics of community rights in this sense often invoke the image of theocratic and patriarchal cultures where women are oppressed and religious orthodoxy enforced as an example of what can happen when the alleged rights of the community are given precedence over those of the individual.

The second kind involves inter-group relations – the right of a particular group against the larger society. This type raises the danger of unfairness between groups. One group may be marginalized or segregated in the name of preserving another group's distinctiveness. Critics of community rights in this sense often cite apartheid in South Africa as an example of what can happen when rights are differentially distributed on the basis of group membership.

To distinguish these two versions of community rights, I call the first 'group rights,' since they affirm the priority of the group over the individual, and the second 'special rights,' since they affirm special status for some groups by according them culture-specific rights.[6] Notice that group rights can exist in culturally homogeneous countries. The desire to protect cultural practices from internal dissent exists to some extent in every culture, even homogeneous nation states. Special rights, however, can arise only in plural societies, since they protect a particular culture from the destabilizing influence of the larger society.

The two kinds of rights need not go together, although they often do. One can accept that a community has special rights against the larger society without accepting that it has rights against its own members. Conversely, one could deny that communities have any special claims against the larger community but affirm that they have wide powers over their own members.[7]

Of these two types, special rights are the most important in Canada. The Québécois, Aboriginal peoples, and the ethno-cultural communities are concerned primarily with ensuring that the larger society does not deprive them of the conditions necessary for their survival. Generally speaking, they are not concerned with controlling the extent to which their own members engage in untraditional or unorthodox practices.

These special rights take a number of forms, depending on what kind of economic or political pressure the minority community faces from the larger society and on how that pressure can be counteracted. These rights may take the form of special representation of the minority community within the political institutions of the larger society (for example, guaranteed representation for Aboriginals in the Senate or for francophones on the Supreme Court), devolution of powers to the minority community (as in giving jurisdiction over immigration to Quebec or control of education to Aboriginal communities), or direct protection of the resources or practices on which the minority community depends (as by protecting minority-language rights or Aboriginal land claims and hunting rights or by subsidizing multicultural activities). Each of these measures helps reduce the vulnerability of minority communities to the decisions of the larger society.

There are also some group rights in Canada, although their scope is less clear. For example, Québécois and Aboriginal leaders have sought qualification of, or exemption from, the Canadian Charter of Rights and Freedoms.[8] These limits on the Charter create the possibility that individuals or groups within Quebec or Aboriginal communities could be oppressed in the name of group solidarity or cultural purity.

This concern that internal minorities might be oppressed first became prominent during the Meech Lake debate (1987–90), when some women's groups (mostly from outside Quebec) worried that the Quebec government might use the 'distinct society' clause to impose oppressive family policies on women (such as restricting birth control or abortion to maintain a high birth rate). Whether this is a realistic worry is debatable. Women's groups within Quebec were quick to reject the idea that community rights for Quebec were a threat to their equality.

More recently, the concern has been expressed that Aboriginal women might be discriminated against under certain systems of Aboriginal self-government, if these are exempt from the Charter. This concern has been expressed by women's organizations both inside and outside Aboriginal communities. Indeed, the Native Women's Association of Canada has demanded that the decisions of Aboriginal governments be subject to the Canadian Charter (or a future Aboriginal Charter, if it also effectively protects sexual equality).

Many Aboriginal leaders, however, insist that this fear of sexual oppression reflects misinformed or prejudiced stereotypes about Aboriginal cultures. They argue that Aboriginal self-government needs to be exempt from the Charter of Rights not in order to restrict the liberty of women within Aboriginal communities but to protect the special rights of Aboriginals vis-à-vis Canadian society as a whole. Aboriginals' special rights to land, or to hunt, or to guaranteed representation, which help reduce their vulnerability to the economic and political pressure of the larger society, could be struck down as discriminatory under the Charter.[9] Also, Aboriginal leaders fear that white judges may interpret certain rights (such as democratic rights) in ways that are culturally biased.[10] Hence they seek exemption from the Charter but at the same time affirm their commitment to the basic human rights and freedoms that underlie the Charter.

These examples suggest that while the potential for group rights exists in Canada, there is little public support for the exercise of such rights even in minority communities. Instead, most community rights are defended in terms of, and take the form of, special rights against the larger community. Insofar as potential group rights are present in Canada, they are often defended as unavoidable by-products of special rights, rather than as desirable in and of themselves.[11] There is little enthusiasm for what we might call 'pure' group rights – protecting the historical customs of a community through limitations on the basic civil liberties of its members. For example, there is little public support for restricting freedom of religion in the name of protecting the religious customs of a community.[12]

Unfortunately, much of the philosophical and popular debate seems to equate community rights with group rights. Hence many people think that the debate over community rights is essentially equivalent to the debate between 'individualists' and 'communitarians' over the relative priority of the individual and the community. Individualists argue that the individual is morally prior to the community: the community matters only because it contributes to the well-being of the people who compose it. If those individuals no longer find it worthwhile to maintain existing cultural practices, then the community has no independent interest in preserving those practices and no right to prevent individuals from modifying or rejecting them. Hence individualists reject the idea that communities have rights.

Communitarians, however, deny that a community's interests are reducible to the interests of the members who compose it. They put the rights of the community on a par with those of the individual and defend them in a parallel way. Theories of individual rights begin explaining what an individual is, what interests she has qua individual, and then derive a set of individual rights that protects those interests. Similarly, communitarians begin by explaining what a community is, what interests it has qua community, and then derive a set of community rights that protects those interests. Just as certain individual rights flow from each person's interest in personal liberty, so certain community rights flow from each group's interest in self-preservation. The community's rights must then be weighed against those of the individuals who compose it.

This debate over the reducibility of community interests to individual interests dominates the literature on community rights.[13] But it is largely irrelevant to community rights in Canada. The claim that communities have interests independent of their members is relevant to group rights – it would explain why members of a community are obliged to maintain cultural practices. But it cannot explain special rights – why some rights are unequally distributed between groups. Communitarians seek to identify rights that all communities have as communities. But in Canada, certain communities are asking for special rights not accorded to all communities. For example, Aboriginal peoples have hunting rights denied to other Canadians. They also have the right to limit the mobility of other Canadians into their homelands. But no one believes that English Canadians should restrict the freedom of Aboriginals to leave their communities and enter the larger society. Similarly, Quebec's government limits the amount of English on commercial signs. But few people think that Alberta should limit the use of French on signs in that province.

Most claims for community rights in Canada are asymmetrical in this way. What we need, therefore, is an explanation of why some communities need special rights. The communitarian approach seeks to explain why communities can have rights independent of their individual members. But it cannot explain why the members of different communities have different rights – why the rights of Aboriginal peoples are different from those of English or French Canadians.

The fundamental issue, therefore, is whether it is acceptable to accord rights to some people on the basis of their cultural membership, rather than to all people universally. Once we see that this is the issue, a familiar misunderstanding can be laid to rest. Many people assume, naturally enough, that community rights must be accorded to and exercised by the community as a whole, rather than its individual members.[14] But in fact, community-specific rights can be ascribed to individuals, or to the community, or even to a province or territory within which the community forms the majority.

For example, francophones' right to use French in federal courts is accorded to and exercised by individuals. Their right to have their children educated in that language is slightly different: it is exercised by individuals but only 'where numbers warrant.' The special hunting rights of Aboriginal people, in contrast, are usually ascribed to the community. For example, an Aboriginal band council has the right to determine what hunting will occur. An Aboriginal whose hunting is restricted by her band cannot claim that this is a denial of her special rights, because Aboriginal hunting rights are not accorded to individuals. The right of the Québécois to preserve and promote their culture, as affirmed in the distinct society clause, is yet another case: it is exercised by the province of Quebec, whose citizens are predominantly francophones but also include many non-francophones.[15] These are all special rights, since they are accorded on the basis of cultural membership. But some are accorded to individuals, some to the community, some to a province or territory, and some where numbers warrant.

The case of hunting rights shows that what matters is not whether the right is 'communal' (as opposed to individual) but whether it is 'special' (as opposed to universal). Those people who object to the fact that Aboriginals have special hunting rights would not be appeased if these rights were accorded to individuals rather than to the band. They object to the fact that rights are accorded on the basis of group membership, thereby giving Aboriginals special rights and special status. Whether these culture-specific rights are attributed to individual Aboriginals or Aboriginal communities is, for critics, largely irrelevant.

Two Arguments for Special Community Rights

So the basic question raised by community rights in Canada is that of 'special status.' Since most community rights are special rights, not group rights, they cannot be defended by showing that communities have interests apart from their members. How can we defend special rights for particular communities? Two basic arguments are often raised in the debate: equality and historical agreement.

Equality

According to one popular argument, special rights are needed to ensure that all citizens are treated with genuine equality. On this view, 'the accommodation of differences is the essence of true equality,' and special rights are needed to accommodate our differences.[16]

However, this notion of equality is rarely explained in detail. This is unfortunate because many people believe that special status is the antithesis of true equality, which requires equal rights for each individual regardless of race or ethnicity. Among many English Canadians in particular, it is the universal rights enumerated in sections 1–15 of the Charter that have come to define their sense of equal citizenship.

How do special rights promote equality? Special rights are said to help 'accommodate differences,' which is the essence of true equality. But critics respond that a system of universal individual rights already accommodates cultural differences, by allowing each person the freedom to associate with others in the pursuit of shared religious or ethnic practices. Freedom of association enables people from different backgrounds to pursue their distinctive ways of life without interference. Every individual is free to create or join various associations and to seek new adherents for them, in the 'cultural marketplace.' According to this view, giving political recognition or support to particular cultural practices or associations is unnecessary and unfair. It is unnecessary, because a valuable way of life will have no difficulty attracting adherents. And it is unfair, because it subsidizes some people's choices at the expense of others.[17]

An equality-based argument for special rights, therefore, must show that some groups are unfairly disadvantaged in this cultural marketplace and that political recognition and support rectify this disadvantage. I believe that this can be shown.[18] Minority cultures are often vulnerable to economic, cultural, and political pressure from the larger society. This makes it difficult for them to sustain their community. The members of majority cultures do not face this problem. Special rights (for example, local autonomy, veto powers, guaranteed representation, land claims, and language rights) can help alleviate this vulnerability. The exact nature of these rights will vary with each culture. Aboriginal groups are more vulnerable than the Québécois and so need greater protection (such as restrictions on the mobility of non-Aboriginal Canadians onto

Indian reservations). Indeed, some people believe that the francophone culture in Quebec is now fully secure.

These rights mean that minority cultures are publicly supported, while the cultural practices of the majority must fend for themselves in the cultural marketplace. But this arrangement should not be seen as unfairly subsidizing some people's choices at the expense of others. Membership in a culture is qualitatively different from membership in other associations, since our language and culture provide the context within which we make our choices. Loss of cultural membership, therefore, is a profound harm that reduces one's very ability to make meaningful choices. Hence special rights compensate for unequal circumstances which put the members of minority cultures at a systemic disadvantage in the cultural marketplace, regardless of their personal choices in life.[19]

Historical Agreement

The second argument for special community rights is that they are the result of historical agreements, such as the treaty rights of Aboriginal peoples or 'the original bargain of Confederation.' Again, this argument is rarely explained in detail. Why do such agreements justify special rights? Surely some of them are out of date, while others are patently unfair, signed under duress or ignorance. As Prime Minister Trudeau put it in explaining his government's 1969 proposal to eliminate the treaty rights of Indians, 'we can only be just in our time.'[20] Why shouldn't governments do what principles of equality require now, rather than what outdated and often unprincipled agreements require?

One answer is to reconsider an underlying assumption of the equality argument – that the state must treat its citizens with equal respect. But there is the prior question of determining which citizens should be governed by which states. For example, should Ottawa have the authority to govern the Inuit, or are they self-governing?

Under international law, all 'peoples' are entitled to self-determination – an independent state. However, this principle is not reflected in existing boundaries, and it would be destabilizing, and indeed impossible, to fulfil. Moreover, not all peoples want their own state. Thus it is not uncommon for two or more peoples to decide to federate. And if the two communities are of unequal size, it is not uncommon for the smaller culture to demand various special rights as part of the terms. Forming a federation is one way for a community to exercise its right of self-determination, and the terms of agreement reflect its judgment about how best to exercise that right. The special rights accorded francophones in the Constitution Act, 1867, and the special rights accorded Indians under various treaties reflect the terms under which these communities joined (and helped create) Canada.

This historical argument may justify the same rights as the equality argument. For example, the special right to local autonomy for Aboriginal communities could be grounded on the equality argument, if it helps the federal government to show equal concern for the members of those communities. Autonomy could also be justified on the historical argument, if Aboriginal peoples never gave the federal government jurisdiction over certain issues. It is likely that the two arguments will yield similar policies. If autonomy is required to ensure that members of a minority are treated with equal concern, then it is likely that the minority would have demanded autonomy as part of the terms of federation (had the negotiations been fair).

However, the equality and historical arguments are distinct. According to the latter, the question is not how the state should treat 'its' minorities but rather under what terms two or more peoples decided to become partners. The issue is not how the state should act fairly in governing its minorities but the limits to its right to govern them.[21]

One difficulty with the second argument is that historical agreements are often hard to interpret. For example, defenders of the 'distinct society' clause say that Quebec's 'right to be different' was implicitly recognized in the Constitution Act, 1867.[22] But others deny this and insist that Confederation was a union of provinces, not a compact between two cultures. Similar disputes arise over some Aboriginal treaties. Moreover, some Aboriginal communities did not sign treaties or signed them under duress. Where historical agreements are absent or disputed, communities are likely to appeal to equality. Thus status Indians, who have clear treaty rights, often rest their claim of special status on historical agreement; other Aboriginal groups who did not sign treaties are more likely to appeal to the equality argument. Likewise, some francophone communities (as in Manitoba), and some immigrant groups (such as the Hutterites), can appeal to explicit historical agreements, while other francophone and immigrant groups cannot. It is often quite arbitrary whether a particular group happened to sign a particular agreement. However, the equality argument can help those groups that, for whatever reason, lack historical rights.

In assessing claims to special community rights, therefore, we need to know whether the rights being claimed are rectifying disadvantages or recognizing historical agreements arising from the terms of federation. Both of these are legitimate grounds for special rights, I believe, but both raise difficult issues. For example, in terms of the equality argument, it seems that some immigrant groups face the same disadvantages in the 'cultural marketplace' as some Aboriginal and francophone communities. Yet Canadian law draws a sharp distinction between the national rights of Aboriginal peoples and French Canadians (to some form of self-determination) and the multicultural right of immigrant groups (to be free to maintain their heritage). The answer here, I believe, lies in the fact that immigrants chose to come to Canada and thereby relinquished some of the rights to cultural protection that they may have had in their homeland. But it is not clear which rights they can be said to have relinquished and which they retain.[23]

Recognizing historical agreements raises other issues. For example, how should we respond to agreements that are now unfair, because of changing conditions? The land claims recognized in treaties may be too much, or too little, given changes in the size and life-style of Aboriginal communities.

Even if the equality or history arguments can be defended, there will still be those who reject community rights, for a number of reasons. For example, Premier Clyde Wells of Newfoundland argues that special status is inconsistent with federalism, which requires equal rights and status for all citizens and provinces. Others claim that special rights are divisive, because they emphasize differences over commonalities. These critics argue that while community rights may be fair on equality or historical grounds, they are unworkable.

This suggests that it was a strategic, as well as an empirical, mistake for proponents of community rights to claim that they are distinctive to Canada. Critics worry that community rights cannot be accommodated within the liberal, democratic, and federalist institutions that we share with many other countries. The claim that community rights are distinctive to Canada just reinforces this fear. It is important, therefore, to show that community rights are in fact quite common throughout the world. They can create problems of representation of federal systems and can cause ethnic tensions. But Premier Wells's claim that a federal system cannot survive if it accords special status is refuted by the experience of many countries.[24] These critics are prisoners of their own a priori definitions of federalism or a priori assumptions about the possible basis of unity. A quick survey of other countries shows that special status is workable and indeed can help keep a country together.

Conclusion

In explaining his opposition to special status for Quebec, Pierre Trudeau said that he believed in 'the primacy of the individual.' He insisted that 'only the individual is the possessor of rights. A collectivity can exercise only those rights it has received by delegation from its members.'[25] Many proponents of special status have responded by arguing for 'the primacy of the community' and by claiming that communities can have interests or rights that are not derived from their members.

This argument over the primacy of the individual or the community is an old and venerable one in political philosophy. But it should now be clear, I hope, how unhelpful it is for evaluating community rights in Canada. Most such rights in this country concern not the primacy of communities over individuals. Rather, they are based upon the idea that justice between communities requires that the members of different groups be accorded different rights. The issue, therefore, is whether rights should be community-specific or universal. I have discussed two arguments why justice between groups requires community-specific, rather than universal rights – namely equality and historical agreement. Both are controversial. However, I believe that both provide grounds for accepting a wide range of community-specific rights.[26]

Notes

This paper is based in part on a study commissioned by the Institute for Research on Public Policy. I would like to thank Alan Cairns, Sue Donaldson, Peter Heap, and Wayne Norman, for helpful comments on earlier drafts.

1 Government of Canada *Shaping Canada's Future Together: Proposals* (Ottawa, September 1991) 10, 3.
2 Ibid, 10.
3 Ibid, vi, 5. Throughout this chapter, I use 'Québécois' to refer to the French-speaking majority in the province of Quebec.
4 For a survey, see Jay Sigler *Minority Rights: A Comparative Analysis* (Westport Conn.: Greenwood 1983).
5 This view is clearly present in the passage from the federal proposal quoted at the outset. It describes community rights as those 'accorded to *individuals as members of certain communities*' and says that these rights are necessary because 'it has not been enough to protect only *universal individual* rights.' In other places, however, the proposal seems to invoke the first view of

community rights, according to which individual rights exist alongside community rights.'

6 For a helpful discussion of these two kinds of rights, see Denise Réaume 'Individuals, Groups, and Rights to Public Goods' *University of Toronto Law Journal* 38 no. 1 (1988) 17. Réaume calls the former 'group rights' and the latter 'collective rights.'

7 I defend the former opinion in *Liberalism, Community, and Culture* (Oxford: Oxford University Press 1989). Chandran Kukathas supports the latter option in 'Are There Any Cultural Rights?' *Political Theory* 20 no. 1 (1992) 105–39; cf. my 'The Rights of Minority Cultures: Reply to Kukathas' in the same volume, 140–6.

8 The 'distinct society' clause qualifies the Charter, in the sense that it instructs the Supreme Court of Canada to interpret the Charter 'in a manner that is consistent with the preservation and promotion of Quebec as a distinct society.' The potential impact of this interpretive clause was unclear, but many people worried that it would weaken protection of the rights of individual Quebecers. Some Aboriginal leaders have argued that Aboriginal self-government should be entirely exempt from the Charter.

9 For example, Aboriginal peoples may acquire the right to guaranteed representation in the Senate, which helps to ensure that they are not outvoted on decisions that are crucial to their communities' existence. However, this guarantee could be seen as violating the equality rights of the Charter, as could restrictions on the mobility rights of non-Aboriginals into Indian reservations.

10 For example, traditional Aboriginal methods of consensual political decision making could be seen as denying the democratic rights guaranteed in sections 3–5 of the Charter. These traditional decision-making procedures do not violate the underlying democratic principle of the Charter – namely, that legitimate authority requires the consent of the governed, subject to periodic review. However, traditional Aboriginal practices use not the particular method for securing the consent of the governed envisioned by the Charter – periodic election of representatives – but rather certain time-honoured procedures for ensuring consensual decision making. Aboriginal leaders worry that white judges will impose their own culturally specific form of democracy, without noticing that traditional Aboriginal methods are an equally valid interpretation of democratic principles.

11 Another example of the way in which group rights and special rights are combined is the language laws in Quebec. This example is complex, since the laws distinguish among different kinds of language use (government services, education, workplace, and commercial signs) and different groups

(resident anglophones, anglophones who move to Quebec from other provinces, francophones, and immigrants). The primary justification for these laws is to ensure equal opportunity for francophones against economic and political pressures of the anglophone majority in Canada (and North America). As such, they have been quite successful, particularly in enabling francophones to use French in the workplace. However, some aspects of these laws involve group rights. For example, the law not only guarantees that commercial signs are available in French but also restricts the availability of signs in English, thereby preventing francophones from voluntarily choosing to use English. This is partly a group right, since it is designed partly to protect the stability of Québécois society from the choices of its own members. It also partly an over-restrictive special right, since it unnecessarily restricts the freedom of anglophones to use their own language. See Robert Yalden 'Liberalism and Language in Quebec: Bill 101, the Courts and Bill 178' *University of Toronto Faculty of Law Review* 47 supp. (1989) 973–94.

12 This does occur, however, in some American Indian reservations. See William Weston 'Freedom of Religion and the American Indian' in R. Nichols ed *The American Indian: Past and Present* (New York: John Wiley and Sons 1981).

13 For representatives of the 'individualist' camp, see Jan Narveson 'Collective Rights?' (329–45) and Michael Hartney 'Some Confusions Concerning Collective Rights' (293–314), both in *Canadian Journal of Law and Jurisprudence* 4 no. 2 (1991). For the 'communitarian' view, see Michael McDonald 'Should Communities Have Rights?' in ibid 217–37. See also Ronald Garet 'Communality and Existence: The Rights of Groups' *Southern California Law Review* 56 no. 5 (1983) 1001–75; Vernon Van Dyke 'Collective Entities and Moral Rights: Problems in Liberal-Democratic Thought' *Journal of Politics* 44 (1982) 21–40, and Darlene Johnston 'Native Rights as Collective Rights' *Canadian Journal of Law and Jurisprudence* 2 no. 1 (1989) 19–34.

14 The federal proposal made the opposition mistake. It defined community rights as 'rights accorded *to individuals* on the basis of cultural membership,' as opposed to 'universal *individual* rights.' This definition correctly focuses attention on the group-specific nature of special rights but incorrectly suggests that such rights are accorded always to individuals.

15 Similarly, Inuit leaders have proposed creating a new territory of Nunavut within Northwest Territories, whose population would be predominantly Inuit. Granting special rights or powers to a province or territory dominated by a particular community may be easier than granting rights or powers to the community itself, since it takes advantage of the pre-existing structures of federalism rather than establishing entirely new political structures outside the federal division of powers.

There is, however, a danger in giving special rights to a provincial or territorial government, since it may create the impression that that government primarily or exclusively serves the interests of the dominant group. It is one thing to say that the Québécois constitute a distinct cultural community entitled to special rights or powers and that the provincial government of Quebec is the most appropriate body to exercise those rights. But there is a danger that this may lead to something else – the very different idea of 'Québec au Québécois,' as if non-francophones were not equally full members of the province. See Robert Howse and Karen Knop 'Federalism, Secession, and The Limits of Ethnic Accommodation: A Canadian Perspective' *New Europe Law Review* 1 no. 2 (1993) 269–320.

In principle, it might be preferable if special rights were always exercised directly by the members of the community, rather than indirectly through a provincial or territorial government. However, this is not always possible, given the federal division of powers, nor desirable, since it might generate constant conflict about who is or isn't a member of the community. The issue of who should exercise special rights – individual members of a community, the community as a whole, or a province or territory – often depends on practical considerations about the efficacy and flexibility of different institutions.

16 Government of Canada *Shaping Canada's Future Together* 3, quoting the judgment of the Supreme Court of Canada in *Andrews v. Law Society of British Columbia* (1989), 10 CHRRD/5719 (SCC).

17 See R. Knopff 'Language and Culture in the Canadian Debate' *Canadian Review of Studies in Nationalism* 6 (1979) 23–39; and F.L. Morton 'Group Rights versus Individual Rights in the Charter' in N. Nevitte and A. Kornberg eds *Minorities and the Canadian State* (Toronto: Mosaic Press 1985) 71–85.

18 I develop this argument in *Liberalism, Community, and Culture* chaps. 7–8.

19 This is similar to the debate over another group-specific policy: affirmative action for women or people with disabilities. Like special community rights, affirmative action programs distribute rights or opportunities asymmetrically, on the basis of group membership. Proponents argue that these policies are required for genuine equality. Critics respond that the economic marketplace (like the cultural one) already respects equality, by treating job applicants without regard to group membership. However, an equality-based argument for group-specific affirmative action can be made if the actual operation of the economic marketplace works to the disadvantage of certain groups. As with special community rights, the equality argument for affirmative action seeks to show how the structure of universal individual rights is intended to treat all people equally but in fact works to the disadvantage of the members of a particular collectivity. Many group-specific claims can be

seen in this way – as compensating for the disadvantages and vulnerabilities of certain groups within the structure of universal individual rights.

Of course, affirmative action policies for women or people with disabilities differs in many ways from community rights for minority cultures, since the two are compensating for different kinds of injustices. The former are intended to help disadvantaged groups integrate into society, by breaking down unjust barriers to full integration. The latter are aimed at helping cultural communities maintain their distinctiveness, by protecting against external pressures to assimilate. The former are thus (in theory) temporary; the latter are permanent, unless there are dramatic shifts in population. Because they aim at integration, affirmative action policies, by emphasizing group differences, are vulnerable to the charge that they exacerbate a problem that they are intended to correct. This criticism makes no sense vis-à-vis community rights, although it is frequently made.

20 P.E. Trudeau, speech of 8 August 1969, reprinted as 'Justice in Our Time' in Eldon Soifer ed *Ethical Issues: Perspectives for Canadians* (Peterborough Ont.: Broadview Press 1991) 295–7.

21 The two arguments generate different attitudes to federal funding of community rights. The equality argument says that fairness may require a positive right to state support for the measures required to maintain a group's distinctiveness. The historical argument, however, may generate only a negative right to non-interference from the federal state. If the members of the minority did not give the federal government responsibility for governing them in certain areas, that government is unlikely to be responsible for funding their self-government in those areas. It is interesting to note that many Aboriginal groups insist that their demands for federal funding are limited to historical compensation. See Noel Lyon *Aboriginal Self-Government: Rights of Citizenship and Access to Government Services* (Kingston, Ont.: Institute of Intergovernmental Relations 1984) 13–14.

22 Government of Canada *Shaping Canada's Future Together* vi.

23 I discuss some of the differences between the rights of national minorities and those of immigrant ethnic groups in 'Liberalism and the Politicization of Ethnicity' *Canadian Journal of Law and Jurisprudence* 4 no. 2 (1991) 239–56.

24 Clyde Wells 'The Meech Lake Accord: An Address to the Canadian Club of Montreal' 19 January 1991 (St John's: Government of Newfoundland and Labrador 1991) 11. For a survey of federal regimes that contain various forms of special status, see Daniel Elazar *Exploring Federalism* (Tuscaloosa: University of Alabama Press 1987) 54–7. Wayne Norman and I discuss the impact of community rights on social unity and civic identity in 'Return of the Citizen' *Ethics* 104 no. 2 (1994) 352–81.

25 P.E. Trudeau 'The Values of a Just Society' in Thomas Axworthy ed *Towards a Just Society* (Toronto: Viking Press 1990) 363–4.
26 For further discussion of community rights, and their relation to liberal democratic theory, see my 'Two Models of Pluralism and Tolerance' *Analyse & Kritik* 14 no.1 (1992) 33–56; 'Group Representation in Canadian Politics' in Leslie Seidle ed *Equity and Community: The Charter, Interest Advocacy, and Representation* (Montreal: Institute for Research on Public Policy 1993) 61–89; and *Multicultural Citizenship* (Oxford: Oxford University Press, forthcoming). See also Avigail Eisenberg 'The Politics of Group and Individual Difference in Canadian Jurisprudence,' forthcoming in *Canadian Journal of Political Science*, and Thomas Isaac 'Individual versus Collective Rights: Aboriginal People and the Significance of *Thomas v Norris*' *Manitoba Law Journal* 21 no. 3 (1992) 618–30.

2

Group Inequality and the Public Culture of Justice[1]

MELISSA S. WILLIAMS

As recent Canadian and European experience demonstrates all too poignantly, a central problem confronting contemporary democratic societies is how to constitute themselves as unitary political communities in the face of a teeming pluralism of social groups. The amplification of the political claims of ethnic and other ascriptive groups – groups in which membership is given by birth rather than by choice – has unsettled the techniques of accommodation that democratic states have relied upon in recent decades. The strategies that worked well to absorb the political pressures asserted by voluntary associations (or 'interest groups') have proven inadequate to answer the political claims of ethnic and cultural minorities. In particular, both the theory and the practice of interest-group liberalism, in which a political marketplace of free associations allocates resources according to principles of fair competition, have failed to satisfy demands by ascriptive groups. For groups in which membership is not voluntary, and whose minority status guarantees that they will lose in any competition for political resources, the legitimacy of the state's authority over them is itself cast into doubt.

Most critics of interest-group liberalism's failure to accommodate historically defined ethnic and cultural minorities have focused on the individualistic presuppositions of liberal theory. By assuming that all politically relevant groups are voluntary aggregations of individual interests, they argue, liberalism fails to comprehend the ways in which individual identity is shaped by membership in broader historical communities whose well-being is inseparable from our good as individuals. Consequently, liberalism also fails to recognize the moral claims that communities, as such, may make. Liberal theorists, in response, have tended to argue that only individuals may rightly be considered the bearers of valid moral claims.

The terms of this debate have recently been altered by Will Kymlicka's path-breaking defence of community rights from within liberal theory.[2] Kymlicka's creativity and originality lie in his insight that collective rights can be understood as emanations of the duties that we owe to individuals. His argument centres on the claim that membership in certain kinds of groups – cultural communities – is a defining element of individual identity and moral agency. As he puts it, 'human freedom and personality are tied to membership in a culture.'[3] Liberalism's concern to protect the conditions under which individuals can exercise their moral agency thus entails a commitment to recognize individuals' membership in cultural communities, as this is one of the most important of such conditions. In particular, Kymlicka argues, when members of minority cultures face loss of their cultural community through involuntary assimilation, principles of liberal justice can uphold extraordinary measures to prevent it.

I sympathize deeply with Kymlicka's argument for recognition of groups particularly with the connection that he draws between group membership and individual agency. Moreover, I think that liberals cannot easily reject the central premiss of his argument – that cultural membership is, in some sense, central to individual identity – and that they must therefore reckon with his defence of collective rights. However, Kymlicka has not made it clear why or how his understanding of liberal justice, with its recognition of cultural membership, can or should be authoritative for culturally plural political communities. The issue arises because of the ambiguity surrounding Kymlicka's view of the foundations of liberal justice.

This ambiguity is particularly worrisome in the light of recent arguments by thinkers ranging from John Rawls to Michael Walzer to Richard Rorty that liberal justice is itself rooted in a broad (but not universal) culture of Western democratic thought and practice.[4] If these people are right, then it is not clear why a liberal conception of justice can or should regulate the relationship between cultures in a society that includes non-Western as well as Western cultural communities. Yet most of the cases that Kymlicka discusses involve Western majority cultures and non-Western minority cultures. If Rawls and the others are correct, these are cases in which the majority culture against which Kymlicka wishes to protect minority cultures is the source of the conception of justice through which he defends minority rights. In short, this argument puts Kymlicka in the position of using the distinctive values of a majority culture to defend the minority against it. At the very least, this strategy courts paradox.

The foundations of a liberal conception of justice – the reasons why we should regard it as authoritative for a particular political community –

are important because they determine how we conceive of the political community itself. If it is culturally plural, there seem to be three ways of construing the bonds among its cultures, and thus three ways of justifying the authority of a liberal conception of justice for it. First, it may be understood best as a federation of cultural (and perhaps other, such as territorial) groups, united (perhaps only provisionally) by a convergence and their diverse interests in cooperation. In this case, a liberal conception of justice would be authoritative because it is the conception that members of the different groups agree best satisfies their convergent interests in association. What makes the conception of justice authoritative in this case is the fact of agreement based on interest alone. Second, it may be seen as a moral community in which the different cultural communities are bound to one another by their agreement on fundamental moral principles. There, a liberal conception is authoritative because the moral principles agreed upon support it. Third, it may be a purely legal and territorial entity, created not by prudential or moral agreement but by the contingencies of history. To claim the authority of a liberal conception of justice for such communities, bound together neither by shared values nor by interest, one would have to posit principles that are morally binding for all peoples and states and that they are captured best by such a conception. The foundations of liberal justice would thus have to be universally valid moral principles.

For reasons outlined below, I believe that only the second, moral view is theoretically coherent and practically sustainable. Yet Kymlicka seems strongly to resist grounding liberal justice in moral agreement. At the same time, he does not explain why liberal justice can be authoritative for a political community lacking such agreement. As I argue, some strands in his arguments suggest his implicit agreement with some form of moral universalism. But he does not explicitly defend this choice, nor can I conceive of defensible arguments on its behalf.

My project in this chapter is to trace the problem of foundations that runs through Kymlicka's liberal accommodation of minority cultures' claims to protection – in particular, whether liberal conceptions of justice must rest on substantive normative foundations that exist independent of agreement or whether agreement among those who are to be governed by a conception of justice is a constitutive element of the validity of that conception. Ultimately, Kymlicka comes down in favour of the former, and I argue for the latter. Although I agree with Kymlicka's conclusions regarding the rights of cultural minorities, I do not believe that they go far enough. The logic of his critique of prevailing conceptions of liberal justice ought to lead us not only to a reconceptualization of the substantive requirements of justice (in which, for example, minority cultures receive protection) but also towards a transformation of the process by which we articulate and define justice-based obligations towards members of marginalized groups in general. Because of the partiality of the social perspectives from which we theorize justice, I argue, the definition of the requirements of justice towards marginalized groups must not be confined within a 'juridical' model characteristic of liberalism, in which justice and rights are defined prior to politics. Rather, the content of justice must also, and perhaps most important, be articulated through a 'political' approach in which members of marginalized groups regularly participate. Addressing the justice-based claims of vulnerable groups requires revitalizing the sphere of the political within liberalism and reexamining the liberal inclination to shelter justice from politics.

The Liberal Rights of Minority Cultures

Since Kymlicka offers his defence of collective rights for minority cultures as distinctively liberal, it is worth noting at the outset what he believes distinguishes his argument as liberal. The defining feature of contemporary liberal morality, Kymlicka maintains, is the claim that 'our essential interest is in leading a good life, in having those things that a good life contains.'[5] This simple idea yields more that may first appear because of two aspects of the human condition. First, our lives are never improved by living according to principles that are forced upon us rather than endorsed by us, so this essential interest in living a good life means that we must live according to our own judgments about the good, leading our lives 'from the inside.' Second, since human judgment is imperfect, we may make mistaken judgments about what constitutes a good life. Consequently, our interest in leading a good life requires the freedom to revise our judgments and to act upon those revisions. Combined, these two facts mean that liberalism necessarily carries with it a corollary commitment to the liberties that are essential to our capacity to live according to our conceptions of the good.[6] Liberalism's core is completed by the principle of equality, which Kymlicka (following Ronald Dworkin) characterizes as an essential premiss of any plausible political theory in the modern world.[7] In its general form, egalitarianism holds that 'the interests of the members of the community matter, and matter equally.'[8] According to Kymlicka, the distinctively liberal interpretation of equality holds that 'since our most essential interest is in getting [our] beliefs right and acting on them, government treats people as equals, with equal concern and respect, by providing for each individual the liberties and resources needed to examine and act on those beliefs.'[9]

Kymlicka's defence of collective rights for minority cultures begins with a distinction between political communities, which are defined both territorially and by a regulative conception of liberal justice, and cultural communities, which are defined by such things as a shared history and language. Although the two types of community sometimes overlap, they play different roles in the lives of individuals: political communities define the sphere within which individuals 'exercise the rights and responsibilities entailed by the framework of liberal justice,' whereas cultural ones provide the context 'within which individuals form and revise their aims and ambitions.'[10] Kymlicka's argument for recognition of cultural membership within the framework of a liberal conception of justice turns on his claim that such membership is an essential component of individuals' moral agency – of their ability to identify and pursue a way of life that they can affirm as good. This is so, he argues, because cultural structures provide the context that gives meaning to specific ways of life and define the understandings of the good life that will resonate with individuals' self-understandings: 'It's only through having a rich and secure cultural structure that people can become aware, in a vivid way, of the options available to them, and intelligently examine their value.'[11] Viewed in this way, Kymlicka argues, cultural membership is such an important prerequisite of individuals' ability to pursue a conception of the good that it should be regarded as primary good in the Rawlsian sense, a good whose equal enjoyment by all citizens should be assured by a liberal conception of justice.[12]

Unfortunately, the importance of cultural membership has been neglected by liberal theory because of an unexplained assumption that the political communities to be regulated by liberal conceptions of justice are culturally homogeneous nation-states. In fact, most contemporary political communities contain a number of cultural communities, so that we cannot assume an easy harmony between the rights and responsibilities of the political community and the definitive characteristics of cultural communities. In practice, Kymlicka argues, two central features of a liberal order stand in some tension with the security of minority cultures: the liberties of the market and the rights of the political process both function (albeit unintentionally) to erode minority communities' ability to sustain themselves as distinct. Because liberal freedoms make it possible for members of the majority to move into and gradually take control of the land and resources that are the lifeblood of minority cultures, they make it difficult, if not impossible, for minority communities to sustain their distinctive traditions and practices. Liberal freedoms tend to press minorities towards assimilation into the majority culture and so gradually destroy a minority's distinctness as a culture.[13] Without some adjustment of liberal principles – some qualifications of standard liberal rights and freedoms – members of minority cultures enjoy the primary good of cultural membership to a lesser degree than do members of the majority culture, who can (and do) take the survival of their culture for granted. Moreover, because cultural membership is given generally by birth rather than by choice, individuals should not be held morally responsible for their unequal possession of this good.[14] Members of minority cultures thus have a strong justice-based claim for measures to protect their cultures from destruction, even if such measures would qualify or amend rights hitherto viewed as definitive of a liberal order.

But Kymlicka insists that the valid claims of minority cultures to protection from external social forces do not entail rights to limit the autonomous moral choices of their own members.[15] In discussing a case involving the Pueblo Indians, whose political organization is quasi-theocratic, Kymlicka argues that his defence of cultural rights does not justify the Pueblos' restriction of their members' religious freedom. The claim to cultural membership does not carry with it a right to prevent change within the cultural community. Indeed, time will inevitably bring changes within cultures, but cultural change is not equivalent to cultural dissolution (notwithstanding arguments such as Lord Devlin's that shifting moral standards within a society threaten its very survival as a society).[16] Although there may be rare cases where internal forces will fatally undercut a given community's cultural structure, as a general matter there is nothing in the liberal view of cultural membership to justify restriction of members' religious freedom, since 'there is *no inequality in cultural membership to which it could be viewed as a response.*'[17] Because it strikes me as a tricky bit of surgery so neatly to separate religion from culture, I am not fully persuaded by Kymlicka's argument on this score. But for purposes of this chapter, the relevant point is this: Kymlicka holds that a liberal justification of group rights requires a distinctively liberal definition both of the duties of the majority culture towards minority cultures and of the latter's duties towards their own members.

Persuasive as this account of minority rights may be to liberal readers, it leaves us uncertain as to Kymlicka's reasons for believing that his interpretation of liberal justice can and should be authoritative for culturally plural societies. In particular, it leaves open the question of what, if any, relationship exists between the values affirmed within different cultural communities and those that underlie liberal justice. In fact, I perceive two divergent but undeclared understandings of the relationship between culture and liberal justice in Kymlicka's work to date. In some arguments, Kymlicka suggests that a liberal conception of justice is historically situated within a broad but distinctly Western cultural tradition, which clearly excludes some of the minority communities that most concern Kymlicka. In others, he implies that justice lies beyond culture, or above it. But before we turn to contrasting these two strands in Kymlicka's argument, let me briefly review the reasons why one might believe, with Rawls, that there is an important relationship between a conception of liberal justice that can effectively regulate relations between members of a particular culture and the moral values affirmed within that culture.

Political Culture and Liberal Justice

Much of Rawls's recent work focuses on the manner in which the modern fact of moral pluralism – the existence within single societies of a diversity of incommensurable conceptions of the good life – constrains the outlines and content of a workable conception of justice. Given the fact of pluralism, no scheme of justice defined from within any one of these conceptions of the good will be acceptable to those who subscribe to contrary views. The task, then, is to define principles of justice that are acceptable from within any (or virtually any) of these conflicting conceptions of the good; a workable conception of political justice must not rest on controversial philosophical or moral foundations. Rawls's strategy is to try to locate a set of ideas and principles on which there is broad moral agreement and to construct from those ideas a public conception of justice. Broad agreement on the principles from which the conception of justice is constructed makes it possible for the resulting view to command an 'overlapping consensus' among people who affirm a range of conceptions of the good life.[18]

The idea of culture enters into this project because, Rawls argues, it is the political culture within a liberal democratic society that provides the shared beliefs from which an acceptable scheme of justice can be developed: 'We look, then, to our public political culture itself, including its main institutions and the historical traditions of their interpretation, as the shared fund of implicitly recognized basic ideas and principles. The hope is that these ideas and principles can be formulated clearly enough to be combined into a conception of political justice congenial to our most firmly held convictions.'[19] Moreover, although Rawls leaves open the question of whether a conception of justice so developed could be applied outside its society of origin,[20] he gives us good reason for initial modesty about the range of applicability. Considered convictions on certain moral and institutional ideas and principles that are shared within the public cultures of liberal democratic societies – convictions about, for example, the importance of religious toleration and the injustice of slavery – are the products of several centuries of political thought and institutional practice. In large part, it is the experience of the broad success of certain democratic ideas in practice that supports general social agreement upon them and creates a source of moral agreement independent of any particular comprehensive conception of the good.[21]

Several considerations stand behind the belief that a workable conception of liberal justice must be grounded in moral agreement among those governed by it. First, no regulative regime can survive over the long term without the willing consent of those who live under it.[22] In addition, there is the moral concern that we should not impose limits or burdens on people for reasons that they could not affirm as valid, for to do so demonstrates disrespect for their moral agency and treats them as means rather than as ends in themselves.[23] Both of these reasons speak to the need for agreement; but why does Rawls believe that the agreement that undergirds justice should be a moral agreement rather than a modus vivendi based on a convergence of self-interests? The answer is stability: while a modus vivendi is preferable to no agreement at all, it is inherently less stable than an agreement on moral principles. The circumstances that make cooperation prudent at one time may change, whereas the moral principles and ideas that undergird justice are regarded as 'values that normally outweigh whatever other values might oppose them, at least under reasonably favorable circumstances.'[24] Moreover, assuming that moral reasons provide a significant source of human motivation for action, a conception of justice based on moral agreement offers greater security against 'free riders' than does one grounded in self-interest alone.[25]

This analysis leaves open the issue of whether moral agreement supportive of a liberal conception of justice can be located in societies without a liberal tradition or across liberal and non-liberal cultures. Given Rawls's account of the special historical circumstances that make it possible to locate an overlapping consensus on principles that can be affirmed independent of particular conceptions of the good, we should at least be circumspect in our expectations that liberal justice can regulate relations between different cultural communities.

These conclusions raise important concerns about the promise of Kymlicka's liberal defence of minority culture rights, as many of the cultural communities that he is concerned to protect lie outside the Western intellectual and political traditions that offer support for a liberal conception of justice. In fact, Kymlicka's argument is addressed especially towards the circumstances of Aboriginal communities that exist within the boundaries of liberal democratic regimes. Yet the values affirmed by many of these communities are often viewed as contradictory to central liberal principles.[26] In particular, many of these groups affirm a communal morality – a commitment to the idea that the needs of the community take priority over the claims of individuals – that would appear to contradict the notions of individual autonomy and agency that lie at the heart of liberal theory.[27] One group of Aboriginal leaders stated that it cannot accept a program that 'seeks to promote the individual, which is contrary to the communal spirit of our peoples.'[28]

Now, it may be the case that a liberal majority culture owes protection to a minority culture even when there is no moral agreement on liberal principles between the two. We might hold that this is a matter of moral consistency: we owe to others the moral obligations that we affirm, even if they do not affirm them, so long as we do them no harm.[29] (It is at least doubtful, however, whether such moral duties could rightly be characterized as duties of justice rather than moral duties of some broader sort. One's answer would depend on whether one regards reciprocity as a defining element of the concept of justice itself.)[30] But given the moral reasons for refusing to impose a conception of justice upon persons who could not agree to it, there seems to be no ground for holding non-liberal minority cultures accountable to liberal standards of individual rights and liberties in the treatment of their own members. If a minority culture's practices do violate some members' essential interests as liberalism understands them, perhaps by denying equal status to females, or, as in the Pueblo case, by denying membership rights to those who reject the community's principal religion, it would seem to be impossible to develop a liberal justification for measures to protect the culture from dissolution.

Of course, even where there are no grounds of moral agreement between a liberal majority culture and an illiberal minority culture, the majority may none the less be in a strategic position to extract liberal protections for members of minority cultures within their own communities in exchange for offers of protection against the loss of the minority culture. That is, assuming members of the liberal majority culture were persuaded by Kymlicka's liberal argument for minority protection, they might have a strong moral interest in preserving minority cultures, even if that meant restricting some of their own freedoms. And minority cultures threatened with dissolution clearly have a strong interest in measures to preserve their integrity as communities, which might make it worth their while to give some ground on the rights of individuals within community boundaries. The possibility of this sort of compromise rests, however, on Kymlicka's assertion that minority cultures' protection of the liberal rights of their members only rarely conflicts with the culture's capacity to survive.[31] Otherwise, a modus vivendi based on liberal principles would either put the majority in the position of protecting illiberal practices in the name of liberal justice or place the minority culture in the position of paying for its survival as a community with its survival as a distinct culture.

Kymlicka on Moral Agreement

One of the prominent stands in Kymlicka's arguments tends to support the current wisdom that liberal justice is culturally situated and that a regime of liberal justice that can effectively and stably regulate relations between majority and minority cultures depends on a degree of moral consensus on central liberal principles. Indeed, the cultural locatedness of liberal values is implicit in the use of 'liberal' and 'illiberal' as predicates of 'culture,' a usage that Kymlicka occasionally employs.[32] Further, although he makes the remark in the course of an argument against the notion that political communities are relevant loci of moral agreement, Kymlicka does state that 'Western democracies ... share the same concept of justice.'[33] Again, Kymlicka's statement leaves us unsure whether the Western concept of justice has any relevant continuities with non-Western notions of justice or whether it can be authoritative for non-Western cultures. But it does suggest that different understandings of justice are expressed within different cultural traditions. More to the point, Kymlicka has recently made explicit his view that there is no liberal justification for imposing liberal constraints on those who do not agree with them: 'Relations between majority and minority cultures should be determined by peaceful negotiation, not force. This means searching for some basis of agreement. The most secure basis would be agreement on fundamental principles. But if two cultures do not share basic principles and cannot be persuaded to adopt the other's principles, they will have to rely on some other basis of agreement, such as modus vivendi.'[34]

In much of his discussion, Kymlicka seems to assume that minority cultures' willingness to agree to liberal constraints will be driven by interest rather than by their moral principles. Aboriginal communities with non-liberal reasons for valuing self-government have a strong political interest in distinctly liberal arguments for cultural rights because, 'for better or worse, it is predominantly non-aboriginal judges and politicians who have the ultimate power to protect and enforce aboriginal rights, and so it is important to find a justification of them that such people can recognize and understand.' Since the 'experiences and traditions' of these judges and politicians arise within the liberal tradition, Kymlicka implies, Aboriginal peoples will profit from framing arguments for minority rights in liberal terms that such power-holders can accept.[35] Although these passages stand in some tension with Kymlicka's statements elsewhere that relations between cultures 'need not (and should not) be governed only by "mutual accommodation", rather than "positive justice,"'[36] their general force is to affirm that moral agreement is stronger within than across cultural boundaries and that the kind of moral agreement that supports liberal justice is most likely to be found within Western cultural communities. Nonetheless, these points stop short of the claim that moral agreement provides the foundation for an authoritative conception of liberal justice.

Kymlicka on Liberal Foundationalism

Another strand in Kymlicka's thought is powerfully resistant to the idea that justice is culturally situated and to the notion that the authority of liberal justice depends on moral agreement among those whom it is to regulate. This strand is most evident in his critiques of theorists who maintain a connection between justice and moral agreement. Three such critiques are particularly revealing: those of Michael Walzer's *Spheres of Justice*, Brian Barry's *Theories of Justice*, and Charles Taylor's *Sources of the Self*.[37] More explicitly, in a recent article, Kymlicka rejects Rawls's argument for a 'political liberalism' based on moral consensus in favour of a 'comprehensive liberalism' based on moral foundations that stand independent of agreement.[38]

Briefly, Walzer argues that the specific content of a conception of justice must be developed in accordance with, and as an interpretation of, the shared meanings found within particular political communities. Any attempt to locate principles of justice outside or above specific communities does violence to persons' equality as 'culture-producing creatures'; equal respect for all persons thus entails, by Walzer's view, respect for communities' claims to work out the requirements of justice according to their own traditions and values.[39] Kymlicka objects that modern political communities are not characterized by the kind of 'collective consciousness' or 'shared meanings' on which Walzer's argument rests. Rather, communities defined by shared meanings are often smaller than political communities (such as cultural communities) or larger (such as the 'Western intellectual tradition').[40] Kymlicka protests that, given the plurality of communities of shared meanings that exist within particular political communities, particularly the plurality of cultural communities, Walzer's approach means that, in practice, interpretation of the requirements of justice will 'reflect, by default, the meanings of the majority culture, which could ... violate the shared meanings of minority cultural communities.'[41] Kymlicka's critique of Walzer assumes that a politics focused on the interpretation of justice in light of shared meanings will inevitably be one in which the power of the majority overwhelms that of minorities. Such a politics 'leaves the defence of minority cultural membership to the vagaries of majority sentiment.'[42]

Here, Kymlicka clearly does not believe that shared meanings or values are a necessary or appropriate basis for the definition of justice. Rather, he argues, 'People do think there are standards independent of their own shared meanings which are authoritative for the different cultural groups.'[43] Yet it is not clear from his argument where these standards come from or what makes them authoritative. In a note, he employs the concept-conception distinction to explain his meaning, arguing that although members of different cultures do not have the same views of the specific obligations and rights commanded by justice – i.e. they do not share the same conception of justice – they none the less share a single concept of justice.'[44] Kymlicka offers the following as the concept of justice that they might share: 'the system of entitlements on the basis of' which people can demand social recognition of their legitimate claims.' But as Kymlicka acknowledges, views as divergent as Karl Marx's and Robert Nozick's may be counted as different conceptions of this single concept. Whatever the taxonomical merits of this point, it makes clear that such a concept of justice is far too general and abstract to be 'authoritative for the different cultural groups.' Certainly, there is nothing within such a broad concept of justice that can defend a claim for minority cultural rights against its critics. Agreement on such a concept of justice as Kymlicka presents it means no more than that the different cultures agree, unlike Hobbes's Foole, that there is such a thing as justice.[45] There is nothing in that agreement to provide a starting point for reaching agreement on what the content of justice is, no shared premiss about what justice requires of us, that could narrow the distance between the different conceptions.[46] In any event, Kymlicka makes clear that, to the extent that any kind of agreement is necessary to establish the authority of liberal justice, it is not the sort of agreement that we find within particular political communities: 'Political philosophers would do best by forgoing such vague claims about "shared meanings"... and sticking closer to the actual terrain of moral beliefs ... The opportunities for, and also the limitations on, meaningful argument do not coincide in any interesting way with discrete communities, and are not specifiable in advance anyway.'[47] Kymlicka thus suggests that the moral agreement that matters is not that among members of a single political community but that which proceeds from critical philosophical reflection on shared intuitions about justice.[48]

More recently, in a discussion of Brian Barry's *Theories of Justice*, Kymlicka again asserts that justice can be defined independent of agreement. Barry's central point in this book is to distinguish theories that ground justice in mutual advantage from those that ground it in the notion of impartiality. Whereas the former approach explains the duties of justice in terms of the demands of self-interest, the latter regards justice as motivated by a 'desire to find principles which others similarly motivated could not reasonably reject.'[49] Kymlicka agrees with Barry's distinction and with his argument that justice is a coherent concept only when viewed in terms of impartiality rather than mutual advantage. Nonetheless, Kymlicka disagrees with Barry's specific interpretation of impartiality. Barry is mistaken, he argues, to define it in terms of what people could agree to, or, to put it negatively, 'could not reasonably reject.' Justice as impartiality is not grounded in agreement, even in abstract standards of rational or reasonable agreement, but it is fully captured by the commitment to give equal weight to each person's legitimate interests. Agreement may play an important role in the practical application of justice. But 'at the deepest level, justice is about the equal consideration of our legitimate interests, and the many virtues of agreement are assessed by reference to that underlying idea, not vice versa.'[50] Moreover – and this seems to be his most powerful reason for rejecting agreement as a standard of justice – Kymlicka argues that the principle of agreement implies that we owe no duties of justice towards those who are incapable of rational agreement, such as children. Yet our intuitions tell us that our duties of justice are strongest precisely towards persons whose lack of developed capacities makes them especially vulnerable. Instead of translating impartiality as agreement, we should recognize that 'we give moral consideration to children because they can suffer or flourish, because their lives can go better or worse, and because we think their well-being is of intrinsic importance ... Some beings with moral status can be given a justification, others can't.'[51]

Clearly, conceiving of moral duties towards children and other dependents remains difficult and elusive within moral theory. In particular, liberalism defines many of the requirements of justice on the basis of the moral premium that it places on agency, as is evident from Kymlicka's own account of liberalism's core commitments. It is difficult to know precisely our duties towards those whose agency is impaired or undeveloped, but we should not take children's relative incapacity for rational agreement as evidence for the claim that justice is not based on agreement at all, as Kymlicka does. By radically separating the definition of justice from moral agreement, he fails to address the reasons why so many theorists believe that agreement is important: it balances our agency with that of others and refuses to favour our moral judgments over theirs in matters that concern us equally. Respect for others' moral agency entails that we heed their judgments of what impartial justice requires, and this commitment means that we should keep watch for reasons why others might reject our own judgments. A standard of rational agreement, or of 'reasonable rejection,' thus seems inseparable from the liberal commitment to treat others as equals.

Of course, Kymlicka is correct to note that there are classes of people whose agreement may not be an appropriate measure of the moral rectitude of a particular act or principle. Children may often fall within this class, as may the mentally ill. But these exceptions establish the rule that, in general, justice requires us to regard others as equal moral agents: to the extent that we rely on a standard other than agreement, we are expressing doubts about their moral agency.[52] Such doubts do not cancel our moral responsibility towards others, but they do qualify our regard for others as moral equals. They place us in a paternalistic or trustee relationship towards those whose agency we regard as limited. In other words, while the interests of persons with limited moral agency still 'matter, and matter equally,' it is not the case that we treat such people as equals 'by providing for each individual the liberties and resources needed to examine and act on [their] beliefs.'[53]

There are several reasons why we might want to hold that justice is based on agreement, while acknowledging that we have moral duties towards those incapable of agreement. For example, it is perfectly consistent to hold that we have moral duties towards people incapable of agreement but to deny that those duties are necessarily duties of justice.[54] Indeed, given the idea that, as philosophers ranging from Hume to Rousseau to Rawls have argued, justice is a social and conventional virtue, a species of morality occasioned by the fact that human wants conflict, it would be surprising to discover that justice defined the whole of our moral duties. According to this view, justice concerns the reciprocal obligations that define the terms under which we cooperate with one another in society. But not all moral obligations are conditioned or reciprocal in this way. We may owe some duties towards others that are not at all qualified by their fulfilment of the requirements of social cooperation. Clearly, the obligations that we feel we owe to children or the mentally ill in no way depend on those individuals' performance of any duties towards us. Our duties towards them are certainly binding, but they are not necessarily duties of justice.

Kymlicka's objection to Barry leaves unresolved whether, at least with regard to competent adults, he believes that the idea of impartiality as reasonable agreement is part of liberal justice. He does not address this matter directly, although he does imply that agreement and consent hold a central and perhaps indispensable position within any theory of justice that claims to be liberal. In fact, he accuses Barry of surreptitiously turning all impartial theories of justice into liberal ones by assuming that they insist on reasonable agreement as a standard for evaluating the justice of principles or policies.[55] It is clearly plausible, he argues, for a benevolent dictator to be committed to treating each person's interests equally without getting any input on what people think their interests actually are. But while this connection between agreement and liberal justice is implicit in his discussion of Barry, he stops short of grounding the authority of liberal justice in moral agreement.

In contrast to his critique of Walzer, Kymlicka's discussion of Barry distinguishes more sharply between liberal and non-liberal justice. But his analysis of Barry brings to the surface a view that is only implicit in his defence of minority culture rights: that what gives content to a liberal conception of justice is not the set of principles or values that can command broad agreement within a society but rather substantive liberal principles whose moral weight can be discerned independent of a society's shared values. The idea of justice as impartiality separates the idea of treating people as equals from the need for agreement within a political community.

This distance between justice and agreement becomes even greater in Kymlicka's discussion of Charles Taylor's *Sources of the Self*. There, Kymlicka responds to Taylor's concern that we moderns have grown too distant from and too sceptical of the moral sources that can undergird the high moral standards of justice and benevolence to which we hold ourselves and that consequently we may be 'living beyond our moral means.'[56] Kymlicka disagrees with Taylor's location of 'moral means' within individual agents – his conviction that individuals' own belief in authoritative 'moral sources' (of which the strong ones, Taylor argues, always, somewhere, involve a god) is what empowers them to live up to moral standards. Instead, Kymlicka argues, we can rely on external institutions, including the 'coercive power of the state,' to 'empower' – to compel – people to act morally when their own beliefs provide insufficient motive. 'Where individuals are unable to comply with moral norms, we do not change the norms, we simply try to ensure that someone else will compel their compliance.'[57] Kymlicka thus implies that the modern ethic of impartiality unproblematically provides the moral norms that should be enforced against those whose moral resources require fortification. Kymlicka sums up his assumptions, and those he ascribes to modern morality in general, in three straightforward points:

(1) People have a natural, pre-moral interest in discovering what is truly fulfilling and worthwhile in life.
(2) Impartiality, or universal benevolence, is a fundamental moral value. Each person, from the moral point of view, matters and matters equally.
(3) Given the genuine value of the goods of ordinary life, and the extent to which these goods may lead away from respect for universal justice, morality may sometimes require more of people than they can voluntarily accept. In these circumstances, it is legitimate for other people, using other means, to compel compliance.[58]

Again, as in his critique of Barry, Kymlicka supposes that impartiality, and thus justice, can be defined independent of individuals' agreement on it. Indeed, he is so confident of the independent moral authority of impartiality that he calls it the ground of '*universal* justice' and approves its coercive enforcement against those who cannot or do not willingly agree to its strictures. The examples that he offers, particularly those of international distributive justice, reinforce the notion that here he does not believe that a conception of justice that can effectively regulate relations among persons (and across cultures) needs to be based on shared understandings among those people.

Clearly, Kymlicka, in his analysis of Taylor, has broken any remaining connection between agreement and the legitimacy of a liberal conception of justice. The only way to avoid this conclusion would be for Kymlicka to assert, as he does not, that those against whom the duties of universal justice are enforced do affirm them as valid moral ideals but lack the moral courage to act on them. But the specific examples that Kymlicka offers as cases of universal justice, particularly those in which he asserts that justice would require redistribution of resources from the developed industrial to the developing world, do not instantiate principles of justice in distribution that would command much agreement among inhabitants of industrial countries – nor, for that matter, among those of developing nations, for whom 'development' would imply destruction of highly valued ways of life. This is true not merely because international redistribution would not serve the selfish interest of members of advanced industrial societies, but because of the controversial character of the implicit claim that duties of redistributive justice extend across international boundaries.[59] It seems impossible to argue that enforcing Kymlicka's principles of universal justice against these people would in fact be a case of forcing them to conform to the moral law that they affirm for themselves (to paraphrase Rousseau).

Certainly, it is open to Kymlicka to claim, as an article of faith or belief, that impartiality provides the foundation for universal justice. But without addressing the liberal concerns about the moral as well as practical importance of agreement on principles of justice, Kymlicka has not shown why others should accept his 'universal justice' as authoritative. He has not demonstrated why *his* resort to universalistic moral foundations for a conception of justice that may be coercively enforced is defensible in a way that reliance on other such foundations – such as the belief that justice is defined by the Koran, or by the Old Testament, or by natural law – is not.

This is not to say that all moral universalism is per se indefensible. There may be, and I believe that there are, moral standards against killing, cruelty, and severe deprivations of freedom, as well as a sense of the positive duties of aiding those in distress, that are widely affirmed across cultural and state boundaries. But these human rights, or 'natural duties' (as Rawls calls them),[60] are too thin to support the kinds of cultural rights that Kymlicka wants to defend. His view of cultural rights requires significant sacrifices by members of the majority community, including giving up the freedom of mobility that some regard as a fundamental human right. Adjudication among individuals' conflicting but essential interests that Kymlicka's approach would require is much more subtle and complex than can be managed by any widely affirmed notion of human rights. 'Basic' human rights may indeed exist, but they are not up to the task of supporting Kymlicka's defence of collective rights.

Despite his resistance to agreement as the foundation of justice, Kymlicka has given us no principled answer to the arguments in favour of grounding justice in agreement, and I fail to see any alternative. This does not mean – nor can it ever be the case – that full moral agreement exists or can be reached on the various interpretations of justice, either for purposes of administering justice in particular cases or in definition of broad schemes of rights and principles of distribution. But without some foundation of agreement at the level of basic premises, rational evaluation of alternative interpretations of justice cannot even begin. In liberal orders of justice, whether created for homogeneous or for heterogeneous political communities, agreement must run at least as deep as a commitment to the idea of the individual as equal and autonomous. Kymlicka is correct, I think, to identify a commitment to individuals' equal moral claims to pursue their understandings of the good life as the core of any distinctly liberal interpretation of justice. As I argue above, a political community governed by liberal principles of justice must therefore be a moral community defined by broad consensus on these core ideas. To the extent that it is not, its prospects for stability – and its capacity to fulfil the requirements of liberal justice – are doubtful.[61]

Protecting the Vulnerable, Empowering the Weak

Why, then, does Kymlicka resist grounding liberal justice in agreement? The reasons, it appears, arise out of his concern to promote justice for the groups that are most vulnerable to injustice. In his critique of Walzer, his arguments turns on his view that justice based on moral agreement will promote the values of majority cultures at the expense of minorities' chances of cultural survival. His discussion of Barry refuses to locate justice in reasonable agreement because to do so suggests that we have no duties of justice towards those incapable of reasonable agreement, or those who may be pushed into agreeing to principles that do not protect their legitimate interests. In his discussion of Taylor, Kymlicka's idea that universal justice can and should be imposed on those who do not comply with it is illustrated by examples defending the justice-based claims of the world's economically downtrodden against those who are privileged in the international distribution of resources. In each case, the logic of his argument is to insulate justice from arenas in which competing interests are worked out, for those forums are likely to work to the advantage of the relatively privileged. In each argument, Kymlicka's central worry seems to be that making justice contingent on agreement will function to deny equal consideration to the groups that most need it, either because there is no moral agreement between these groups and the dominant ones, or because the imbalance of power between the groups will result in agreement that works to the advantage of the dominant groups.

Seen in this way, Kymlicka's defence of impartial justice bears important similarities to his defence of the neutral state against the communitarian vision of the political sphere as a sphere of deliberation about the common good. While Kymlicka agrees that collective deliberation may be an essential element of individuals' ability to live lives that they affirm as good, the work of the liberal state is to protect their right to engage in such deliberation within the institutions of civil society rather than directly to create opportunities for collective inquiry.[62] Kymlicka's principal concern is that devoting the political sphere to deliberation about the good – what he calls 'state perfectionism' – would 'serve to distort the free evaluation of ways of life, to rigidify the dominant ways of life, whatever their instinctive merits, and to unfairly exclude the values and aspirations of marginalized and disadvantaged groups within the community.'[63] On the latter point, Kymlicka argues that political deliberation about the good would result in the 'dictatorship of the articulate,' which is dangerous for those disadvantaged groups – cultural minorities, recent immigrants, women, blacks, Hispanics – whose oratorical skills have been developed with fewer resources than those of more privileged groups: 'State perfectionism intensifies these problems, since it dictates to minority groups when and how they will interact with majority norms, and it dictates a time and place – public deliberation over state policy – in which minorities are most vulnerable. State neutrality, on the other hand, gives culturally disadvantaged groups a greater ability to choose the time and place in which they will confront majority sensitivities and to choose an audience with whom they are most comfortable.'[64] That place, in Kymlicka's view, is within a civil society.

But as we have already seen, Kymlicka's defence of the neutral state does not translate neutrality as colour- or difference-blindness. Rather, he incorporates within the idea of neutrality or impartiality the notion that individuals' equal right to cultural membership should be protected by the state, if necessary through extraordinary legal rights. And because his conception of neutrality rules out political deliberation about the common good, he seems to suppose that the rights of minority cultures can be defined and administered without any institutionalized setting for political deliberation about the content of those rights or the manner in which they should be balanced against one another. We are to presume, it seems, that the impartial judges and other agents of the neutral state are well-positioned to identify and enforce the requirements of justice towards minority groups in the absence of 'political deliberation over state policy.' As with Kymlicka's views of impartial justice as independent of moral agreement, this reasoning functions to insulate justice from politics, to leave interpretation and administration of justice in the capable hands of the agents of a neutral state.

But the logic of Kymlicka's own critique of contemporary liberal theory should guide us in a different direction – not to separate justice from politics, but to democratize interpretation of justice. Kymlicka's central insight into the weakness of contemporary liberalism, particularly that of Rawls and Dworkin, is that it ignores or overlooks the perspectives of cultural minorities as it constructs theories of justice. As Kymlicka argues in a recent article, there are a number of historical reasons why Post-Second World War liberalism has tended to reject minority rights, in contrast to the earlier liberalism of, say, Hobhouse.[65] But it also seems relevant to ask what makes it possible for recent liberal theories to overlook the importance of cultural membership, and here the answer seems clear: philosophers such as Rawls and Dworkin have failed to perceive the centrality of cultural membership to individual identity because they are themselves members of the majority culture. The importance of cultural membership to individual agency becomes vivid only when looked at through the eyes of members of minority cultures threatened with cultural extinction.[66] Of course, failure to take up that perspective in constructing principles of justice is not a reflection of malicious intent. Rather, it simply demonstrates the inescapable partiality of human knowledge and experience.

This insight into the partiality of prevailing understandings of justice – which Kymlicka shares with feminist theorists who focus on the exclusion of women's distinctive perspectives from liberal constructions of justice[67]

– leads Kymlicka to correct the omission at the level of principles. This he accomplishes by showing why, in Rawls's view, cultural membership should be regarded as a primary good, and how, in Dworkin's scheme, being a member of a minority culture is something against which his desert islanders would purchase insurance.[68] Kymlicka's approach seems to be that once these correctives are made, liberal theories of justice will no longer systematically work to the disadvantage of cultural minorities. The work of justice thus becomes a problem of application, of balancing out the competing principles affirmed within the conception of justice, a project that Kymlicka has not yet addressed in any depth. Many of his remarks suggest that this effort is most likely to be undertaken by those agents of the state described above, the 'judges and politicians,'[69] the 'political elite,'[70] whose judgments about what impartiality requires will be newly informed by the value of cultural membership. Admittedly, Kymlicka has not yet publicly articulated his vision of what the process of interpreting justice should be, since his concern has been 'with what the principles being enforced ought to be – not with who ought to have the power to determine, interpret, and enforce those principles.'[71] Without further elaboration, however, Kymlicka's significant critique of Rawls and Dworkin leaves intact their treatment of justice as a moral concept that can be defined analytically and applied juridically.

In my opinion, Kymlicka's insight into the partiality of prevailing understandings of justice should lead us in a different direction, towards the epistemological limitations of any construction of justice that is developed from a particular social position, as all understandings of justice are.[72] It should remind us that every interpretation of the values of individual equality and autonomy is just that, an interpretation, and cannot, without public consideration, debate, and acceptance, be regarded as an authoritative conception of justice. Kymlicka's understanding should lead him to see that even the interpretations of our society's pre-eminent philosophic minds are socially situated in this way, notwithstanding their veils of ignorance and hypothetical contract situations. (In fact, these constructions and metaphors may illustrate the nature of those social situations.) And given that the social position that makes such theorizing possible is a privileged one, the perspectives that are most likely to elude these theorists are those of society's disadvantaged or marginalized. These perspectives are not those of Rawls's 'least advantaged member of society' in the abstract but are informed by the actual experience of radical social, political, and economic inequality in contemporary liberal democracy.[73]

If we are dedicated to a justice that does not exclude the voices and viewpoints of disadvantaged groups, articulation of its content must proceed through political as well as philosophical argumentation. I take the existence of vulnerable groups as a signal that their voices need to be heard within a public discourse about justice, not a reason for protecting justice from the political fray. Although Kymlicka is right to draw our attention to the vulnerability of such groups in public forums, I believe that the proper response is to create public institutions of representation that do not systematically advantage privileged groups. By providing spaces in which representatives of marginalized groups can articulate their distinctive understandings of the requirements of justice, their competence in presenting their views will develop quickly, as indeed it has for those groups that have entered political life. Kymlicka's worries about the 'dictatorship of the articulate' are not insurmountable.[74]

Now, it is open to Kymlicka to argue that I am here conflating two distinct processes: that of defining justice and that of implementing it.[75] It is perfectly reasonable, he might claim, to believe that the process of defining justice should be independent of the political process but that interpretation and implementation of the resulting conception should be informed by the perspectives of vulnerable social groups. Kymlicka's view may not necessarily entail insulating justice from politics altogether; it leaves a great deal of room for political deliberation at the stage of interpretation and implementation.[76]

But what would it mean for members of marginalized groups to participate in the interpretation of principles of justice that they had had no role in defining? This approach has two important flaws, a practical one and a moral one.[77] The practical flaw concerns our ability to distinguish a genuine moral community from a mere modus vivendi based on interest or concealed coercion. A group's participation in interpreting of principles might indicate nothing more than an effort to glean what it could from existing arrangements, but it might be interpreted mistakenly as moral assent to those arrangements. Cooperation in the interpretation of principles of justice might obscure deeper moral disagreement about what justice requires. A policy-level analogue might be women's involvement in deliberations about legislation on work hours in an attempt to institute flexible schedule arrangements so that they can get care for their children. Their activity might be taken incorrectly for willing acceptance of a structure of the workplace which, by failing to provide on-site day care for children, continues to assume implicitly that employees have wives who care full-time for their offspring, an assumption that disadvantages workers who are the children's primary caregivers. By allowing for groups' participation in interpreting but not in defining principles or, analogously, in choosing specific policies but not in determining the political agenda, this approach might lead to false assumptions of the moral legitimacy of the prevailing conception of justice.

Willingness to politicize interpretation but not definition of justice contains a moral flaw, for it fails to treat citizens as equals. The definition of justice is not delivered to a political community from the hand of God but must be articulated by some human agent. What is it that qualifies that person to define justice, but other citizens only to apply it? Citizens who help interpret justice without having the opportunity to agree or disagree with its principles are not on a moral par with those who have helped define it in the first place.

As a matter of fact, when Kymlicka introduces the perspectives of members of minority cultures into a reconsideration of liberal justice, he does so at the stage of definition of principles. As we have seen, within Rawls's scheme of liberal justice, Kymlicka argues, cultural membership should be regarded as a primary good. But the definition of the primary goods that should be distributed in accordance with the principles of justice is not a problem of application but a central part of the definition of justice. Kymlicka's insight should be generalized so that the process of defining principles of justice is opened to marginalized groups in a manner not contingent on a theorist's chance noticing of a group's novel or challenging understandings. Genuine neutrality among citizens would leave philosophy only disciplining arguments and offering alternatives for debate, not defining justice.

Certainly, I agree with Kymlicka that the definition of justice should not depend on a standard of agreement that systematically disadvantages members of marginalized groups. But the ideal should be one of moral agreement across group lines on what justice requires. The agreement that I have in mind goes beyond actual agreement to moral agreement. In other words, it does not accept coercion in any form. If members of disadvantaged groups are not persuaded by the arguments of the majority, then the majority's conception of justice should not be regarded as authoritative for them, and vice versa. Agreement on many issues of justice would likely be provisional, subject to revision.

When justice is viewed in this way, as informed by rather than shielded from the play of different social perspectives, Kymlicka's sharp distinction between the justice of Aboriginal claims and notions of colour or gender-blind justice loses its edge.[78] In fact, it suggests that a rigid policy of colour-blind justice may be no more appropriate for African Americans, and that gender-blind justice may be no more appropriate for women, than culture-blind justice is appropriate for Aboriginal peoples. As Kymlicka himself suggests, a commitment to the equal protection of citizens' capacity to pursue their conceptions of the good life may, without contradiction, lead us to endorse both school desegregation for American blacks and special cultural rights for Aboriginal communities. Cultural membership and citizenship are not, as Kymlicka argues, different sources of our claims to equal recognition; the equal recognition owed to citizens sometimes requires acknowledgment of the differences among them that arise from their membership in certain kinds of groups.

This argument certainly does not privilege marginalized groups' interpretations of justice as the ones that should be authoritative for a particular political community; their judgments, too, are partial. Moreover, criticisms of impartial justice mean not that we cannot aspire to and even approximate impartiality in our judgments about justice, but merely that we should not presume that we have achieved it in any final sense. We should, instead, adopt a stance of epistemological humility in our judgments about justice, maintaining careful awareness that there may be social perspectives that we wrongly exclude from our deliberations. And we should devote theoretical and practical energy towards restructuring our political and judicial institutions so as to reduce the likelihood of such exclusion.

In practice, I believe, this must mean revitalizing the sphere of the political within liberalism, reconsidering the liberal inclination to shelter justice from politics. To say this is certainly not to advocate majoritarian politics or to make citizens' fundamental rights and liberties contingent on shifting public opinion. I am in complete accord with Charles Taylor when he writes that 'the participatory society doesn't exclude the entrenching and security of rights.'[79] Rather, we must acknowledge that justice-based concerns permeate our everyday policy decisions and that the different viewpoints of marginalized ascriptive groups yield varying interpretations of what justice requires of us in these decisions. In fact, some of Kymlicka's own arguments point unmistakably in this direction, as when he argues that we cannot give all disadvantaged citizens the same rights 'because they suffer different *kinds* of disadvantage and so require different *kinds* of rights.'[80] Treating persons as equals requires awareness of the particular forms that their disadvantage takes, and those forms are inseparable from the meanings attached to their group characteristics by the privileged or majority members of society.

Conclusion

It is clear from the foregoing that the discursive definition of the content of justice must rest on an understanding of political community defined by moral agreement on certain principles. The process of deliberating about the requirements of justice must be construed as one of interpreting principles on which the interlocutors agree but whose requirements in particular cases are indeterminate. Most fundamentally, such a discourse could occur only in a place where all participants reciprocally affirmed each others' equal standing as members. The only hope for the definition of a liberal conception of justice that can be regulative for any society, including one with a plurality of cultural communities or ascriptive groups, is some consensus on the values that define the core of liberalism. And it is only from such consensus, thin as it may be, that citizens will feel bound to take seriously each others' admittedly partial understandings of the requirements of justice. The obligation of majority and minority, privileged and disadvantaged, to observe principles of justice arises out of their joint membership in a political community defined by respect for individuals as free and equal citizens. Individuals are bound to one another by a shared public culture of justice, whose contours they participate in reshaping as the sources and nature of inequality are illuminated through public discourse.

According to this view of liberal justice, the problem of illiberal minorities cannot be resolved from within a conception of justice. Instead, relations between illiberal cultural communities and surrounding liberal societies must be regulated by a modus vivendi of some sort, or by international law. In other words, an illiberal cultural community surrounded by a larger liberal society presents a circumstance for which, in my opinion, 'political community' is a misnomer.

Notes

1 I would like to thank the Department of Political Science, University of Toronto, for funding this project. I am especially grateful to Joseph Carens for helpful discussion and comments on earlier drafts of this chapter and to Will Kymlicka for his generous and thought-provoking remarks on an earlier version. I also wish to thank Judith Baker, Victoria Kamsler, Annabelle Lever, and David Welch for their insightful comments and suggestions.

2 Kymlicka's view is laid out in his *Liberalism, Community, and Culture* (Oxford: Clarendon Press 1989) and elaborated in a number of subsequent articles,

including 'The Rights of Minority Cultures: Reply to Kukathas' *Political Theory* 20 no. 1 (1992) 140–6, 'Liberalism and the Politicization of Ethnicity' *Canadian Journal of Law and Jurisprudence* 4 no. 2 (1991) 239–56, and chapter 1 in the present volume.

3 Kymlicka 'Liberalism and the Politicization of Ethnicity' 256.

4 See John Rawls 'Justice as Fairness: Political not Metaphysical' *Philosophy and Public Affairs* 14 no. 3 (Summer 1985) 228; Michael Walzer *Spheres of Justice* (New York: Basic Books 1983) especially 312–14; Richard Rorty 'The Priority of Democracy to Philosophy' in M.D. Peterson and R.C. Vaughan eds *The Virgina Statute for Religious Freedom* (Cambridge: Cambridge University Press 1988) 257–82.

5 Kymlicka *Liberalism, Community, and Culture* 10.

6 Ibid 11–13.

7 Kymlicka *Contemporary Political Philosophy* (Oxford: Clarendon Press 1990) 4–5.

8 Kymlicka *Liberalism, Community, and Culture* 13, quoting Ronald Dworkin 'In Defense of Equality' *Social Philosophy and Policy* 1 (1983) 24–40. More recently, Kymlicka states the principle of egalitarianism even more broadly, eliminating the phrase 'in the community': 'each person is equally worthy of moral consideration, each person is an end in herself, whose interests must be given equal consideration.' 'The Ethics of Inarticulacy' *Inquiry* 34 no. 2 (June 1991) 159.

9 Kymlicka *Liberalism, Community, and Culture* 13.

10 Ibid 135.

11 Ibid 165.

12 Ibid 166. Rawls defines primary goods as 'things that every rational man is presumed to want. These goods normally have a use whatever a person's rational plan of life.' *A Theory of Justice* (Cambridge, Mass.: Harvard University Press 1971) 62.

13 The economic liberties that erode minority cultures (particularly the Aboriginal cultures with which Kymlicka is principally concerned) include the rights to buy and sell property, which may, for example, transfer control of tribal lands to members of the majority culture. On the political side, mobility and voting rights may mean that members of the majority culture will gradually become an electoral majority in a region, again wresting control over the fate of the community from members of a minority culture. For further discussion, see Kymlicka *Liberalism, Community, and Culture*, 146–9.

14 This is the flip side of the idea that we are morally responsible for the choices that we make and for the burdens that they impose on others. The

notion of responsibility for our ends is what leads liberal thinkers such as Rawls and Dworkin to favour resource rather than welfare-based theories of justice. For Kymlicka's lucid discussion, see ibid 184–7 and his *Contemporary Political Philosophy* 73–5. This logic entails that we should not hold members of any ascriptive group responsible for their group membership.

15 See Kymlicka *Liberalism, Community, and Culture* 195–8; Kymlicka 'Reply to Kukathas' 142 ('A liberal conception of minority rights ... will endorse special rights for a minority culture against the larger community but not against its own members'). In the language of his chapter, Kymlicka wishes to defend 'special rights' but not 'group rights'; see p. 19, above.

16 Kymlicka *Liberalism, Community, and Culture* 168–9. The reference is to Patrick Devlin's well-known critique of the Wolfendon Report, *The Enforcement of Morals* (London: Oxford University Press 1965).

17 Kymlicka *Liberalism, Community, and Culture* 196.

18 See Rawls 'Political not Metaphysical' 225–6 and 'The Idea of an Overlapping Consensus' *Oxford Journal of Legal Studies* 7 no.1 (Spring 1987) 2–5.

19 Rawls 'Political not Metaphysical' 228.

20 Rawls 'Overlapping Consensus' 3 and note 3; Rawls 'Political not Metaphysical' 225.

21 Rawls 'Overlapping Consensus' 2.

22 See, for example, Stephen Salkever *Finding the Mean: Theory and Practice in Aristotelian Political Philosophy* (Princeton, NJ: Princeton University Press 1990) 144.

23 This Kantian idea permeates contemporary liberal theory. See, for example, Thomas Nagel 'Moral Conflict and Political Legitimacy' *Philosophy and Public Affairs* 16 no. 3 (Summer 1987) 238; Ronald Dworkin *A Matter of Principle* (Cambridge, Mass.: Harvard University Press 1985) 205; and Rawls *Theory* 338.

24 Rawls 'Political not Metaphysical' 250.

25 On morality as a source of motivation, see T.M. Scanlon 'Contractualism and Utilitarianism' in Amartya Sen and Bernard Williams eds *Utilitarianism and Beyond* (Cambridge: Cambridge University Press 1982) especially 103–6. On the greater stability of a conception of justice based on moral agreement as compared with modus vivendi, see Rawls 'Political not Metaphysical' 250. On the need for moral reasons rather than reasons of self-interest to support an effective conception of justice, see Brian Barry *Theories of Justice* (Berkeley: University of California Press 1989) 282–92.

26 However, as Kymlicka noted in his comments on an earlier draft of this chapter, liberal principles admit of a much wider range of interpretation than they are usually given, and consequently the conflict between native

community values and liberal principles is often less stark than is commonly assumed.

27 As Frances Svensson puts it, 'Most Indian societies [are] communal in the sense that the responsibilities of individuals toward the community are stressed over the claims of 'rights' that individuals are viewed as having against the community in Anglo-American society. Members of the community are expected to participate in communally-oriented functions, and to respect the authority of the community and its traditions and values; withdrawal from participation is equated with withdrawal from the community, since membership can mean nothing other than participation.' 'Liberal Democracy and Group Rights: The Legacy of Individualism and Its Impact on American Indian Tribes' *Political Studies* 27 no. 3 (1979) 431. See also Chandran Kukathas 'Are There Any Cultural Rights?' *Political Theory* 20 no. 1 (February 1992) 120–1.

28 Quoted in Vernon VanDyke *Human Rights, Ethnicity, and Discrimination* (Westport, Conn.: Greenwood Press 1985) 83.

29 See, for example, Nagel 'Moral Conflict' 222.

30 See, for example, Rawls *Theory* 102–3.

31 Kymlicka *Liberalism, Community, and Culture* 171, 198.

32 See, for example, Kymlicka 'Reply to Kukathas' 143, 145.

33 Kymlicka *Liberalism, Community, and Culture* 235 note 1.

34 Kymlicka 'Reply to Kukathas' 144–5; see also his 'Two Models of Pluralism and Tolerance' *Analyse & Kritik* 13 (June 1992) 52–3.

35 Kymlicka *Liberalism, Community, and Culture* 154.

36 Ibid 229.

37 Charles Taylor *Sources of the Self* (Cambridge, Mass.: Harvard University Press 1989).

38 Kymlicka 'Two Models of Pluralism and Tolerance' *Analyse & Kritik* 13 (June 1992) 33–56.

39 Walzer *Spheres of Justice* 314.

40 Kymlicka *Liberalism, Community, and Culture* 222–3, 234–5 note 1.

41 Ibid 223.

42 Ibid 233.

43 Ibid 231.

44 Ibid 234 note 1.

45 'The Foole hath sayd in his heart, there is no such thing as Justice; and sometimes also with his tongue.' *Leviathan* [1651], ed C.B. Macpherson (London: Penguin Books 1985), chap. 15, p. 203.

46 It is clear from Dworkin's own discussion of the distinction between concepts and conceptions that the former are too empty of content to provide a guide

to action. It is only when we develop them into particular conceptions that specific actions are recommended or discounted. 'When I appeal to [the concept of] fairness, I pose a moral issue; when I lay down my conception of fairness I try to answer it.' *Taking Rights Seriously* (Cambridge, Mass.: Harvard University Press 1978) 135.

47 Ibid 235 note 1.

48 'If a theory of justice matches our considered intuitions, and structures them so as to bring out their internal logic, then we have a powerful argument in favour to that theory.' Kymlicka *Contemporary Political Philosophy* 7. It is not clear, however, to what extent 'our' intuitions coincide because 'we' are members of the same culture.

49 Barry *Theories* 284; see also 8, 290–1. Barry's interpretation of justice as impartiality is drawn explicitly from T.M. Scanlon's view of contractualism in 'Utilitarianism and Contractualism.'

50 Kymlicka 'Two Theories of Justice' *Inquiry* 33 (March 1990) 112.

51 Ibid 111.

52 Indeed, one could argue that we have a moral obligation to respect the (limited) moral agency that children and the cognitively impaired do possess when we define the justice-based claims that can be made on their behalf. For example, the fact of a psychiatric patient's objection to incarceration or to certain modalities of treatment should be given moral weight in evaluating what constitutes just treatment, not only because of concern to avoid the cruelty involved in using force against such a person but also because impairment of judgment does not mean that a person has lost moral agency altogether. Judith Failer advocates this position in 'Who Qualifies? Rights Talk and the Mentally Ill' Paper presented at Annual Meeting, American Political Science Association, Chicago, 3–6 September 1992.

53 Kymlicka *Liberalism, Community, and Culture* 13.

54 As this suggests, I believe not that such obligations are duties of justice, as Kymlicka wishes to argue, but that they are part of the broader moral duties that include fundamental human rights, or what Rawls refers to as our 'natural duties.' *Theory* 114–17. Of course, this is to say not that they are not morally binding but merely that their observance is not contingent on others' agreement in the same way that justice-based obligations are.

55 Ibid 113.

56 Kymlicka 'Ethics of Inarticulacy' 172.

57 Ibid 174.

58 Ibid 178.

59 For further discussion of justice beyond borders, see David A. Welch *Justice and the Genesis of War* (Cambridge: Cambridge University Press 1993) chap. 7.

60 Rawls *Theory* 114–17.

61 In a detailed and generous response to an earlier draft of this chapter, Kymlicka comments that I conflate two distinct senses of the 'authority' of standards of justice. First, standards of justice can possess 'epistemological authority,' which concerns the grounds on which individuals believe their conceptions of justice to be true. Second, principles of justice can be 'politically authoritative,' that is, they can be regarded as legitimate grounds for coercive state action. Kymlicka says that these are separate issues and that we might regard a conception of justice as epistemologically authoritative (based on a moral truth) without being willing to use state power to impose it on those who do not affirm it. This distinction is implicit when he speaks of 'identifying' and of 'imposing' a defensible theory of liberal justice; see 'Two Models' 52–3 and 'Reply to Kukathas' 144–5.

Appealing as this distinction may appear, I am not persuaded that it resolves the problem of foundations in Kymlicka's work, for he has neither identified nor defended the 'moral truth' that undergirds the epistemological authority of liberal justice. Whose judgment establishes such authority? In short, his distinction tends to confirm my conclusion that his claims for liberal justice rest on a foundationalism that remains unarticulated.

Moreover, I believe that the distinction between the epistemological and the political authority of a conception of justice is unsustainable here. The latter is indistinguishable from political legitimacy, which is defined precisely in terms of a people's voluntary acquiescence in or agreement to abide by the laws of a particular political order. Such agreement may be forthcoming for reasons of rational self-interest (as in a modus vivendi), but, as discussed above, p. 41, stable political authority must be based on reasons or principles that the people living under it are willing to accept. Significant dissent over the validity of those reasons or principles undermines a state's political legitimacy. As Jürgen Habermas puts it, 'legitimacy, the belief in legitimacy, and the willingness to comply with a legitimate order have something to do with motivation through "good reasons." But whether reasons are "good reasons" can be ascertained only in the performative attitude of a *participant* in argumentation, and not through the neutral *observation* of what this or that participant in a discourse holds to be good reasons.' 'Legitimation Problems in the Modern State' in *Communication and the Evolution of Society* trans Thomas McCarthy (Boston: Beacon Press 1979) 200. The political authority (though not necessarily the power) of a regime thus rests directly on the people's regard for the epistemological authority of the principles that it propounds and defends.

62 Kymlicka 'Liberal Individualism and Liberal Neutrality' *Ethics* 99 (July 1989) 896–8.

63 Ibid 900.

64 Ibid 901.

65 Kymlicka 'Liberalism and the Politicization of Ethnicity.' Kymlicka identifies three features that have contributed to the contemporary liberal rejection of collective rights for minorities: Nazi manipulation of the League of Nations' minority rights schemes, the movement for racial desegregation in the 1950s and 1960s in the United States, and the 'ethnic revival' among US immigrant groups.

66 As Charles Taylor says in relation to French Canada, 'Since English is virtually the world hegemonic language today, it is difficult for those who speak it even to understand what it could be to live under linguistic threat.' 'Alternative Futures: Legitimacy, Identity and Alienation in Late Twentieth Century Canada' in Alan Cairns and Cynthia Williams eds *Constitutionalism, Citizenship, and Society in Canada* (Toronto: University of Toronto Press 1985) 216. In his comments on an earlier draft, Kymlicka expressed his agreement with this point.

67 See especially Susan Moller Okin *Justice, Gender and the Family* (New York: Basic Books 1989) chap. 5; Iris Marion Young *Justice and the Politics of Difference* (Princeton, NJ: Princeton University Press 1990); and Martha Minow, *Making All the Difference* (Ithaca, NY: Cornell University Press 1990).

68 Kymlicka *Liberalism, Community, and Culture* 166–9, 187–9. Dworkin uses the idea of a desert island as his hypothetical agreement situation in 'What Is Equality? Part II: Equality of Resources' *Philosophy and Public Affairs* 10 no. 4 (1981) 283–345.

69 Kymlicka *Liberalism, Community, and Culture* 154.

70 Kymlicka 'Liberal Individualism and Liberal Neutrality' 902.

71 Kymlicka *Liberalism, Community, and Culture* 197.

72 Young's work has influenced my views on this issue. See especially her discussion of the impossibility of impartiality, *Justice and the Politics of Difference* 102–11.

73 On correctives to partiality within the judicial sphere, see Minow 'Making All the Difference' 389.

74 Kymlicka 'Liberal Individualism and Liberal Neutrality' 900.

75 In fact, Kymlicka does so argue in his response to an earlier draft of this chapter.

76 In his critique of an earlier version, Kymlicka expresses his enthusiasm for minority participation in the interpretation and application of principles of justice.

77 I am grateful to David Welch for pointing out that moral and practical flaws are distinct.

78 See, for example, Kymlicka *Liberalism, Community, and Culture* 214–26.
79 Taylor 'Alternative Futures' 209.
80 Kymlicka 'Reply to Kukathas' 141.

3

Collective Rights and Women: 'The Cold Game of Equality Staring'

SHERENE RAZACK

'The cold game of equality staring makes me feel like a thin sheet of glass: white people see all the worlds beyond me but not me. They come trotting at me with force and speed; they do not see me. I could force my presence, the real me contained in those eyes, upon them, but I would be smashed in the process. If I deflect, if I move out of the way, they will never know I existed.' So observes Patricia Williams in *The Alchemy of Race and Rights*.[1]

For me, collective rights are fundamentally about seeing and not seeing, about the cold game of equality staring. I experience talking about women's lives in the language of rights as a cold game indeed, played with words and philosophical concepts that bear little relationship to real life. In spite of these doubts, the game is always enticing, perhaps because it seems to hold out the promise that something about the daily realities of oppression will eventually emerge from under the ice. Equality staring, however, as Williams poetically describes, is a 'no-win' situation. The daily realities of oppressed groups can be acknowledged only at the expense of dominant groups. Unlikely to confront their own domination, dominant groups merely deny that such realities exist. The idea of rights, turning as it does on notions of individual freedom and autonomy, helps to regulate what can be seen and acknowledged in women's lives; rights rhetoric masks how highly organized and constrained individual choices are, hence how restricted is the information that dominant groups have about the lives of oppressed groups.

In one way, this chapter is yet another lament about the constricting features of rights discourse, and this is where I begin, with the question: 'What's Wrong with Rights?' It is also, however, an exploration of how we might seek more fruitful ways to acknowledge the realities of women's oppression and of the legitimacy of their group-based claims for justice, themes that I pursue in the second half of the essay.

What's Wrong with Rights?

I first came to think about rights as a human rights educator. Without a theoretical background, but compelled none the less to talk about the problems of women and minorities within a framework of rights in law, my first workshops (and the manuals that emerged from them) consisted of squeezing the realities of daily life into a rights framework and realizing somewhat belatedly that not only was it difficult to obtain a fit but any experiences that could be taken up within a rights framework were hardly ever the ones that were most relevant for evaluating claims for justice. Let me illustrate this first encounter.

Working with a paradigm that I now know to be common to many liberal thinkers but which I then knew from a booklet written by Alan Borovoy called *The Fundamentals of Our Fundamental Freedoms*,[2] I began with the notion that we all have rights as rational human beings. Primarily, we possessed the right to pursue our own interests. As a woman, I have never found this to ring true for me, but I usually played along with the game to level 2: in the event that my interests collided with anybody else's, we were each entitled to equal consideration. Finally, at level 3, no one's interests should inflict harm, and, when harm was unavoidable, the individual whose claims inflicted the least harm won the right to assert her claim. In my classes with trade unionists and community human rights activists, we usually viewed this three-step model as impossibly abstract. What was harm? What was equal consideration? More fundamental, the idea that a human being was, above all else, a rational person entitled to pursue his or her own interests seemed unrelated to our daily lives. Perhaps we did not appreciate the more sophisticated connection between freedom to pursue the goals that we thought worthwhile and individual autonomy.

In the activist classroom, we would often debate some classic examples of conflicts in rights in an effort to make the 'model' work. Should the police have the right to bug the homes of the members of an allegedly violence-prone Black Panthers group in Nova Scotia? Even when the threat to national security is overemphasized in the example, most trade union and community activists introduce into the rights balancing process their scepticism of police allegations and their sense that to be Black in Nova Scotia was to be overwhelmingly disadvantaged at any point in the justice system. It made little sense to us to evaluate abstractly whose rights were most important in the example, given that neither the police nor the public whom they are meant to be protecting could be disentangled from the racism that pervades Canadian society. It was more important to us to identify how the racism limited what could be known about Black Panthers.

When my students tried to work out conflicts in rights involving groups, the bearing that existing relations of domination have on the rights balancing process became even clearer. For instance, in deciding whether or not Quebec's Bill 101, which limited the rights of individuals to attend English-language schools, was justifiable in order to protect the francophone collectivity in Quebec, many English-speaking activists abandoned their characteristic identification with the 'oppressed' group largely because they did not believe that French-speaking Quebecers were an oppressed group. They would not grant collective rights if they could not 'see' the oppression. Similarly, men (and some women) who rejected affirmative action for women and minorities did so on the basis that such groups were not oppressed. If there is no harm, then there need not be a remedy. The granting of special rights in these examples turned on whether or not the collective realities of the groups in question were acknowledged to be under oppression. The subject position of those 'granting' special rights considerably affected how these realities were perceived. Those who stood in a dominant position to the groups requiring special rights often had difficulty perceiving oppression.

I later came to review the exercises on rights conflicts in an academic context. I took the concerns of my activist students and used them to lay the basis for a critique of liberalism and of 'rights discourse.' I began, as most scholars do, with the limitations of liberalism, using Michael Sandel as well as several feminist scholars to make the point that the liberal self is a being without defining links to a community – that is, someone who is not socially constituted. My complaints were that liberalism, as I understood it from Rawls and Dworkin among others, isolated the individual from his or her various communities to the point that one could no longer see how group membership altered or constrained individual choices and opportunities. I wrote then of the difficulties that seemed to flow from this premiss: I was bothered primarily by the individualized view of power relations that lurked within the concept of free, autonomous individuals:

In sum, the concept of an independent, decontextualized individual functions to suppress our acknowledgment of the profound differences between individuals based on their situation within groups and the profound differences between groups. Without a theory of difference, we also cannot make clear what the relationship is between groups or communities. Finally, what this notion most inhibits is our understanding of power as something other than the power of one individual to assert his or her claim over another's. It is difficult to explain oppression, that is the consistent dominance of the claims of one group over another with this one-dimensional and individualized view of power. Further, it is a framework that effectively shuts out opportunities to propose new relationships not predicated on the concept of individuals in competition for pieces of the pie.[3]

It is tempting, in making this critique of liberalism, to invent 'a liberalism eerily unified and unchanging over time, denuded of any ethical dimension or indeed of any ability at all to see beyond the virtues of self-interest.'[4] Even without straw men, however, finding a way out of individualism from within liberalism is difficult. Theoretical efforts to contextualize individuals in their communities and thereafter to deal with their rights claims floundered for a number of reasons. First, Kenneth Karst (and others) tried to work from a premiss of the interdependence of individuals, but this did not enable him to establish the boundaries to caring and thus to work out either where self ends and community begins or the relationship between communities. Second, communities have often been oppressive places for women, and we ignore at our peril what happens to individuals within communities. Third, feminist efforts to talk about the community of women encouraged a universalizing of women's experience that left unexamined the realities of poor women of colour, lesbians, and women with disabilities.[5]

Some liberals have thought carefully about the self's relationship to community, and what they have to say has been used to acknowledge collective realities and thus to make a case for collective rights. Specifically, as Will Kymlicka has argued in *Liberalism, Community and Culture*,[6] even if one begins with the basic liberal premiss that what is most important in a society committed to justice is that individuals enjoy the maximum in personal autonomy, one can still find the space to honour minority rights. As I understand it, the argument is that individuals have choices for which they are held responsible, but if those choices are constrained by factors not of their own choosing, they are entitled to rights that correct the situation and effectively bring them to a point where they might be said to be exercising freedom of choice. Moreover, freedom of choice enables individuals to pursue what is most important to them.

This argument has held great attraction for feminists. Defenders of affirmative action use it to talk about bringing women up to a 'level playing field.' Scholars such as Martha Minnow, Ann Scales, and Elizabeth Wolgast argue that special rights for women are simply a route to treating men and women equally.[7] Kymlicka himself proposes (in this book) that such special rights are justifiable for two reasons: in the interest of equality and in order to honour historical agreements. Difficulties persist with this approach, however, that have to do with how constraints on choice are understood. The breakdown occurs in much the same way that it did in the rights-balancing exercises in my classroom of activists. If the contexts in which individuals must make their choices are not carefully deconstructed, we easily deny rights to those whose realities we do not wish to, or are ill-equipped to, acknowledge. For example, it is often argued that immigrant groups are not entitled to the same rights as the French and the English collectivities in Canada.[8] Immigrants choose to come here, and they thereby relinquish their right to the conditions under which their cultural identities might flourish. Such an argument denies the conditions under which most of us become immigrants, and it sidesteps the point that immigrants seek protection from oppression perhaps more than they seek the right to their own culture. How much of a choice is it to flee poverty and starvation in lands ravaged by a global economy dominated by the first world? Who is ultimately responsible for such flight?

The question of when historical accountability begins – one that plagues Canada's constitutional struggles – must be confronted when we justify the granting of special rights based on bargains struck at an earlier time. The terms of the bargain become all-important, as Kymlicka and others recognize, but not only in the sense of determining who agreed to what. We have to examine such bargains on the basis that they were not only or even primarily rational agreements between equally free parties. Autonomy and freedom have the combined effect of distracting our attention from the terms and conditions under which many bargains are made – the historical conditions, that is, under which individuals and groups 'choose' their own destinies.

Oppression and Group Rights

Constraints on Choice and on Women

What is and isn't of our own choosing? In mapping out for a court's benefit women's group-based realities, feminists have found that many of

their difficulties begin around the proof required to answer this question. For instance, when a male judge considers an incident of sexual
harassment to be about the attraction of one individual to another, and
takes lightly the consequences in the workplace of this so-called attraction, it may involve an enormous conceptual leap for him to the feminist
position that what happens between individual men and women on the
job has a great deal to do with their respective socialization and status in
society as members of different and unequal groups. Women who argue
along this line are often told that they could have exerted their individual agency and say 'no.' Individual choice is even further obscured in
rape cases, where the meanings of consent and resistance change if one
takes into account men's social power and the deeply sexualized forms
that this takes in society. While it has certainly been possible – and the
successes of the Women's Legal Education and Action Fund illustrate
this[9] – to introduce context, hence to argue that women share a group-
based oppression that alters their opportunities, such an approach has
simply not worked when the group-based reality in question is too unseemly to stomach (for example, the extent of violence against women)
or too costly to acknowledge (domestic workers who do not enjoy the
same employment rights as others). In the end, group-based constraints
on choice are simply not acknowledged in these situations, mainly, I
think, because of the implications that this would have for fulfilling the
requirements of justice.

The recent case of Nancy B., paralysed from the neck down and living
on a respirator, dominated the news for a few days and acted to remind
me what happens when individual freedom and autonomy are our starting points at the expense of what we know to be the deeply embedded
ways in which choice is constrained. Nancy B.'s individual right to choose
life or death[10] precluded discussion of the circumstances under which
she made her choice. Few commentators pointed out that real societal
constraints (such as lack of provision for full attendant care), not her
physical condition itself, may have greatly influenced her wish to die.
The able-bodied privilege that enabled many of us to see Nancy B.'s life
as one not worth living was, in this instance, well-served by the liberal
rhetoric around individual agency. Jenny Morris, commenting on similar
American cases, notes: 'The question is, in such a context, is the wish to
die a so-called rational response to a physical disability? Or is it a desperate response to isolated oppression? As Ed Roberts, head of the World
Institute on disability said, "It's not the respirator. It's money."'[11] Would
Nancy have wanted to live had she had the quality of attendant care

necessary to live a better life? We don't know because we never asked. We, able-bodied, preferred to talk about her courage and mourn her death. That the concepts of freedom and autonomy can be so easily harnessed in the interests of dominant groups should serve as a powerful reminder to question their construction in the first place.

Scholars who have questioned the origin and constructions of freedom, choice, and autonomy have invited us to consider whether we would still want to rely on these notions even in the absence of the societal constraints that we know to be there. For instance, Carole Pateman has taken issue with the original premiss of the social contract at the heart of liberalism by arguing that the problem of political freedom has effectively fore-closed any discussion about domination. That is, the free, autonomous individual who acts in his or her own self-interest can do so only while standing on the back of someone else. That someone is usually a woman. She notes, too, that whites have stood on the backs of blacks. As she says: 'Contract always generates political right in the form of relations of domi-nation and subordination.'[12] I take this statement to mean that in order to have your own way, you have to suppress someone else's: concretely, someone else takes care of the kids. Developing the idea that in contract theory the individual is owner, Pateman outlines in ways more compli-cated than I suggest here how a sexual (and a slave) contract supports the whole notion of individual freedom. In any discussion of rights, it will therefore be exceedingly difficult to introduce the notion of oppres-sion of women by men (and whites by non-whites) because this oppres-sion is the hidden cornerstone on which rests individual autonomy.

A scholar working in the area of schooling, Valeria Walkerdine, sheds light on the idea that the price of autonomy is the enslavement of others, notably women. Tracing the history of the concept of the 'natural child' in schooling, Walkerdine observes that the child freed from coercive education became in effect more subtly regulated into 'normalcy' through a variety of pedagogical practices. The teacher, typically a woman, contains the child's irrationality and manages the production of the natural child. Female teachers get caught 'inside a concept of nurturance which held them responsible for the freeing of each little individual, and therefore for the management of an idealist dream, an impossible fiction.'[13] What we see made invisible and pathologized in this scenario of covert regulation are oppression and powerlessness.

Patricia Williams, with whose words I began, is concerned also with the fiction of choice that lies at the heart of the social contract. She reminds us, as does Pateman, of the subtexts, the knowledge that is suppressed in contracts. The constraints on individual choice are in reality far more pervasive and deeply embedded that we realize. We would be wise to explore how constraints on individual choice shape what kind of contract is possible. Such an exploration helps to identify whose interests are being served in any one context; it serves, in effect, to place the emphasis on domination.

The Habit of His Power, the Absence of Her Choice

To talk about constraints on individual choice within a framework of autonomous individuals and with an individualized view of power relations is difficult. For instance, to say that we decide how to live our lives but that we do so within certain cultural and linguistic narratives is to avoid asking how those narratives are organized in the interests of some and not others. Women clearly have not enjoyed the same options as have men within these narratives, and to understand where their personal agency ends and the narratives take over is no easy task. Patricia Williams uncovers some of these deeper levels of constraints when she pursues the point that freedom is either a contradictory or a meaningless concept given that one person's freedom is another's loss of freedom. She writes: 'In our legal and political system, words like "freedom" and "choice" are forms of currency. They function as the mediators by which we make all things equal, interchangeable. It is, therefore, not just what "freedom" means, but the relation it signals between each individual and the world. It is a word that levels difference.'[14]

Freedom, choice, and autonomy are all concepts that impose a particular kind of order, a structure that violently suppresses those details that do not fit – in particular, the details surrounding the persistent domination of men over women, rich over poor, and whites over blacks. When my students and I complained that the rational, autonomous individual seemed irrelevant, we were trying to identify what is not said: such an individual can exist only at the expense of the individual defined by responsibilities to other, defined by emotion – in short, by all that cannot be expressed 'in the language of power and assertion and staked claims.'[15] Williams makes these ideas of absence-defining presence, ideas central to postmodern thinkers such as Foucault, concrete when she considers her own family history. Her great-great-grandmother was purchased at the age of eleven by her great-great-grandfather, a white slave owner. She illuminates the meaning of freedom and autonomy:

I track meticulously the dimension of meaning in my great-great-grandmother as chattel; the meaning of money; the power of consumerist world view, the deaths of those we label the unassertive and the inefficient. I try to imagine where and who she would be today. I am engaged in a long-term project of tracking his words – through his letters and opinions – and those of his sons who were also lawyers and judges – of finding the shape described by her absence in all this.

I see her shape and his hand in the vast networking of our society, and in the evils and oversights that plague our lives and laws. The control he had over her body. The force he was in her life, in the shape of my life today. The power he exercised in the choice to breed her or not. The choice to breed slaves in his image, to choose her mate and be that mate. In his attempt to own what no man can own, the habit of his power and the absence of her choice.

I look for her shape and his hand.[16]

We must begin with the relationship that is the habit of his power and the absence of her choice, for this was not only the context in which the concepts of freedom and choice were developed (as Pateman shows) but is still the situation for Black women today. We ought to be aware that his habit of power depends on the absence of her choice. The most obvious difficulty to emerge is how communities are going to recognize and make allowances for circumstances beyond an individual's or a group's choosing when to do so is to subject one's own privilege to scrutiny. To force one's presence is to be smashed in the process. The discussion around rights will therefore remain where it began for my human rights students. What is harm? What is equal consideration? Privilege will prove to be the major stumbling block, as popular educators have acknowledged in our work in the classroom. Women and minorities will simply not be seen to deserve collective rights. Their realities will not be admissible within the construct of rights.

This perspective is cripplingly bleak, and we must, if we are to find a practical way out (for hope is also tied to interest!), devise ways to interrogate ourselves about what we see and don't see. This is why I maintain that the major stumbling block to collective rights is not simply the failure of their advocates to present the case within liberalism but the way in which the discussion is regulated to obscure relations of domination. Liberal whites who cannot accept Aboriginal self-government do not fear that it may lead to apartheid; the security of dominant groups makes this seem highly unlikely to me. Rather, they correctly fear that they will lose privileges and that they will do so to a group undeserving of these fruits. Racism joins self-interest, as it usually does, and the rhetoric of rights serves well to camouflage what is going on. However, as many others have seen, it is not satisfactory to refuse to play rights games altogether simply because of their built-in limitations.[17] The games are in fact thrust upon us. In playing them, we can make use of the idea that they impose a particular kind of order and violence on experience. We can anticipate, then, that collective realities of oppressed groups will be barely visible for the simple reasons that they implicate dominant groups and are hidden under the layers of constructed meanings designed to suppress knowledge of their existence. We ourselves participate in the construction of these meanings. One strategy is to insist on descriptions of the realities of oppressed groups that bring the relations of domination and submission to the surface, as feminists working in law have done. A second is to be ever mindful of what can be heard in any given context. A third is to use advisedly concepts such as rights in reference to such realities as violence against women and children and the genocide of a people. The idea of rights regulates the discussion and hides 'the complex, multi-faceted structure of domination in modern patriarchy.'[18] We shall need to find new concepts to talk about the way in which power works that can describe oppression – the consistent and organized domination of one group over another.

On Dispensing with Autonomy

Feminist thinkers remind us that women have only recently been thought to be the makers of their own fate; we ought, therefore, to think twice about dispensing with the value that liberals place on freedom and autonomy. We may come to see women, as Jane Flax puts it, as 'acted upon beings'[19] and thus leave little room for resistance to oppression. Dwelling on the apparent contradiction between saying that the concepts of individual freedom and autonomy presuppose relations of domination and claiming that women are oppressed because they do not have the freedom and autonomy, I returned to Foucault's work. In 'Two Lectures,' he elaborates on his understanding of how power works, noting, in language akin to Pateman's concept of the individual as owner, that power is not something one 'possesses, acquires, cedes through force or contract.'[20] Instead, power is a relation of force. The system of right, which relies on the idea that individuals possess their autonomy, invites us to consider, then, the legitimacy of one claim over another, rather than 'the methods of subjugation that it instigates.'[21] If in fact we turn our attention to methods of subjugation, we are taken back to Pateman's idea that a sexual and slave contract underpins the whole notion of individual freedom. The individual, then, doesn't simply possess power but is constituted by a set of power relations cast like a net over how we see and think. It is precisely these power relations that are observed when we balance competing claims. The individual can, however, resist these relations at nodal points along the net.

Drawing on Foucault, as I have done, Valerie Walkerdine makes the important observation that when we work with a concept of liberation as personal freeing (from constraints), hence with a notion of power as a fixed possession, we focus on the lifting of those overt constraints that we experience as repressive. Freedom becomes freedom from overt control, and our attention is taken away from the many covert ways in which we are regulated.[22] This has been my argument about understanding collective rights. Unless we come to terms with covert regulation, with power as an effect, we will be unable to determine who is being oppressed and what should be done about it. Oppression, in liberalism, means imposition of unjust constraints. When one departs from the notion of choice and freedom that is the beginning of this particular story – the 'contract-oppression scheme,' to use Foucault's words – and comes to see power as a net organizing how individuals are constituted in any one context, oppression becomes a story of 'struggle and submission,'[23] of how what is present is made possible by what is absent. I believe this to be a useful political direction in which women might travel in their quest for justice. We might make use of the notion of autonomy and perhaps return to oppression as the absence of choice as a matter of strategy so as not 'to make the question of women's oppression obsolete,'[24] but in doing so, we ought to be aware that women could emerge as individuals 'further implicated in the patriarchal and logocentric tradition which proposes the bourgeois individual as guarantor of the new order.'[25] Jennifer Nedelsky's proposal – that we consider autonomy not as an essence innate to us but as a capacity that must be nurtured through relationships with others – will not suffice if we forget to examine how nurturing is accomplished.[26] It is thus imperative to ask about how relationships are structured. It becomes necessary, in other words, to put oppression back into the picture.

Jane Flax offered the following observations about the fourfold task of feminist theory: 'We need (1) to articulate feminist viewpoints of and within the social worlds in which we live, (2) to think about how we are affected by these worlds, (3) to think about how our thinking about them may itself be implicated in existing power/knowledge relationships, and (4) to think also about the ways in which these worlds ought and can be transformed.'[27]

Her advice applies equally to those of us either theorizing and/or organizing for collective rights. We need to ground discussion of collective rights in concrete social realities. We need to think about how these realities affect women. We need to think especially about what we know and can know how those realities before we begin to evaluate claims for justice. These prescriptions amount, in my view, to a search for the patterns and consequences of domination, which begins with acknowledgment that women live a collective reality of oppression in which their individual choices are seriously constrained. We ought to use with care any rhetoric that does not begin there.

Notes

1 Patricia Williams *The Alchemy of Race and Rights: Diary of a Law Professor* (Cambridge, Mass.: Harvard University Press) 222.

2 Alan Borovoy *The Fundamentals of Our Fundamental Freedoms* (Ottawa: Canadian Labour Congress 1979).

3 Sherene Razack 'Revolution from Within: Dilemmas of Feminist Jurisprudence' *Queen's Quarterly* 97 no. 3 (Autumn 1990) 401.

4 Joan C. Williams 'Culture and Certainty: Legal History and the Reconstructive Project' *Virginia Law Review* 76 no. 1–4 (1990) 719.

5 See Razack 'Revolution' for a fuller discussion.

6 Will Kymlicka *Liberalism, Community, and Culture* (Oxford: Clarendon Press 1989).

7 Sherene Razack *Canadian Feminism and the Law: The Women's Legal Education and Action Fund and the Pursuit of Equality* (Toronto: Second Story Press 1991) 23.

8 See, for example, Kymlicka's chapter (no. 1) in this collection.

9 Razack *Canadian Feminism.*

10 Rhéal Séguin and Rod Mickleburgh 'Nancy B. Judge Balanced 2 Codes' *Globe and Mail* (Toronto) 7 January 1992, A4.

11 Jenny Morris *Pride against Prejudice* (London: Women's Press, 1991) 42.

12 Carol Pateman *The Sexual Contract* (Stanford, Calif.: Stanford University Press 1988) 8.

13 Valeria Walkerdine *Schoolgirl Fictions* (London: Verso 1990) 19.

14 Patricia Williams *Alchemy* 31.

15 Ibid 21.

16 Ibid 19.

17 See the discussion of Robert Williams and Elizabeth Schneider in Razack *Canadian Feminism* 17.

78   Sherene Razack

18 Pateman *Sexual Contract* 16.
19 Jane Flax *Thinking Fragments: Psychoanalysis, Feminism and Postmodernism in the Contemporary West* (Berkeley: University of California Press 1990) 181.
20 Michael Foucault *Power/Knowledge: Selected Interviews and Other Writings 1972–1977* ed Colin Gordon, trans Colin Gordon, Leo Marshall, John Mepham, and Kate Soper (New York: Pantheon Books 1980) 88–9.
21 Ibid 96.
22 Walkerdine *Sexual Fictions* 18.
23 Foucault *Power/Knowledge* 92.
24 Martin Biddy 'Feminism, Criticism, and Foucault' in Irene Diamond and Lee Quinby eds *Feminism and Foucault* (Boston: Northeastern University Press 1988) 17.
25 Walkerdine *Sexual Fictions* 36.
26 Jenifer Nedelsky 'Law, Boundaries and the Bounded Self' *Representations* 30 (Spring 1990) 169.
27 Flax *Thinking Fragments* 182.

4

Towards a Philosophy of Federalism

WAYNE J. NORMAN

Introduction: Group Rights and Federalism

Demonstrating that some group is entitled to some genuine collective rights is only half the intellectual battle.[1] Various kinds of abstract collective rights have little meaning or content until they are brought to life by some concrete institutional mechanism. While individual rights are often defined (and justified) wholly by their correlative duties imposed on others, collective rights are more likely to be characterized by forms of control over or representation in political institutions. Thus Will Kymlicka's list of typical 'special' rights for minority cultures includes rights to local autonomy (the right to exercise a range of powers within a community) and guaranteed representation and veto powers within the larger community's legislature and supreme court.[2] The second half of the battle in arguing for any particular collective right, then, involves designing and justifying the institutions through which it is exercised. In this chapter, I am concerned almost exclusively with this latter task. More specifically, I discuss the idea of federalism as a system of political institutions for satisfying some important claims to collective rights within a multinational, liberal democratic society.

Typically, federal arrangements allow a minority within a large domain to be a majority within a smaller, territorial sub-unit. Within the sub-unit, that minority-turned-majority can exercise a range of powers to protect its special needs and promote its special interests (be they linguistic, religious, ethnic, cultural, or economic); and the sub-units themselves, or the members thereof, are entitled to various forms of representation in, or influence over, federal institutions at the centre. So conceived, federalism as such provides no magical defence against many of the forms of oppression, disempowerment, and injustice threatening minorities in modern states. Consider two conspicuous gaps in the protection that it offers. First, it provides no special mechanisms for assisting members of groups that are not territorially concentrated. These may include scattered linguistic, religious, or ethnic minorities, as well as women, the disabled, and so on. And second, by according majoritarian powers to a national minority within a sub-unit, a federal system almost inevitably creates new minorities (for example, those who are not members of the federally protected national minority) within the same sub-unit.

So for those concerned about justice in general, and group rights in particular, in the words of Alan Cairns, 'federalism is not enough.'[3] A just federation requires other mechanisms for protecting individual and collective rights. (Many of these, discussed elsewhere in this volume, are equally applicable to non-federal states.) Recent Canadian experience highlights the significant role that a charter of rights can play in protecting certain minorities, especially if bolstered by effective race-relations boards, fair-employment legislation, limitations on abusive speech and publication, and a political culture in which an ethic of racial and cultural pluralism is deeply rooted.[4] Another way of closing the gaps in the protection that a federal system offers to non-territorially based minorities is to extend some of the logic of federalism beyond its territorial roots. In certain special cases, some form of federal partnership, including the exercise of powers and representation in federal institutions, could be granted to groups lacking a near-exclusive geographical location. So while Inuit and Indians on reserves could participate as new kinds of partners in a territorial federal system in Canada, non-status Indians – who share cities and towns with other Canadians – might nevertheless be 'intraterritorial' or 'consociational' federal partners with control over, say, their own schools, hospitals, and social welfare system.

Now one must not underestimate the theoretical and practical difficulties of wedding an orthodox federal system with either a charter of rights or an extra dimension of consociationalism. As Cairns has argued, for example, the seemingly innocent insertion of a charter of rights into a federal constitution (as happened in Canada in 1982) can establish a competing and in some sense contradictory locus of sovereignty: where the people are supreme in matters covered by the Charter of Rights and Freedoms but governing elites maintain the ultimate power, through the amending formula and the 'Notwithstanding clause,' to abrogate or override citizens' rights.[5] The theoretical task of making sense of such a hybrid is all the more difficult when we consider that we are not really in possession of a sophisticated normative theory for one of its component parts: it is not overstatement to suggest that there does not exist in any detail an adequate political philosophy of federalism itself. (As far as I am aware, for example, no English-speaking philosopher has ever devoted a book to the subject.[6]) In this chapter, I take some tentative steps in that direction by trying to explain why we might need such a theory, by showing what we might reasonably expect from it, and, finally, by sketching what a normative theory of federation might look like.

Why federate?

While federalism is not enough, in many situations it is almost certainly indispensable. That is, while it does not in itself address the needs and rights of many kinds of minority groups, it does offer potentially ideal protection and opportunities to a few very important classes of minorities – including national groups or 'peoples' and distinct geographical or politico-economic regions, roughly, the sorts of groupings that might have a valid claim to secede from a state. National identities have profound moral significance in individuals' lives; indeed, it is something of a commonplace for sociologists to argue that national identities are in general people's most significant identities.[7] Moreover, as Kymlicka has argued so persuasively, membership in the culture of one's nation (where one's nation is not always one's country) is morally vital and qualitatively unlike membership in other groups or associations, insofar as one's language and culture provide the context within which one makes one's choices.[8] Well-designed federal systems offer the possibility of protecting sub-national cultures at least as well, if not better, than would states in which each of these nationalities formed a majority. But these are not the only advantages that a world of federations has over a world of genuine nation-states.

By some estimates, more than 90 per cent of existing states contain a plurality of national, ethnic, or linguistic groups; in other words, less than 10 per cent are actually the classical nation-states that most political philosophizing seems to presuppose. In 1983, Ernest Gellner judged there to be five potential states to each actual state in the world 'in terms of the number of ethnic and linguistic enclaves within existing states that originally had just as good a claim to separate statehood as those which did achieve it.'[9] That we do not have five or six hundred members in the United Nations today is explained largely by the fact that few of these nations ever consented to sharing states with their neighbours, and few have been allowed democratic opportunities to leave. The break-up of the Soviet Union and Yugoslavia – first along 'republic' boundaries, then further into nervous enclaves of ethnic minorities – are ominous precedents. These facts suggest that some compelling 'negative' reasons for seeking out federal solutions to the problems of multinational states. The world surely has little to gain from being divided into 600 states (with 600 tetchy armies and who knows how many ethnic and religious militias), and still less from going through the 'liberating' process (Yugoslav-style) of fighting to become 600 states.

There are also, however, attractive positive reasons for seeking federal and quasi-federal arrangements between neighbouring polities. These are exemplified best by the remarkable political fusion taking place in western Europe, an experiment that is likely to be emulated to varying degrees in almost every region of the globe over the next generation or two. To begin with, there are often material advantages to the citizens of the suitor nations from tighter economic integration – and, according to the new orthodoxy, deep and successful economic union requires some form of political and social union. But still more can be said for the political culture that might emerge in any successful poly-national federation, where ethnic pluralism and diversity are not just tolerated but celebrated, and where confident linguistic and cultural communities thrive in part because their virtues and artefacts are appreciated by members of neighbouring communities. Of course, countries such as Canada and Belgium, stand as reminders of how difficult such federal utopia may be to achieve, even among tolerant and democratic peoples. But, as with democracy and social justice, an ideal is not necessarily tarnished by its being, as yet, rarely and incompletely realized.

Now all of these virtues of federation are premised on the possibility of identifying and developing a 'well-designed federal system.' A poorly designed federal system may well serve no participating nation's long-term interests. In what follows, I attempt to 'unpack,' and then assemble in the form of a theory, the complex of normative and empirical factors involved in evaluation and design of a federal arrangement.[10]

Towards a Theory of Federative Justice

Until recently, federal arrangements, like the international relations, were thought to be primarily matters that were appropriately determined by pragmatic rather than moral considerations. (This is at least part of the explanation for why political philosophers have largely ignored both of these domains[11] preferring instead to take the frontiers of the near-mythical nation-state to be the boundaries of their discipline.) In Canada, at least, this is clearly no longer the case. All major constitutional proposals – including Quebec's demands for 'distinct society' status and veto power over institutional change, Aboriginal claims to an inherent right to self-government, and outlying provinces' desires for a so-called Triple-E senate – are now argued for explicitly on moral grounds. A normative theory of federation (or theory of federation justice – I use these terms interchangeably) is an attempt to evaluate and systematize these sorts of moral claims.

The approach that I outline here is contractarian. Roughly put, it recommends federal principles and institutions if they would have been selected by enlightened federal partners interested in developing a stable, mutually beneficial federation for the long haul. In ways that become clear below, this framework has the virtue of deriving realistic normative recommendations from largely empirical considerations – federal justice from mutual, national self-interest. This is because (again, very roughly) unjust federal arrangements are likely to be unstable in the long run. Such a contractarian approach, outlined below, enables us to organize and to balance the sorts of empirical considerations that are crucial to any design of political institutions. Of course, our knowledge of the relevant empirical facts is often sketchy and conjectural at best. For example, it is often impossible to say with a great degree of confidence what will be the likely effects on the political culture of the introduction of some new institution (such as Triple-E Senate or recognition of Quebec as a distinct society). But a comprehensive normative theory will enable us to see what is at stake when an institution has this or that effect.

Interlude: Some Preliminary Objections to Contractarian Federal Theory

Now students of political philosophy and students of history are likely to have two different sets of worries about the sort of federal contractarianism just sketched. Philosophers might voice two complaints. First, there are many types of contractarian theories: for example, some (such as Rawls's[12]) work from idealized bargaining situations involving rigorous constraints on information so that the hypothetical parties are prevented from tilting the contract unfairly in their favour; others (such as T.M. Scanlon's[13]) assume ordinary people with ordinary interests and knowledge who try to reach agreements that none of them could reasonably reject. More-over, while both Rawls's and Scanlon's theories try to model the idea of justice as impartiality, other contractarians, such as David Gauthier,[14] think of justice as mutual advantage and therefore see nothing inherently unjust about stronger parties bullying weaker parties into accepting an unequal deal. Different forms of contractarianism will result in very different sorts of principles, but it is not yet clear which sort of contract theory is being proposed here for a normative theory of federalism. Second, contractarianism as a moral methodology has not fared particularly well since it was revived by Rawls. It is criticized typically for giving a superfluous account of moral justification. Why then should it be reintroduced here?

Let me respond very briefly to these challenges, in part by accepting their criticism. In general, I believe that we are at such an early stage in understanding and systematizing the moral principles of federalism that high-level distinctions and debates imported from theories of justice are still largely irrelevant. (It is important for the history of aviation that the Wright brothers got a plane off the ground, but this did not require their understanding the aerodynamics necessary to break the sound barrier). At any rate, I think that there is reason to expect a fair bit of convergence on the sorts of federal principles that various contract models would elicit, although of course this would have to be demonstrated.

It can also be granted that even if the contract argument is superfluous for ultimate justification it is still useful for helping us to organize our moral intuitions and draw consistent inferences about principles and institutions from them. This, in effect, is how Rawls views the role of his social contract argument.[15] Further, even if contract arguments were misleading for theories of justice (because we never actually had or consented to a social contract), they might nevertheless be especially helpful in cases such as federal and international relations because these arrangements are usually the results of bargaining processes. A contract argument then will enable us to mirror closely the kinds of considerations that federating polities actually do take seriously, while allowing us to abstract away from obvious moral defects in real-world negotiations – such as short-sighted political expediency, lack of empirical and historical knowledge, and unfair bargaining strengths.

Historians are likely to have rather different concerns, they will rightly question the presumption that actual federations have usually been enlightened pacts between consenting polities. Often, as Robert Howse puts it, federalism is understood best 'as a political result born of necessity rather than choice – a stand-off between ethnic groups with claims on the same territory; a solution imposed on a weaker nationality by a stronger one; or a pact between communities who feared a common enemy even more than they distrusted one another.'[16]

All contractarian arguments are hypothetical. They assist us in organizing our intuitions about what is fair by referring to what would have been chosen by fictional parties in the appropriately described initial bargaining situation. Hence, it is irrelevant in the first instance whether there actually was a contract. This is not to deny, of course, that when evaluating the institutions and arrangements of any actual federation we must look at historical pacts, treaties, and traditions. Here, however, I sketch the basic structure of a normative theory for any modern, pluralistic, democratic federation. I treat as the basic case the situation of independent nations negotiating to form a just and stable federation.[17] Applying such a general theory to an actual federation will involve balancing its recommendations with the moral force of historical agreements.[18]

Historians and political sociologists may have an additional worry about the effects of having a contractarian theory of federalism current in the political culture of a poly-national federation. Many English-Canadian historians would point to what they believe have been the pernicious consequences of the myth of confederation as a pact among provinces or between 'two founding peoples.' This myth, they will argue, not only boosts the egos of provincial premiers but it develops a federal culture of 'elite accommodation' that ill serves the interests of the citizens of the federation.

With such critics I share the belief that a normative political theory is seriously compromised if the currency of its language and patterns of argumentation would be dangerous in a political culture.[19] In this case, however, it is not a normative theory that is alleged to corrupt the political culture, but rather a supposedly mistaken view of history and constitutional law. At any rate, the normative language of a contractarian theory will be not necessarily that of a compact but rather that of the federal principles that the contract argument generates (for example, Rawls would have citizens arguing from his two principles of justice, not from the original position).

End of Interlude: Agreeing to Just Terms of Federation

An adequate normative theory of federalism must be able to answer two questions. What terms should federal partners accept as the basis of their federation? And what should be their grounds for accepting these terms?

The relevance of the second question may not be immediately apparent. But as I argue, an answer is crucial to the success and stability of a pluralistic federation. Consider the analogy of a marriage. There are certain terms and obligations, legal and otherwise, that partners accept when they wed. But their accepting these terms at that time is obviously no guarantee that the union will be long or successful. It matters how and why they accept the contract. A partner marrying for money will be unwilling to stay when the money runs out. A union is more likely to survive if based on true love and mutual respect. Similarly, the terms of a federal union must be accepted on the basis of some analogue of true love and mutual respect. The parallel need not be very direct. Flemings and Walloons don't have to love each other or each other's cultures. Without some moral or quasi-moral bond between federating polities, however, one side or the other will quickly sour of the relationship when short- to medium-term considerations suggest that it could be doing better out of the federation. Failure to recognize or appreciate the need for this moral bond has, I believe, been the great shortcoming of much of the theory and practice of federalism around the world.

In order to develop a language and a normative framework for evaluating the grounds or bases of federal marriages, I recommend adapting a version of Rawls's recent overlapping consensus theory of justice.[20]

Federalism as Overlapping Consensus

It is not necessary for me to explain in much detail, let alone to defend, Rawls's own overlapping-consensus theory of justice. Rawls does not apply this model to the problems of federalism.[21] In adapting it for the case of federalism, it is an open question whether I am applying and extending his theory or developing an analogous one. Given more space, I would argue for the latter interpretation, and thus this theory of federative justice will sink or swim on its own, regardless of the truth or falsity of Rawls's more general conception of justice. In fact, the new federal theory should be able to overcome at least some of the criticisms directed at Rawls's theory – for example, that it is overly concerned, as a theory of justice, with the problem of stability. Surely nobody would deny that stability is a primary requirement for a well-functioning federation. Given the enormous political energy and will that a successful federation requires – not to mention the possibility of major economic adjustments – potential partners have little motivation to federate if they cannot reasonably expect the relationship to thrive.

For Rawls, consensus around a liberal conception of justice is the only

viable basis for a stable social union in modern democratic societies characterized by what he calls the fact of pluralism. This fact of commonsense
sociology is that citizens have, and will continue to have, competing,
comprehensive moral conceptions that involve different convictions about
what makes life valuable and what metaphysical, religious, or moral theories ground such beliefs. The fact of pluralism, then, rules out the first of
three possible bases of social union – universal acceptance of some particular comprehensive moral doctrine. Such agreement would require
state coercion incompatible with democracy. A second possibility would
be modus vivendi agreement on basic principles of cooperation between
groups of individuals with differing comprehensive moral doctrines,
adopted by each party on the basis of its self- (or group) interest. Rawls
does not deny that this basis is consistent with the demands of democracy. But he argues against such a conception of justice because it is
inherently unstable, given its dependence on 'happenstance and a balance of relative forces.' As the history of international relations demonstrates so clearly, such agreements tend to evaporate when changes in
relative strength make breaking them more advantageous than keeping
them.

Rawls's third possible basis for social union borrows the best from the
other two. This is the idea of finding an overlapping consensus around a
political conception of justice. Unlike a modus vivendi, an overlapping
consensus is a moral commitment to social union and thus less prone to
desertion when it is to one party's advantage. And unlike a comprehensive moral doctrine, it demands only limited moral commitment. It can
be adopted by people with differing comprehensive doctrines and justified varyingly, according to those same doctrines.

In adapting overlapping-consensus theory for federal relations, we retain the following key elements and motivations of Rawls's theory. First,
we attempt to find just rules to serve as a stable basis of cooperation (now
and between federal partners), given the fact of pluralism (the persistence
of divergent conceptions of citizenship and cultural membership based,
for example, on national, linguistic, ethnic, or regional identities, affiliations, or concerns). Second, we identify three types of federal commitment – 'comprehensive,' 'modus vivendi,' and 'overlapping consensus' –
which are analogous to Rawls's.

Let us assume that democratic states (or potential states) would not
band (or remain) together in a federation if they did not perceive it to
be to their mutual advantage. It does not follow, however, that federal
relations are nothing more than a modus vivendi. In fact, for reasons

parallel to those advanced by Rawls, it is reasonable to suppose that a federation based merely on a modus vivendi – one in which pan-federal identifications and solidarity do not develop – will remain inherently unstable: a partner that had for generations been a net beneficiary might defect the moment it felt called upon to be a net contributor.

At the same time, federations differ from unitary states because federal partners (and their citizens) did not want to relinquish all of their autonomy, sovereignty, and identity. This is already a reason to believe that federal partners do not have to or wish to accept deep, monolithic conceptions of citizenship and identity as the basis of their union. We can go further and say that they do not all have to share the same reasons for accepting the federal union and their citizens do not have to identify with the federal state in the same way or to the same extent. The most suitable basis for a just and stable federal union will thus be some form of overlapping consensus that demands more of federal partners and their citizens than a modus vivendi, but less than a comprehensive, monolithic conception of shared identity and citizenship.

Overlapping-Consensus Theory in Canadian Federalism

I believe that it is something close to a necessary condition for the acceptability of an overlapping-consensus theory of federation that it be able to categorize the principles used in actual debates in actual federations according to Rawls's three bases for union (or types of federal commitment). If classes of important normative arguments for federal arrangements cannot even be recognized by this conceptual scheme, then it is defective. If it turns out that competing federal principles do fit fairly neatly into these three slots, and if seeing them in this way helps to clarify federal debates, then I would count this as a significant achievement for the theory. In this section, I suggest that there are encouraging reasons to believe that Canadian constitutional discussions are explicated by Rawls's categories.[22] In sketching how that may be so, I also try to clarify a bit more the distinction between these three kinds of federal commitment.

The three possible bases for social union, along with a preference for overlapping consensus, seem to be summed up elegantly, for example, by Henri Bourassa, in 1904, in his reply to the nationalist editor of *La Vérité*, J.-P. Tardivel: 'We also want to "defend and develop our own [French-Canadian] nationality"; but we think that is only part of our job; we believe that this special development can and must come about in conjunction with the development of a more general patriotism *that unifies us, without fusing us*, to "the other elements that make up the population of Canada.'"[23] Bourassa is, in effect, denying Tardivel's false dichotomy between the modus vivendi of French-Canadian nationalism[24] and loss of French-Canadian identity to a monolithic, pan-Canadian nationalism. The more desirable alternative, for Bourassa, is a 'general patriotism' based on an overlapping consensus that 'unifies us, without fusing us.'[25]

I am fairly confident that Canada's most recent constitutional contortions fall easily along this grid. Overlapping consensus represented the official rationale of the most committed supporters of the Meech Lake Accord of 1987 (although there is no reason to believe that overlapping-consensus theory would necessarily have required supporting Meech). The accord, they claimed, would allow Quebecers to embrace Canada and its constitution 'with honour and enthusiasm' – a clear moral or quasi-moral step beyond modus vivendi – while recognizing, in effect, their divergent conception of citizenship and national identification.[26] It would permit, even encourage, Quebecers to be Canadians, but of a distinct type. Similar sorts of accommodation had been urged by the (Laurendeau-Dunton) Royal Commission on Bilingualism and Biculturalism (1963–71) and the (Pepin-Robarts) Task Force on Canadian Unity (1977–9) and would be recommended again, after the collapse in 1990 of Meech Lake, by the Spicer Commission.

Not all opponents of the accord were against overlapping-consensus federalism. Some may have been supporters of such a principle but opposed Meech Lake for other reasons (its rigid amending formula, its symmetrical decentralization) or because they believed that it would only fuel the kind of nationalism in Quebec that could never see relations with the rest of Canada as more (and often less) than a shrewd modus vivendi. These critics were not, however, the most vocal opponents. Historians will no doubt emphasize the role played by Pierre Trudeau, Clyde Wells, and their followers and advisers, who opposed the accord because their commitments to normative federal principles of a more comprehensive type precluded the idea of an overlapping consensus.[27] Comprehensive principles are also claimed by Quebec nationalists, among others, to lie at the heart of the Constitution Act of 1982: its Charter of Rights and Freedoms, they claimed (usually without supporting argument), defines too deep a common standard of citizenship for all Canadians.

Modus vivendi principles were not prominent during the Meech Lake debate. I suppose this would have been the best way to characterize the lukewarm reaction of the Parti québécois, which saw the accord as at best an absolute minimum demand from the point of view of Quebec's interests. Nevertheless, such a conception of 'Quebec-Canada' relations (the emergence of this expression is itself revealing) struck with a vengeance after the death of Meech Lake in June 1990. It rang clear as a bell in the Quebec's Allaire and Bélanger-Campeau reports and is heard increasingly from those, especially in western Canada, who have grown impatient with what they see as futile attempts to accommodate Quebec.

Overlapping Consensus about What?

The survey in the preceding sub-section was intended only to suggest that the three categories of federal commitment are useful in mapping out debates over federal principles and visions. We have yet to examine the ultimate merits of normative theories of federalism based on these different types of commitment. Such a contest is still premature, for we do not yet have a clear idea of what the overlapping-consensus theory would look like and how exactly it is to be distinguished from a more comprehensive theory. In this final sub-section, I begin some of this task of clarification.

In order to develop this theory so that it will have real normative effect, we must begin to identify in a general way the 'content' of the overlapping consensus.[28] What is it that federal partners must be willing to embrace together, and what may they remain free to pursue and develop in their own ways? We can start to answer this question in two stages – this will still amount to little more than a sketch to guide extensive empirical and normative research.

First, we can identify the sorts of concrete institutional arrangements that must be the legal basis of any federation. These include constitutional agreement on division of powers; design and functioning of, and representation in, federal institutions such as legislature, a supreme court, and a central bank; and integration of markets and legal systems. Political scientists and legal theorists who have addressed quasi-normative questions about federal design have tended to focus on such institutional questions.[29] Yet agreement on a constitutional set-up such as this remains neutral among three kinds of federal commitment and hence, if I am correct, fails to deal with some of the most critical considerations relevant to the long-term justice and stability of a pluralistic federation.

Second, we can specify the 'domain' of the overlapping consensus, a more difficult task. Let us think first of the most basic case – a federation among previously independent nations. And again, although such nations will have decided to federate probably for reasons of mutual self-interest, they must also realize that such a modus vivendi will be unstable.[30] They must, therefore, be willing to commit themselves to various measures to encourage development out of this modus vivendi of a moral commitment to the new federal state. These measures form the second layer of the overlapping consensus. How are they to be identified? We can consider a positive and a negative route to the same end. On the one hand, we can imagine of what this moral commitment might positively consist. We may think of it as, say, a developing sense of solidarity among the citizens of the new federation or as emergence of a new pan-national identity. We could then identify the domain of the overlapping consenses by considering what sorts of institutions and policies are necessary or useful for engendering such sense of solidarity or identity.[31] On the other hand (and this is the strategy that I would recommend), we might begin by enumerating a list of casual factors likely to destabilize a pluralistic federation. (Such a list is fairly easily gleaned from the experiences of unsuccessful and less-than-wholly-successful federations such as Belgium and Canada.[32]) These factors include the perception by the citizens of any sub-unit (in Canadian terms, a province) that it is unfairly disadvantaged in the federation or that it is under-represented in key federal institutions; mutual lack of understanding among citizens and political elites of different regions or provinces of each others' political, economic, or cultural situation; divergent perceptions of the history and prehistory of the federation; mutual distrust concerning, say, the use by other federal partners or their politicians of federal institutions; and resentment by one national, ethnic, linguistic, or religious group that is a majority in one province concerning treatment of its own people who are a minority in another province. Many of these factors are, of course, related. Lack of mutual understanding and mutual mistrust, for example, feed on each other. A successful federation will be one that anticipates these potential federation-busters and develops concrete institutions and policies, and, less concretely, a federal political culture, that lessen their impact. This, in short, is how I suggest that we can most realistically expect to specify in a general way for all or most pluralistic federations, and in a specific way for any particular federation, the content of the overlapping consensus.

'Nation-building' in a modern democratic federation – one that is not forged by war or coercive homogenization – is a matter largely of visionary anticipation of federal frictions, combined with pragmatic, cooperative measures to smooth them out. These measures need not all be considered negative and defensive; some may be positive or 'pre-emptive.' It is an interesting question none the less (albeit one that I cannot pursue here[33]) what sorts of positive steps in forging a pan-national identity of patriotism the liberal federal state may or may not be permitted to take. The ultimate hope of the builders of a poly-national federal nation must be that if peoples live, work, and vote together long enough, in a political culture that avoids unnecessary ethnic conflicts, they will come to feel at home with each other and part of a common destiny. While this hope may seem unrealistic in a world with resurgent nationalism and ethnic particularism, rarely has a pluralistic federation been designed with the sort of foresight that facilitates relatively frictionless coexistence – certainly Belgium, Canada, Czechoslovakia, the Soviet Union, and Yugoslavia were not.

To understand how the content of overlapping consensus helps us to organize and clarify what is morally important in the design of a federation, consider the following two cases: the role of a language policy and control of nationalism.

Language Policy

In a linguistically diverse federation, language policy can be employed against several of the above-listed potential federation-busters.[34] Absence of a lingua franca and substantial bilingualism (or multilingualism) will render systematic mutual misunderstanding and mistrust probable; a common culture is unlikely to develop, since citizens of different languages will not read the same newspapers or books, idolize the same celebrities, or laugh with the same humorists; there is potential for injustice in allocation of jobs and key decision-making roles in the federal bureaucracy; and diverse battles may be fought over rights for minority-language services and education. Federal partners in such a state, then, clearly have both a material and a moral obligation to develop a language policy that will mitigate these factors which both threaten development of a stable overlapping consensus and lead to specific injustices. Of course, exactly which language policy any given multilingual federal state ought to develop is an open and difficult question: a policy that works reasonably well in the political culture of one country would often prove disastrous in another.[35]

Control of Nationalism

Another example concerning the terms of the federation that demonstrates some of the moral bite of the overlapping-consensus model is found in the problem of nationalism. When its appetite is sufficiently whetted, nationalism, almost by definition, is sated with nothing less or more than a nation-state. Its hunger is generated by, and it in turn encourages, many of the conditions isolated above as federation-busters. Hence federating partners must treat the fact and potential of nationalism seriously and search, from the outset, for institutions that will help to deprive it of sustenance. Again, in the aftermath of the break-up of the Soviet Union and Yugoslavia, and potentially of Belgium and Canada, we cannot underestimate how resistant and persistent a menace nationalism is to a federation. I do not presume that any of this is surprising.

The contractual model that I am proposing here may, however, have an interesting implication for nationalism. It would seem to show why it is morally incumbent on any nation wishing to enter or remain in a federation that it or, properly speaking, its government pledge to do what it can to discourage nationalist sentiment in its domain. Otherwise it would be, at the very least, entering into (or remaining in) a mutually beneficial federal arrangement in bad faith. This is certainly the case, in normal circumstances, if a provincial government actually works to encourage such nationalist sentiments, say, as a way of driving a harder bargain with its federal partners. It is, I believe, a virtue of a normative theory of federation that it enables us to see the peculiar form of injustice in such a situation. (It goes without saying that we would need many more details, both in the theory and in a historical situation, to make a judgment against any specific government at a particular time.)

Of course, I do not mean naively to suggest that nationalism can be turned on or off by disputes or agreements among polities' elites. Nationalism is an extremely complex sociological phenomenon that is generated and sustained by a wide range of factors in the political institutions and culture of a state. It differs from nation to nation and evolves markedly over time. Controlling nationalism within a tolerant, culturally plural federal state will always be potentially tricky, because it is often not easy for people to recognize the subtle but crucial distinction between the task of preserving languages and cultures that is one of the raisons d'être of the federation and the nationalist's desire to have sovereign control over the territory in which the nation is a majority. The contract model suggests that federating parties must recognize and appreciate the threat of nationalism not only to the continued unity of the federal state but also to its effective governance, since continued rearguard action to preserve the state siphons political energy and attention from other concerns, and they must use any (unfortunately limited) knowledge afforded by history and political sociology to design institutions that will forestall the attractions of nationalism. Some (especially from the United States) might argue that the latter provision requires visionary resolve to implement assimilationist policies that will lead to elimination of strong sub-national identities. Louisiana, they might note, does not cause the United States the sorts of 'problems' that Quebec causes Canada. It is unlikely, however, that the contract model would sanction the assimilationist's terms. For one thing, it is empirically unsound, in most situations, to assume that attempts to assimilate linguistic and cultural minorities – a process that, except in the most brutal regimes, takes many generations – will dampen rather than fuel nationalist fervour. And for another, it would be morally unreasonable to demand (on whatever time-frame) that a federating partner should have to agree to give up its language and culture. Put another way, one could imagine a federating nation accepting such terms of federation only under the sort of extreme duress that a fair contracting situation would, by definition, not allow.

A more reasonable and just alternative to assimilation would presumably try to asphyxiate nationalism by addressing the genuine fears and insecurities that are its oxygen. This is easier said than done, since nationalism, like other forms of populism, can survive for some time with the artificially supplied oxygen of unfounded or manufactured fears and insecurities. Still, the hope must be that nationalists cannot thrive indefinitely in the face of transparently just arrangements that address the genuine fears and insecurities of members of minority sub-nations (concerning, for example, loss of a language or culture or less-than-equal opportunities for success by members of a minority group). Of course, these fears must be dealt with in a manner that is just, and perceived to be just, by the members of the other federating groups, or frictions will arise. In addition, they must be addressed in ways that will also facilitate the flourishing of pan-national affiliations and identities among national minorities.

Now these three requirements – to assuage national minorities' fears justly, effectively, and in ways that encourage pan-national identities – will demand careful consideration of the division of powers between the central and sub-unit governments. Pierre Trudeau, and more recently Howse, have argued, that nationalism will never be eliminated as long as national minorities look to the government of their sub-unit, rather than to the federal government, for cultural and economic advancement.[36] Although I believe Trudeau and Howse overstate their case, they are certainly right in emphasizing the implications for nationalism of constitutional decisions on the key terms of the federal contract: division of powers and representation of national minorities in federal institutions. Again, I believe that our current, and in all likelihood future, knowledge of political sociology will always be insufficient for predicting accurately the effects of federal institutions on political culture. Still, although we are myopic, we are not blind. It is quite likely that the decisions that actual federating parties take on division of powers, for example, will usually be less than visionary – and ultimately, therefore, less than federally just – given their desire as governing elites in the new sub-units to maintain as much control as possible over the cultural direction of their peoples.

Conclusion

An initial sketch of a theory must arbitrarily end somewhere, lest it begin to resemble a full-fledged portrait – or worse, a doodle. I do not pretend that the outline so far really constitutes much of an argument for a theory of overlapping-consensus federalism. I hope that this discussion encourages at least some readers to see that there are a whole range of normative problems concerning federalism that deserve some kind of systematic philosophical attention. It is a virtue of the overlapping-consensus model recommended here, I believe, that it identifies and deals with normative issues in close conjunction with empirical and historical concerns. A normative theory of federation must respect the fact that well-functioning federal arrangements are likely to vary drastically around the world and across time – much more so, I would guess, than 'regular' democratic institutions. Any normative theory of federation, therefore, that takes, instead, the abstract and universalistic route – for example, by working out ideal principles of federal equality or generalized conceptual and moral relations among notions of cultural identity, sovereignty, national autonomy, destiny, and the like – will vastly underdetermine its applied recommendations. Although we can find much to admire in a universalistic conception of justice, such as Kant's, we could only laugh at a platonic Form of federalism. What we need, rather, is a theory to help us organize and systematize our intuitions about just and appropriate federal relations and to elicit their implications for more complicated cases. In this chapter, I have done little more than propose a research program for developing such a theory.

Notes

I owe more than the usual intellectual debts to Allen Buchanan, Robert Howse, Will Kymlicka, Guy Laforest, Phil Lancaster, Don Lenihan, Ann Levey, Philimon Peonidis, John Rawls, and Don Ross for their comments on earlier versions of this chapter. Parts of it were also delivered to the Department of Philosophy at the Universitat de les Illes Balears, in Palma, Majorca, Spain, and to the annual conference of the Canadian Philosophical Association in Charlottetown in May 1992.

This paper is dedicated to the memory of Pauline Jewett – a great Canadian patriot and federalist and an esteemed colleague of mine for two years at the Network on the Constitution.

1 I completed this chapter one month before the signing of the ill-fated Charlottetown Accord in August 1992. I see that document as grounded in principles similar to those underlying the Meech Lake Accord, which is discussed below in the sub-section 'Overlapping-Consensus Theory in Canadian Federalism.'
2 See Kymlicka's chapter (no. 1) in this volume.
3 See Allan C. Cairns 'The Case for Charter-Federalism' *Network* 2 (Ottawa: Network on the Constitution, June–July 1992) and "Constitutional Government and the Two Faces of Ethnicity' paper presented to the Conference on Federalism and the Nation State, at the Centre for International Studies, University of Toronto, June 1992. The preceding paragraph, and much else in this chapter, owe a great deal to these and other recent writings of Cairns's.
4 See Cairns 'Constitutional Government.'
5 See Alan C. Cairns *Charter versus Federalism: The Dilemmas of Constitutional Reform* (Montreal and Kingston: McGill-Queen's Press 1992) 57, 93ff.
6 The only contemporary book-length study of federalism of which I am aware that contains a substantial contribution by philosophers is Stanley G. French ed *Philosophers Look at Canadian Federation* (Montreal: Canadian Philosophical Association 1979). See also Charles Taylor 'Shared and Divergent Values' in R.L. Watts and D.M. Brown eds *Options for a New Canada* (Toronto: University of Toronto Press 1991) 53–76 and 'The Politics of Recognition' in D.M. Brown, R. Young, and D. Herperger eds *Constitutional Commentaries: An Assessment of the 1991 Federal Proposals* Reflections No. 10 (Kingston: Institute

of Inter-governmental Relations 1991) 67–71. Allen Buchanan's *Secession: The Morality of Political Divorce from Fort Sumter to Lithuania and Quebec* (Boulder, Col.: Westview Press 1991) is a model philosophical contribution to an important aspect of a normative theory of federation (or defederation). Despite some profound disagreements, I find the most impressive marriage of philosophical, legal, and sociological acumen currently being directed at the problems of federalism in the writings of Robert Howse. See his *Economic Union, Social Justice, and Constitutional Reform: Towards a High But Level Playing Field* (North York, Ont.: York University Centre for Public Law and Public Policy 1992) and 'Is Federalism the Future?' paper presented to the Conference on Federalism and Nation State, at the Centre for International Studies, University of Toronto, June 1992. The remarks in the text are not intended to slight theorists from law and political science who have, of course, raised the study of federalism to a high level with no help at all from political philosophers. My only claim is that philosophers should be able to make as significant a contribution to normative federal theories as they have to theories of justice and democracy. Let us not forget that the welfare state was invented, developed, and publicly justified long before most political philosophers took note; but let us also not forget Rawls. Modern federal theory, one might say, awaits its Rawls.

In the history of modern political philosophy, questions of federalism have rarely attracted more than a footnote or a chapter. Cursory discussion can be found in the writings of Bodin, Grotius, Montesquieu, Bentham, Constant, J.S. Mill, and Sidgwick. Rousseau is said to have produced a major work on federation that was destroyed during the French Revolution, leaving nothing from him beyond a few remarks in *Social Contract* and *Government of Poland*. Kant is responsible for the most extensive federal writings by a great philosopher, and the utopian Proudhon devoted a book to the 'federal principle.' There have always of course, been important philosophical contributions by perceptive political sociologists such as Madison, Calhoun, and Tocqueville. For discussions of, and references to, these works, see Daniel J. Elazar *Exploring Federalism* (Tuscaloosa: University of Alabama Press 1987) 115–53 and Murray Forsyth *Unions of States: The Theory and Practice of Confederation* (Leicester: Leicester University Press 1981) 73–159.

7 See Anthony Smith *National Identity* (London: Penguin 1991) 170–6.

8 See Kymlicka's chapter (no. 1) in this volume and his *Liberalism, Community, and Culture* (Oxford: Oxford University Press 1989) chaps. 7 and 8.

9 Ernest Gellner *Nations and Nationalism* (Oxford: Blackwell 1983), quoted in Alan C. Cairns 'Constitutional Government.'

10 I often use terms such as 'federal arrangement' or 'federation' in a broad

sense, which includes a wide range of associations, from Canadian or American federalism to European Community – style confederation and sovereignty-association. It is, in effect, an open question how tight any given federal arrangement ought to be.

11 According to Brian Barry – who ought to know – the first book-length study of the justice of international relations by an Anglo-American philosopher was Charles Beitz's *Political Theory and International Relations* (Princeton, NJ: Princeton University Press 1979).

12 See John Rawls *A Theory of Justice* (Cambridge, Mass.: Harvard University Press 1971). For a helpful survey and critique of social-contract theories, see Will Kymlicka 'The Social Contract Tradition' in Peter Singer ed *A Companion to Ethics* (Oxford: Blackwell 1991).

13 T.M. Scanlon 'Contractualism and Utilitarianism' in A. Sen and B. Williams eds *Utilitarianism and Beyond* (Cambridge: Cambridge University Press 1982).

14 David Gauthier *Morals by Agreement* (Oxford: Oxford University Press 1986).

15 See Rawls *Theory* 18.

16 Howse 'Is Federalism the Future?'

17 Note that while few existing federations may have been formed this way, this may be the wave of the future, led of course by the European Community and followed, potentially, by some successor to the Commonwealth of Independent States.

18 A parallel tradeoff of historical and abstract-egalitarian considerations for Aboriginal rights is discussed by Kymlicka in chapter 1, above.

19 A stock criticism of 'Government House Utilitarianism' raises a similar point in questioning the consistency (and elitism) of those who must urge, on utilitarian grounds, that citizens not be encouraged to apply utilitarian morality. I have discussed other perplexing examples of this general objection in 'Démocratie juste ou justice démocratique?' *Cahiers de philosophie politique et juridique* 19 (1990) 109–24 and in 'Democratic Theory for a Democratising World? A Reassessment of Popper's Political Realism' *Political Studies* 41 (1993) 252–68.

20 The roots of this theory can be found in part 3 of Rawls *Theory*. He develops it explicitly in 'Justice as Fairness: Political not Metaphysical' *Philosophy and Public Affairs* 14 no. 3 (1985) 223–51, 'The Idea of an Overlapping Consensus' *Oxford Journal of Legal Studies* 7 no. 1 (1987) 1–25, and 'The Domain of the Political and Overlapping Consensus' *New York University Law Review* 64 no. 2 (1989) 233–55.

21 Indeed, as an indication of how mainstream political philosophy has ignored problems of federative justice, I know of no place where Rawls has even used the word 'federalism.'

22 Since I am trying to propose a general normative theory of federation – one that would evaluate the justice of federal relations in any modern, pluralistic, democratic federation – it is not of course sufficient to show that it works well for Canadian debate. I would consider the theory to be inadequate if, say, the competing visions of the founders and 'developers' of the European Community could not be explicated by Rawls's categories.

Note: in this section I discuss only one dimension of these debates – relations between French and English Canada, or, latterly, between Quebec and the rest of Canada.

23 J.-P. Tardivel and Henri Bourassa 'A Controversy' in Ramsay Cook ed *French-Canadian Nationalism: An Anthology* (Toronto: Macmillan 1969) 149, my emphasis.

24 Tardivel had claimed that 'our job as French Canadians [is] the defence and development of our own nationality. The other elements [of Canada] are in a good position to defend and develop themselves without our help'; ibid.

25 Bourassa gives substance to these distinctions in his 1902 pamphlet 'French Canadian Patriotism: What It Is, and What It Ought to Be,' reprinted in Cook ed *French-Canadian Nationalism.* See especially the sections 'Duties to Canada and English Canadians' and 'Duties to Ourselves.'

26 For a philosophically sophisticated formulation of this argument, see Taylor 'Shared and Divergent Values' and 'The Politics of Recognition.'

27 There may be subtle but important differences in the motivations of Trudeau and Wells on this point. Trudeau's hatred and fear of Quebec nationalism, and his conviction that there can be no stable Canadian Federation until nationalism is extinguished, hamper our ability to surmise the ultimate rationale for his normative federal principles. Perhaps he could live with significantly distinct status for Quebec if he could be assured that this would not fuel a nationalism content only with independence. Wells seemed, if anything, unalarmed by nationalism. He appeared truly to be surprised by the rise of nationalist sentiments in Quebec after the death of Meech Lake. His opposition to the asymmetry in the accord was derived explicitly from a commitment to principles of equality of provinces and uniformity of citizenship – that we must all define ourselves as Canadians first, and residents of this or that province second. Such a view, it seems to me, is as good a candidate as any in the contemporary debate for the status of what I have been calling a comprehensive federal principle.

28 I say identify in a 'general' way because we will expect any particular federation to be based on quite specific institutional agreements – a certain parliamentary system or language policy.

29 See, for example, the once-standard text, K.C. Wheare *Federal Government* fourth ed (Oxford: Oxford University Press 1963).

30 It is, of course, misleading to think of nations simply deciding to federate. More probably they began by seeking a trade or military treaty – again, for reasons of mutual advantage – only to find that the advantages of such a relation could increase with further political integration. But again, it makes sense to begin by considering the basic case of voluntary federation by previously independent states or colonies.

31 I have examined this strategy at some length in 'Unité, identité et nationalisme libéral' *Lekton* 3 (1994) 35–64.

32 The question of why federations fail is discussed extensively in the literature of comparative federalism. See, for example, Thomas. M. Franck ed *Why Federations Fail: An Inquiry into the Requisites for Successful Federalism* (New York: New York University Press 1968); Elazar *Exploring Federalism* 240–51; and Ursula K. Hicks *Federalism: failure and Success: A Comparative Study* (London: Macmillan 1978).

33 See my 'Unité, identité et nationalisme libéral.'

34 This is not to deny, of course, that there can be more-or-less independent grounds of justice for certain provisions of language policy. See Leslie Green and Denise Réaume 'Bilingualism, Territorialism, and Linguistic Justice' in *Network* 1 no. 3 (Ottawa: Network on the Constitution, July 1991) 9–11.

35 This point is illustrated well by Pierre Laberge in an unpublished paper, 'X devrait-il adopter le modèle linguistique de Y?' See also Kenneth D. McRae, *Conflict and Compromise in Multilingual Societies: Switzerland* (Waterloo, Ont.: Wilfrid Laurier University Press 1983) and *Conflict and Compromise in Multilingual Societies: Belgium* (Waterloo, Ont.: Wilfrid Laurier University Press 1986).

36 See P.E. Trudeau *Federalism and the French Canadians* (Toronto: Macmillan 1968) and 'The Values of a Just Society' in P.E. Trudeau and Tom Axworthy eds *Toward a Just Society* (Toronto: Viking Press 1990) 357–404; and Howse 'Is Federalism the Future?'

5

Internal Minorities and Their Rights

LESLIE GREEN

Because the persecuting majority is vile, says the liberal, *therefore* the persecuted minority must be stainlessly pure. Can't you see what nonsense that is? What's to prevent the bad from being persecuted by the worse?[1]

The Problem: Minorities within Minorities

We acknowledge the rights of minorities in order to protect some of their urgent interests, even against the otherwise legitimate claims of the majority. Thus ethnic, cultural, religious, or sexual minorities end up with rights that are, in a certain way, rights against the majority. But these minority groups are rarely homogeneous; they often contain other minorities. The Scots are a minority nation within the United Kingdom, and the Gaelic-speaking are a minority among Scots. Mennonites are a religious minority, and gays are a minority among Mennonites. In this paper, I want to explore the moral standing of such internal minorities.

The issue is urgent in both theory and practice. Some of the ways in which we try to ensure that minorities are not oppressed by majorities make it more likely that those minorities are able to oppress their own internal minorities. For example, we sometimes accord religious or cultural minorities special rights to self-determination. But as students of international relations know, the right to non-interference in internal matters is the first refuge of a government intent on violating rights. In a parallel way, the special rights of minority groups can empower them to make decisions that persecute their own internal minorities. What then should be done?

This problem is relevant to any political theory that attaches significant weight to the value of personal autonomy, but it is especially important

to modern liberalism. It is often said that liberals are atomistic individualists, concerned to protect people against the predations of the state
and thus blind to important values of solidarity and community. The
picture is familiar enough to need no elaboration. Nonetheless it is wrong.
For the individuals in the historically dominant forms of liberalism are
not isolated monads; they are members of families, churches, ethnic
groups, nations, and so on. Indeed, it was group-based strife – particularly seventeenth-century wars of religion – that gave birth to central
elements of the liberal tradition. The struggles to secure civil liberties,
limit the powers of government, and the like were motivated less by
social atomism than by what we might call molecularism – acknowledgment that among the most significant constituents of civil society are
overlapping social groups. And for liberals this is not merely a brute fact
to be noticed and accommodated; it is something to be fostered and
celebrated, for it is partly through such associations that people find
value and meaning in their lives. Liberals (and even some libertarians[2])
defend political freedom in order to promote experiments in living, but
these experiments are normally joint ventures.

Misguided emphasis on the supposed atomism of the liberal tradition
has thus occluded a more important risk: liberalism may become an un-
critical booster of civil society. So, far from being unrelentingly individualistic, it is prone to a naive collectivism of the middle range. For the social
groups that it protects and promotes can themselves be enemies of liberal
values, as my epigraph from Christopher Isherwood suggests. Liberal theory
and practice secure the family from the interference of the state but rarely
protect women or children from the predations of the family.[3] They
secure religious liberty but permit religions to oppress their minority members. These issues are not framed well in the language of atomism.

Some liberals have noticed the problem. J.S. Mill, for example, was
alive to the risks of social, not just political, tyranny (although, as we shall
see, his response to it was not always adequate). But others have ignored
it. They suppose that if the point of a liberal society is to provide for
conditions of freedom in which diverse social groups may flourish then it
should not interfere with their internal constitutions. Fundamental principles of political morality are thus applied only at the molecular level.
Here, I examine and criticize some sources of that view.

Rights and Minority Groups

To grasp the problem better, it helps to consider the nature of rights. X
has a right, as I understand it,[4] only if X has an interest sufficiently

important to warrant holding others to be under some duties to respect or promote that interest. Rights are thus not merely correlates of duties on the part of others; they are the ground of such duties.

Collective Interests

When we speak of minority rights, whether in morality or in law, we may have in mind one of two things. The first is the rights that people have even when they are in the minority. The rights of communists to organize politically, or of gay men to sexual liberty, are of this sort. The fact that a communist or a gay man is properly held to enjoy these rights is not something that flows in any essential way from membership in a social group; it derives from an urgent, but individuated, interest. To be sure, freedom of political association and sexual liberty are valuable in part because of the forms of social interaction that they make possible. But they are individuated interests inasmuch as the individual's stake in these goods is itself sufficiently important to warrant holding others duty-bound. The interests command respect without waiting on the reinforcement of numbers.

In contrast, the second sort of rights is one that people have only because they are members of a certain minority group. The right of the Aboriginal inhabitants of North America to self-government is of this sort; the value of group membership is part of the ground of the right. Such rights exist because some of our most urgent interests lie not merely in individuated goods such as personal liberty and exclusive property but also in collective goods. These include things, such as clean air and national defence, that are public goods in the economists' sense: they are inexcludable and non-rival in consumption. If they are available for some, then there is no convenient way to prevent others from receiving them, and the quantity consumed by one person does not perceptibly limit the amount available to others. Other collective goods, though excludable, are non-rival in a deeper sense; their collective production or enjoyment is part of what constitutes their value. Self-government is like that, and so is life in a cultured society. These are supplied jointly, but only to those who participate; yet the fact of being in it together is part of their value.

While some theorists deny that collective interests of either sort can ground rights, I do not think that that position can be sustained, and I have argued against it elsewhere.[5] Certainly, there is no ground for the view that collective interests are, as a class, less urgent than individual interests. An individual's interest in some of the most central liberal rights, such as freedom of expression, is often quite weak; most people have greater interests in a healthy physical environment or in a climate of mutual tolerance. It is true that, in the case of collective interests, the benefits of rights are assignable only to a class (so that we cannot give a fully individuated answer to the question, 'For whose sake is this duty imposed?'). But that does not make them weak or diffuse, and the relevant class may be reasonably determinate. In such instances, it is hard to resist the conclusion that collective interests warrant holding others duty-bound and thus that they ground rights.

It is, of course, open to dispute just which collective interests are this important – that is a major question of substantive moral philosophy. I think that there is a moral right to clean air, and to a tolerant society, and sometimes to national self-determination, but not to a tradition of epic poetry or to general cultural survival. It is also a matter for argument whether these are appropriately thought of as 'collective rights.' But we do not need to resolve these issues here. It is enough that individuals have interests as members of a certain social group, in collective goods that serve their interests as members, but the duty to provide which would not be justified by the interests of any one individual taken alone.[6]

It seems to me that membership in some minority groups – for instance, certain ethnic, national, cultural, or religious communities – is bound up with significant collective interests of this kind. In such cases, in addition to the usual individual rights to personal liberty and associative freedom, there are further special rights to powers and resources needed for the existence of the group. Will Kymlicka has given one argument for such rights in the case of cultural minorities.[7] Our most important interest is in leading a good life, and as a necessary component of that we need the capacity to frame, pursue, and revise our conceptions of the good life. Testing and choosing for ourselves among the options are a major part of life's value. But no one chooses the options themselves; no one chooses the context of choice. And that being so, the cultural resources with which we find ourselves are among our unchosen circumstances of life. Through no fault of our own, and sometimes through no fault of anyone, the culture in which we begin provides an insecure foundation on which to build, If, for example, one is born to the cultural resources of most people of Canada's First Nations, one will find much of one's energy just going to secure those forms of community, language, and culture that others are able to take for granted. Even if one will ultimately kick away the ladder on which one has ascended, it must be strong enough to bear the initial weight. The special rights of minority cultures – the powers, liberties, and rights that go to strengthen them – can thus be understood and justified as a kind of ex ante compensation. They are not a compromise with the requirements of justice, but a consequence of them.

Notice that on this argument there is nothing about minority status as such that generates rights. It is just that the most vulnerable are those with the least powers and resources, and they are often, though not invariably, in the minority. Minority status is one imperfect correlate of social marginality. Some minorities, such as the rich, are extremely powerful; some majorities, such as women, are not. (That is why there is an affinity between the rights of women and the rights of minorities.) The main context in which minorities are disadvantaged as such is in majoritarian decision procedures such as voting, and those procedures are usually not the only way of settling things. (So while the rich might be outvoted, they are rarely outbid.)

Protection of Minorities

The argument from the value of cultural membership is one source of the special rights of minority groups; another familiar one is based on the interest in national self-determination. It might be objected,[8] however, that there are lots of cultural, ethnic, and religious minorities, yet we do not want to endorse endless special rights of the sort that we ascribe to Aboriginal peoples. That would be rights inflation, and it would introduce so many constraints on decision making that nothing could get done.

The objection contains both truth and falsehood. Of course, the self-government model is unlikely to be appropriate for all minorities. But that is only one extreme example of the kind of rights at issue. Other options include granting groups limited autonomy in certain areas (for instance, over education), exempting them from certain general obligations (such as military service), giving recognition to their divergent practices (as in marriage), supporting their distinctive institutions, and so on. These lesser forms of protection may not give the minorities everything that they want, or even need. But to have a right, it is not necessary that one have an interest so dominating that it warrants imposing a whole set of duties adequate for sufficient promotion of the interest. (Few rights of any sort are powerful enough to guarantee the interests that they protect.) The definition requires only that it be important enough to warrant imposing some duties on others (or depriving them of some powers, and so on[8]). It is reasonable to suppose that different minorities are in different positions, some entitled to substantial support, others to a minimum. And the minimum might be small enough or of such a character that it would be wrong to institutionalize it in the legal system, for that is always a further question. I am going to say little about these issues here, for we have enough problems just at the level of theory. But it is worth bearing in mind that questions of institutional design always need to be argued separately.

The Rights of Internal Minorities

If minority groups do have such rights, then it might seem that so must internal minorities. It is just a matter of logic: they too are minority groups, and they have two different majorities to contend with. So members of internal minority or marginal groups have, first, individual rights. Aboriginal women, for example, have a right to fair participation in the political institutions that govern them. And second, they may have collective rights as members of an internal minority group: if cultural membership can ground special rights, then so can membership in a sub-culture. Thus English-speaking Quebecers have, in addition to their individual rights of freedom of association and of expression, a collective right to the resources needed for their cultural and linguistic security.

The highly controversial character of the two examples just mentioned should already be enough to suggest that the argument cannot move so swiftly. It is often denied that Aboriginal women or anglophone Quebecers have the moral rights in question: their interests are thought to be embraced or excluded by the rights of the respective minorities of which they form parts. It is said that the patriarchal structure of some bands need not yield to the claims of women or that the visage linguistique of Quebec need not accommodate English. Now, it would be unsurprising if those views came from conservative or traditionalist quarters; what is interesting is that they are also endorsed by some liberals. The latter say that the autonomy of the bands frees them from having to conform to colonial European views about democracy, or that respect for the distinctive character of Quebec's society includes respect for its decisions about how to control its cultural environment. Familiar liberal values thus apply among, but not necessarily within, minority groups. How might liberals defend that double standard?

Two Claims

In both theory and popular ideology, two claims seem to be most persuasive. They centre on purported disanalogies between the situation of minority groups and that of their internal minorities. The first is that if members of internal minorities do not like the way that a minority group is treating them, they can exercise their powers of exit and simply leave the group. Consider the case of Rev. James Ferry, the Canadian Anglican priest dismissed for disobeying his bishop's order to abandon his gay lover. It may be heart-rending that Anglicans are entitled so to discriminate against sexual minorities; but some argue, if gays do not like it, they are free to leave the church. (And often do.) In contrast, a minority group is not free to leave the state or the broader society. Ferry is free to join another church or none; but where are Anglicans as a whole supposed to go?[9] States exercise compulsory jurisdiction, and even when they allow exit, they do so on their own – not necessarily favourable – terms. And one generally leaves a state only to go to another,[10] admission to which is even more closely regulated. In contrast, the minority groups that compose civil society are not like states or inclusive societies; they generally do allow exit, so those who regard themselves as harshly treated by their group are free to disaffiliate or assimilate to the majority. While Anglicans therefore have rights to religious freedom, gay Anglicans have no comparable rights to sexual freedom, at least not if they wish to hold holy office. Because religious liberty properly includes a measure of self-determination for sects, we should tolerate such local illiberalisms, goes the argument.

The second claim is that the internal majority–minority relationship differs from that between minority and majority with respect to relative power. One reason why we want to protect minorities is that they are relatively powerless to protect themselves. The majority is strong; the minority is not. So, while giving the First Nations special rights against the Canadian majority strengthens the weak as against the strong, to give other special rights to, say, Metis or urban Indians is to strengthen them as against an already weak group. Or again, to give the province of Quebec special powers to promote use of French strengthens that minority as against the continental majority; but to give special powers or immunities to Quebec's English would strengthen their hand as against the French, who are a weak group in the continental context.

This objection is frequently voiced by activists who, having suffered the

real consequences of their political vulnerability and internalized an identity of weakness, are now told that they are oppressors of their own
minorities. A lesbian feminist complains of bisexual activists: 'Who or
what has the power in the bisexual vision? Can activists really think that
lesbian feminists *oppress* them? ... Given our vulnerability, the priorities
of bisexual declarations are baffling: do oppression and phobia from the
gay world warrant more attention than, say, Jesse Helms or global capital-
ist patriarchy?'[11] The question of 'priorities' and of what kind of oppression warrants more attention might suggest that it is just a matter of
rank: first we deal with the oppression of minorities, then we get to the
internal minorities. It is understandable why Aboriginal women, Quebec's
anglophones, and bisexual women might not want to wait for self-government, Quebec independence, or gay liberation to have their say. But
in fact the second objection is not intended in this way. The asymmetries
in power are thought to undercut, and not merely delay, the rights of
internal minorities. The belief is that internal minorities should not have,
because they do not need, rights against the minorities themselves.

If these objections hold good, then internal minorities do not have the
same sort of rights as the minority groups themselves. And if that is so,
then a liberal regime is compatible with the existence and protection of
minority groups that treat some of their members badly and that, to be
more exact, act towards internal minorities in ways that would be con-
demned if practised by the larger community against the minorities.
There is no doubt that if Anglicans were subjected to the distress
and humiliation to which they subjected Rev. Ferry, they would regard it
as a clear violation of religious freedom. If the French language were
proscribed in the circumstances in which English is in Quebec, it would
be thought outrageous. If all Aboriginal bands were excluded from
national political power in the way in which the patriarchal bands
exclude women, it would be a corruption of democracy. So we need to
ask: are these objections – the arguments from exit and from relative
power – really compelling enough to deny rights to the internal minorities in question?

Exit and Justice

Let us consider first the argument from exit. Its root appeal rests in the
liberty principle itself: people ought not to be prevented from doing
those things that they freely and competently choose, provided that they

do not harm others. The apparent setback to the interests of internal minorities is thus tolerable, for they freely and completely choose to adhere to the minority groups of which they are members. The harms suffered, if any, are not done to 'others.'

This argument is sound only if members of minority groups do in fact have a fair chance to leave if mistreated. To see how rarely that is the case, one must assess the real prospects for exit.

Consider a clear violation of individual rights by a minority group.[12] David Thomas, a member of the Lyackson Indian Band in British Columbia, was forcibly and without consent captured and initiated into the ceremony of 'spirit dancing,' in the course of which he was assaulted, battered, and wrongfully confined. His captors (all members of other bands) defended their actions on the ground that they had a collective Aboriginal right to continue their traditions of spirit dancing, notwithstanding that this practice violated Thomas's individual rights to personal security. The court did not agree with them, and Thomas won his lawsuit. The judge held: 'He is free to believe in, and to practice, any religion or tradition, if he chooses to do so. He cannot be coerced or forced to participate in one by any group purporting to exercise their collective rights in doing so. His freedoms and rights are not subject to the collective rights of the aboriginal nation to which he belongs'.[13] Setting aside the legal issues, what exactly is the relationship between Thomas and the nation 'to which he belongs'?

Membership in this minority group, like that in many others, is partly ascriptive. Thomas was an Indian within the meaning of the Indian Act, but that was not his doing. He was also recognized by the nation as one of its own, but he testified that he had lived off the reserve most of his life, was not raised in the traditional religion or culture, knew little about it, and did not want to learn any more. And, of course, he did not consent to the initiation ceremony. Nonetheless, his abductors did not think that he had exercised any relevant power of exit: they still saw him as subject to their traditions. But what else could Thomas have done? Left the area? Repudiated his family? When membership is partly ascriptive in this way, exit is difficult and hardly a good substitute for rights.

J.S. Mill encountered this problem in his argument for tolerating the Mormon practice of polygamy, which he thought violated the rights of Mormon women: 'No one has a deeper disapprobation than I have of this Mormon institution; both for other reasons, and because, far from being in any way countenanced by the principle of liberty, it is a direct infraction of that principle, being a mere riveting of the chains of one half of the community, and an emancipation of the other from reciprocity of obligation towards them.'[14] It is important to notice how substantial these vices are. Polygamy violates both liberty and justice because it upsets a fair reciprocity of obligation. That is, it violates women's rights in the only sense of the term that Mill recognizes. But Mill says that the practice should none the less be tolerated, because exit from it is possible: 'Still it must be remembered that this relation is as much voluntary on the part of the women concerned in it, and who may be deemed the sufferers by it, as is the case with any other form of the marriage institution.'[15]

Now Mill was, as we know, not exactly thrilled by the ordinary monogamous marriage, so to say that polygamy is no less voluntary than that is not saying much. (Indeed, he calls women's acquiescence in it 'surprising' and thinks it explained by their belief that any form of marriage to a man is better than being single.) But, provided that Mormons 'allow perfect freedom of departure to those who are dissatisfied with their ways,'[16] they should be tolerated.

To test the force of this argument, we need to notice what Mill means by 'tolerating polygamy.' This does not bring any obligation to recognize Mormon marriages, nor to release others from their own obligations on the strength of Mormon views. Mill merely says, 'I cannot admit that persons entirely unconnected with them ought to step in and require that a condition of things with which all who are directly interested appear to be satisfied, should be put to an end.'[17] That is, he takes the argument from exit to justify tolerating polygamy in the sense of not extirpating it.

That is indeed one kind of toleration; but it is an uninterestingly special case. There are perfectly good reasons for doubting that outsiders should undertake a crusade against polygamy – reasons that have nothing to do with the argument from exit. For example, the crusade may well fail or backfire. In any case, there may be no question of putting polygamy to an end; we might simply be wondering about whether it is permissible to impose restraints and safeguards on the practice – for instance, to ensure that women who refuse it are not shunned or impoverished, to guarantee that men in such unions do fulfil their obligations, and to provide for easy divorce. Any of these limitations would be at odds with Mormon practices of the time; yet all of them would go some way to respecting the rights of Mormon women.

A more interesting question, then, is whether the freedom to exit obviates the rights that these measures would protect. Let us suppose, with Mill, that Mormon women are free to remain unwed and (unlike David Thomas) may leave the jurisdiction of the group. In this sense, then, the church is a voluntary association: one is free to exit. But entry is a different matter. Adult converts are a minority in most religions. So the position of these women is more complex than the notion of 'voluntary association' might suggest. They are not like members of a tennis club who assessed the options and then freely joined and who remain free to resign. On the contrary, they typically found themselves members of an institution whose character is largely beyond their control but that structures their lives.

That being so, the meaning and costs of departure are different from what Mill's argument might suggest. For reasons that Hume gave[18] and with which Mill was certainly familiar, the mere existence of an exit does not suffice to make it a reasonable option. It is risky, wrenching, and disorienting to have to tear oneself from one's religion or culture; the fact that it is possible to do so does not prove that those who do not manage to achieve the task have stayed voluntarily, at least not in any sense strong enough to undercut any rights they might otherwise have.

So the exit argument is a poor one. Mill began by conceding that what is at issue here is justice: polygamy upsets a fair reciprocity of obligation between men and women. But it is no part of a liberal theory that justice can be secured merely by providing for exit. If a certain social structure is unjust, it cannot become just merely by becoming avoidable. True, when exit is unavailable things are even worse, but that does not prove that when exit is available things are all right. What we would have expected here from Mill is not a weak and formalistic appeal to the principle volenti non fit injuria, but rather a rejection of the practice's claim to impose obligations at all, along the lines of his rejection of slavery contracts.[19] That he does not do so results from his identifying toleration of a practice with not eliminating it. Had he considered that the minority might protect the interests of women in other ways, he would have had to confront the conflict more directly.

These examples suggests ways in which the real prospects of leaving a minority group differ from the model of voluntary association. And the examples are not idiosyncratic: the minority groups that are most prized as experiments in living are precisely those in which membership is an 'organic' relation, where entry is not voluntary, membership is partly ascriptive, and exit, when possible, is costly. Under these conditions, internal minorities still need their rights.

Relative Power

Now I turn to the second objection to recognizing the rights of internal minorities – namely, that the groups against which they seek rights are, by definition, weak ones.

The reply here turns on getting absolute and comparative judgments of power into the right perspective. It is true that minority groups often have inadequate resources and that that is a reason for recognizing their special rights to begin with. But although that is so, many internal minorities are even worse off, and in ways that make them vulnerable to the minority.

First, there is a delicate question of political culture. It has often been noted that the disadvantage in which minority groups live is not always a fertile field for tolerance. In Christopher Isherwood's novel *A Single Man*, the gay protagonist puts it this way: 'While you're being persecuted, you hate what's happening to you, you hate the people who are making it happen; you're in a world of hate. Why, you wouldn't recognize love if you met it!'[20] And even in a world of love, Freud thought, hate must find some expression: 'It is always possible to bind together a considerable number of people in love, so long as there are other people left over to receive manifestations of their aggressiveness.'[21]

To be sure, these pessimistic thoughts are speculative, and one cannot discount bias on the part of those who routinely suspect all minorities of intolerance. The capacity for intolerance is quite widely spread; Mill called the tendency to compel social conformity 'one of the most universal of all human propensities.'[22] And not everyone thinks that this tendency is most likely to become malignant in tight-knit social groups. On the contrary, some have argued that such groups actually promote tolerance. Espousing the view that it is in fact an anomic, mass society that nurtures hatreds, Michael Sandel writes, 'Intolerance flourishes most where forms of life are dislocated, roots unsettled, traditions undone.'[23] That might suggest that it is liberal society itself, not the minority groups, that is the problem.

These claims are hard to adjudicate and can rapidly descend into what Robert Nozick calls 'normative sociology' – the study of what the causes of social problems ought to be. Still, I think that there is ground for worry here. If one has learned to expect that one will be attacked from above, it is natural to fear that one may also be assaulted from below and to strike pre-emptively. These fears undermine trust in others, and trust is important in sustaining tolerance. Moreover, it is hard to build defences that shelter from one direction only – institutions and practices that promote solidarity, unanimity, and so on keep both majorities and internal minorities in check, whether that is their intention or not.

So we need not postulate special psychological mechanisms to predict a deficit of internal tolerance among some minorities: the circumstances of their lives simply make it extremely prudent to strive for unity. Inasmuch as there is strength in numbers, the minority will seek to avoid costly internal dissent. And the majority will also find it convenient if there is one authoritative voice that speaks for the minority. As a result, there is strong pressure for minorities to discipline themselves in these ways. And that is in fact what happens. The political development of Aboriginal associations in Canada follows the normal career of modern pressure- group politics, just as the US gay liberation movement formed itself fairly explicitly on the civil rights movement that preceded it. When minorities are thus organized and disciplined, they are given a clear voice and become stronger; but they often silence and disempower internal minorities in doing so.

A probable consequence of this process is that internal minorities will be among the most vulnerable groups in a society. Minorities are badly off, but internal ones are often even worse off. They suffer from being members of minority groups who need to defend themselves not only from the majority but also from other members of their own minority.

The reply to the second objection thus rests on complex factual questions about power and strategy, the answers to which are not always clear. Aboriginal women are doubly marginalized. But what should we say, for example, of anglophone Quebecers? That they were a historically powerful group does not seem in doubt. But are they still? It is sometimes thought that their power is somehow transmitted to them from other English-speaking groups. It is often said, for example, that Quebec is the last hope for the French language in North America, whereas if English were to perish in the province it would still flourish elsewhere. Is that relevant? After all, it is no solace to francophones that their language will always survive in Paris; why should English Montrealers feel reassured that their language will still be spoken in Boston?

These issues are obviously complex. My point is this. Neither the absolute weakness of a minority group, nor its relative weakness vis-à-vis the majority, proves that it is also weak vis-à-vis its own internal minorities. Moreover, there is good reason to suppose that it will often be stronger. I conclude, therefore, that the argument from relative power is no better than the argument from exit and that at least some internal minorities are entitled to rights in just the way that the minority groups themselves are, and for the same reasons.

Conflicts of Rights

If this thesis is correct, then minority rights are more dense than they appear. People have rights as members of a minority group, but members of the minority have rights as individuals *and* sometimes also as members of an internal minority.

The density of these rights makes conflicts among them nearly inevitable. Giving special rights to Indian bands does not have much chance of weakening or diminishing the cultural context of the Canadian majority. But securing the individual rights of native women within an Aboriginal community may well weaken it, as may securing the collective rights of groups within some bands. So here we have a genuine case of conflicting rights, in which to satisfy one is to set back another.

How are these conflicts to be resolved? I can say nothing about it here, and it is silly to look for a general theory. Everything depends on the character and weight of the particular rights involved and on the social context. But I want to stress that the existence of conflicts is what is at issue, for it has significant consequences for the relationship between liberalism and minorities.

Both protection of special minority interests and the limits on that protection flow from a single source. So while liberals can defend, for example, the value of cultural membership – including collective rights in one sense of that term – they cannot defend every culture. It is the liberal hope that people will, through experiments in living, articulate lives that are rich with value and meaning. At the same time, it is a requirement of liberal theory that they do so within the limits imposed by justice. As Kymlicka rightly says: 'Each person should be able to use and interpret her cultural experiences in her own chosen way. That ability requires that the cultural structure be secured from the disintegrating effects of the choices of people outside the culture, but also requires that each person within the community be free to choose what they see to be most valuable from the options provided (unless temporary restrictions are needed in exceptional circumstances of cultural vulnerability).'[24]

I think that is roughly correct but want to raise a question about its implications for the character of minority groups in a liberal society. If internal minorities are to have their rights, will not the whole point of different experiments in living be defeated? Are we to be able to experiment provided that we stay away from the dangerous elements of patriarchy, or nationalism, or homophobia – that is, provided that minority groups remain, so to speak, nice?

Clearly, much variation will be possible; there are many different ways of being nice. But could the Pueblo, for instance, remain theocratic? Kymlicka says that his argument for protecting culture provides no ground for restricting the religious freedom of the Pueblo because they could survive with a Protestant minority. There could be no legitimate reason for restricting religious freedom, since there is no inequality in cultural membership to which it might be a response.[25]

Perhaps the Pueblo could remain Pueblo even with a Protestant minority; but that is only because it is in this case possible to prise apart culture and religion. It is a lucky thing if that is so, but it is easy to think of contrary examples, especially when one looks to cultural or religious minorities that cannot be defined by a certain linguistic or ethnic character. Many religions, for example, simply incorporate as central elements doctrines that are inconsistent with respect for the rights of women, children, sexual minorities, and so on. Here, to liberalize is to change.

Now, it is true that any theory of cultural integrity must allow for a distinction between changes in and changes of a culture. Conservatives often complain that the former amounts to the latter, that any change is a fundamental threat to 'our ways.' That is not a credible position. Many cultures incorporate as part of their fabric disputes about what their ways really are. But still, I think of no way of showing ex ante that the distinction will always fall neatly along the line demarcated by respect for rights. It may just be true of some groups that respect for the rights of their internal minorities would undermine them. And if so, there will be genuine and tragic conflict to face.

There is therefore no doubt that some ways of understanding group life – for example, most types of religious and cultural fundamentalism – will fare poorly under any regime that strives to respect personal autonomy. It is not that such ways of life will entirely vanish, but they will be deeply transformed if they survive, perhaps in the sort of way that Scots Calvinists became moderate presbyterians in North America. That may worry some who believe that a liberal regime must be 'neutral' among competing conceptions of the good. Certainly the consequences of a liberal political order will not be neutral among experiments in living. It is true that the reason that liberty-limiting fundamentalisms (for example) fare poorly is not that the liberal order disapproves of their way of life nor that they refuse to conform to community standards. They fare poorly because they are ill-adapted to the environment of liberal justice. But that distinction, native to modern liberalism, is foreign to them.

Yet without respect for internal minorities, a liberal society risks becoming a mosaic of tyrannies; colourful, perhaps, but hardly free. The task of making respect for minority rights real is thus one that falls not just to the majority but also to the minority groups themselves.

Notes

1 Christopher Isherwood *A Single Man* (New York: Farrar, Straus, Giroux 1964) 72.

2 Robert Nozick *Anarchy, State and Utopia* (Oxford: Blackwell 1974) chap. 10.

3 See Susan Moller Okin *Justice, Gender, and the Family* (New York: Basic Books 1989).

4 I follow Joseph Raz *The Morality of Freedom* (Oxford: Clarendon Press 1986) 166 ff.

5 See Leslie Green 'Two Views of Collective Rights' *Canadian Journal of Law and Jurisprudence* 4 (1991) 316–27. See also Denise Réaume 'Individuals, Groups, and Rights to Public Goods' *University of Toronto Law Journal* 38 (1988) 1–27.

6 The conditions follow Raz *Morality of Freedom* 208.

7 Will Kymlicka *Liberalism, Community, and Culture* (Oxford: Clarendon Press 1989). Kymlicka does not consider the collective character of the interest in cultural survival. He treats it instead as a fully individuated interest in a certain comparative good – not having a worse cultural endowment than others – thus connecting it with a certain doctrine about equality. That thesis is not essential to the present argument.

8 By, for example, John R. Danley 'Liberalism, Aboriginal Rights, and Cultural Minorities' *Philosophy and Public Affairs* 20 (1991) 169, 176, 177.

9 For Ferry's account, see James Ferry *In the Courts of the Lord* (Toronto: Key Porter Books 1993). Anglicans are not, I think, an oppressed minority among Canadian religions and have little incentive to depart. But some religious minorities, such as Puritans, Mennonites, Hutterites, and Doukhobors, did leave oppressive states. Their success in attaining religious freedom elsewhere was mixed.

10 Setting aside the interesting case of carving a new state out of the territory of the old. For a helpful discussion of the issues, see Allen Buchanan *Secession: The Morality of Political Divorce from Fort Sumter to Lithuania and Quebec* (Boulder, Col.: Westview Press 1991).

11 Ara Wilson 'Just Add Water: Searching for the Bisexual Politic' *Out/Look* 16 (1992) 30.

12 *Thomas v. Norris*, [1992] 2 *CNLR* 139.

13 Ibid 162.

14 J.S. Mill *On Liberty* in his *Utilitarianism* ed M. Warnock (London: Fontana 1962) 224.

15 Ibid.

16 Ibid.

17 Ibid.

18 David Hume 'Of the Original Contract' in his *Essays: Moral, Political, and Literary* (London: Oxford Press 1963) 452–73.

19 Mill *On Liberty* 235–6.

20 Isherwood *A Single Man* 72.

21 S. Freud *Civilization and Its Discontents* (Harmondsworth: Penguin 1971) chap. 5.

22 Mill *On Liberty* 216.

23 M.J. Sandel 'Morality and the Liberal Ideal' in J.P. Sterba ed *Justice: Alternative Political Perspectives* 2nd ed (Belmont, Calif.: Wadsworth 1992) 224.

24 Kymlicka *Liberty, Community, and Culture* 198.

25 Ibid 196.

6

The Group Right to Linguistic Security: Whose Right, What Duties?

DENISE G. RÉAUME

Recent debates about the viability of the concept of group rights implicate many important theoretical issues about the nature of rights, of right holders, and of the duties claimed of others. These issues are all important in their own right; however, it is difficult to avoid the suspicion that those arguing against the idea that there are group rights are motivated as much by deep political misgivings about the implications of recognizing this type of right as by strictly conceptual concerns. Their uneasiness has to do with the effects on those on whom duties will be imposed in the name of group rights.

The sceptics fear that the rights claimed by groups sill severely impair the well-being of individuals. As a practical matter, this is a well-founded worry. One need not look far to find examples of group claims that, if honoured, would be seriously detrimental to individuals. However, the fact that unattractive claims have been made shows merely that groups are not immune to hunger for power and self-aggrandizement. No less so than individuals, on whose behalf some equally destructive rights claims have been made. This development has sometimes been used by critics of rights discourse as a reason for abandoning that discourse altogether.[1] That appropriate reply, of course, is that no conceptual tool is incapable of being abused; nor is there any evidence that rights language is more susceptible to abuse than any other way of conceptualizing the moral and political issues at stake. My central concern here will be to explore whether any claims to group rights are valid and what consequences they have for others, not whether unsupportable claims may or are likely to be made.

To consider this question fully would require a comprehensive, substantive account of both the interest at stake in claims to group rights and the interests with which they may conflict, in order that we might begin to assess the respective weights of the two sets of interest. While having no pretensions to that degree of comprehensiveness, I would like to outline an account of one group right – that to linguistic security – and some of its attendant duties in order to explore the cogency of the sceptic's concerns. In a preface to this exercise, I first outline my understanding of what it is to have a group right and attempt to clarify some of the issues in the conceptual debate.[2] Once the right to linguistic security is sketched out, I use the account to illuminate three recent controversies over language rights.

What Is a Group Right?

Individual and Collective Interests

Any analysis of these issues must begin with a definition of rights. I continue to adhere to that offered by Joseph Raz: 'X has a right' if and only if X can have rights, and, other things being equal, an aspect of X's well-being (his or her interest) is a sufficient reason for holding some other person(s) to be under a duty.[3] This focus on the contribution to well-being or interests served by a claim of rights lends itself easily to consideration of different kinds of interests and their implications.

There is an emerging consensus that if there are any group rights, they are rights with respect to the protection of collective interests. By implication, individual rights concern protection of individual interests. 'Collective interest' and 'individual interest' might, however, refer respectively to the interest of a collective or individual agent, or to the interest in a collective or individual good,[4] or to both. The debate encompasses both the kinds of entities that can have rights and the types of goods to which they may have rights. At least three positions are possible. First, one might accept only individuals as holders of rights and dismiss the idea of interests in collective goods. This stance would confine rights to claims by individuals to protection of individual interests. Second, one might acknowledge the existence of collective goods but deny that groups can hold rights . One might then be inclined, with Raz, to consider 'collective rights' to be a mere 'façon de parler,'[5] denoting an individual right to protection of a collective interest. Third, one might argue that groups are the appropriate holders of rights with respect to at least some collective goods. On this view, 'group (or collective) right' refers both to the holder of the right and to an important feature of the good claimed.

Elsewhere, I have argued for a distinction between 'individual interests' and 'collective interests' that distinguishes different kinds of goods and has implications for whose right each can be said to be.[6] An individual interest should be understood as one in a good that is enjoyable by an individual, independent of or in isolation from others. The complementary conception of collective interest is that of one that can be enjoyed only communally. It builds on the difference between private and public goods but focuses on a particular kind of public good. These goods share the standard features of public goods: no one can be involuntarily excluded from them (publicity of consumption), and they frequently require the efforts of many to be produced (publicity of production). But they are also public in a deeper sense: their value lies in the publicity of either or both production and consumption. These are the kinds of goods that I have called participatory[7] and that Leslie Green has referred to as shared.[8]

This distinction between individual and collective interests, when factored into the definition of a right, has implications for which people can hold each kind of right. X has a right if an aspect of X's well-being is sufficient reason to justify imposition of duties on others. This formulation illuminates a feature commonly associated with rights. For example, we often say that X having a right means that certain actions must be performed for her sake, whether or not any other good comes of it. Similarly, the idea of rights as trumps, famously explicated by Dworkin, involves the intuitive idea that X having a right means that her interest in a particular good must be protected even if others are thereby disadvantaged. Both these ideas are contained in the formulation that X's well-being must be sufficient ground for others' duties. To say that something is sufficient reason to require certain actions is to say that no other reason is necessary (the action must be performed for X's sake) and that no contrary reason counts against performance of the action (X's interest trump the competing interests of others).

For an individual to claim a right, it must be the case that her well-being is sufficient reason to hold others under certain duties. It must be for her sake that the duty is imposed in the sense that only the good to her need be considered. And it must be the case that the opposing claims of others cannot defeat the reason for acting in her favour.[9]

Only individual interests – enjoyable by an individual in isolation from others – meet these conditions. The individual's interest in some public goods – namely, participatory ones – cannot be sufficient reason to impose duties on others, precisely because we cannot say that it is for her sake that the duty is imposed. Not only is it impossible to protect such goods for the enjoyment of an isolated individual, but we cannot even understand it as a good except through participation of many in its production and consumption. We can say only that it is for the sake of all, considered as a group, who enjoy it that it is provided. If this understanding is correct, there can be no individual right to a collective good but only a collective right, held jointly by all who share in the collective good. Only this collective interest is sufficient reason to impose duties.

Differentiating Individual and Collective Interests

Beginning from the premiss that rights are grounded in certain interests (those sufficiently important to justify imposition of duties), it is natural to assume that whose interest it is has a bearing on who can have a right to its protection. My approach concedes the obvious, that interest Y must be an interest of agent X in order that X can claim a right to its protection, but it denies that we can simply read off the identity of the right holder from who has an interest in the good claimed. The contrast with two alternative ways of differentiating collective and individual interests will elucidate the significance of this claim. Both alternatives allow for an understanding of collective rights as individual rights to collective goods. Both fail to take account of whether any interest that an individual may have in a collective good is capable of grounding a right to its protection.

First, we might rather simply distinguish between the interests of individuals and those of groups by classifying conditions, goods, and so on into those affecting the well-being either of individuals or of groups. Thus if provision of a good affects a person, it can be said to be in that individual's interest. Coupled with the assumption that having an interest lays the basis for being able to claim status as right holder, this definition casts the net of individual rights very wide indeed. Few would disagree that the kinds of claims that are typically framed as group rights concern practices, behaviour, and the like that affect the well-being of individuals. The contrary argument would have to claim that collective goods benefit only groups considered apart from their members.

However, this definition of individual interest supports the conclusion that collective rights are individual rights to collective goods only if one ignores the comparably broad sense of collective interest – that is, a group has an interest in a certain good insofar as its well-being is affected by provision of the good. To deny this conclusion would be to argue that it is impossible to conceive of the interests of a group as distinct from those of any of its members. Once both sides of the distinction are taken into account, it becomes clear that there is enormous overlap. We may readily concede that individuals can be said to have an interest in collective goods or to have collective interests, but this does not show that groups do not also have an interest in collective goods.[10] Thus this approach, if it is to eliminate the possibility of groups as right holders, must go further and argue that groups do not have interests. Without this premiss, the argument that rights follow the entity that has an interest in a particular good threatens merely to produce parallel sets of individual and group rights with respect to some goods. In addition to failing to eliminate group rights, this way of drawing the distinction between individual and collective interests fails to establish that there can be individual rights to collective goods. Although individuals are affected by provision of collective goods, I argue above that this is insufficient to infer an individual right to such goods.[11] While some collective goods may be enjoyable individually, not all are. If a rights claim requires that the claimant's interests alone be sufficient reason for imposition of duties, only individually enjoyable collective goods can be the subject matter of an individual rights claim.

Second, we may distinguish well-being as an individual from that as a member of a group, equating the former with individual interest and the latter with collective. This distinction might refer to the difference between interests that one has because of one's membership in a group – that is, by virtue of some characteristic that one shares with some others – and those that one has irrespective of any group membership – that is, those that one has simply by virtue of being a human being. On this reading, interests that one has as an individual are universal, and those that one has as a member of a group are particular interests.[12] However, this reasoning appears to lump together, as collective interests, all those that happen to be shared by a number of people. If any collection of people who share an interest can constitute a group, we cannot distinguish between the interests that one has in common with one's fellow stock-market investors and those shared with co-religionists. They all appear equally relevant in building an argument for or against the existence of group rights, making it impossible to distinguish a group right from a set of individual rights. This conclusion is counterintuitive, since the kinds of interests that typically feature in claims of group rights are not the sort that investors share. Any conception of collective interests that renders these indistinguishable will seem the first step towards dismissing group rights by reductio ad absurdum.[13]

More important for us, distinguishing individual from collective interests in this way implies that both are the interests of individuals, although interests as a member of a group are the interests of an individual in a collective good. Raz, for example, characterizes collective rights as individual rights arising out of the interest in collective goods: 'A collective right exists when the following three conditions are met. First, it exists because an aspect of the interest in human beings justifies holding some person(s) to be subject to a duty. Second, the interests in question are the interests of individuals as members of a group in a public good and the right is a right to that public good because it serves their interest as members of the group. Thirdly, the interest of no single member of that group in that public good is sufficient by itself to justify holding another person to be subject to a duty.'[14] Once again, the argument moves too quickly from determination of whose interest it is to that of whose right it is. Raz's third condition recognizes that with respect to these rights any single individual's interest is not sufficient to justify imposing duties on others. How then can an individual be said to have such a right when it is not for that individual's sake that the duties are imposed? Raz's three conditions make sense only if the second is interpreted in line with my conception of collective interest. That is, to have an interest as a member of a group in a public good is to have an interest in a good that derives its value from participation by many in its production and consumption. The third condition then becomes a mere implication of the second, rather than a separate condition. More important, it cannot then make sense to conceive of the right in such a case as one held by the individual. If the right is held by an individual, the third condition must be abandoned altogether, and then there seems no point in using the term 'collective right,' even as a façon de parler.

Both of these alternative conceptions of 'collective interests' fail to make sense of an individual right to their protection because they fail to make the link between an individual's possession of an interest and the standing to make a rights claim with respect to that interest. If collective rights are to be understood as rights with respect to collective goods, the most plausible account is one that restricts collective goods to participatory goods and attributes the rights to the groups that participate in their enjoyment.

Right-Holding Capacity

So far, I have done no more than show that the idea of individual rights to participatory goods is conceptually flawed and that it would make more sense to say that such goods are provided for the sake of the collectivity as a whole. This leaves outstanding the issue of whether groups have the moral standing to be considered right holders. Raz phrases this as the question of the capacity to have rights. He argues that only those whose well-being is of ultimate value, or artificial persons, have this capacity.[15] Groups might be said to have this capacity, then, if either their well-being is of ultimate value or they can be considered artificial persons. Although the propriety of attributing ultimate value to group well-being is an important question, I want to concentrate here on Raz's second ground for recognizing a capacity to have rights and explore briefly one objection to treating groups as artificial persons.

At least one of the chief concerns in according rights to groups is a related set of problems of indeterminacy. First, there may be indeterminacy concerning the group's boundaries, which in turn threatens to give rise to indeterminacy vis-à-vis its interests. Second, it may be difficult to identify group actions and decisions of the sort normally associated with exercising and waiving rights. Since the group consists of individual human beings, each capable of acting and deciding, how are we to tell what count as the actions and so on of the group as opposed to those of an individual member or subset of members?

To constitute the group as an artificial person is to create a set of rules that determine what shall count as an action or decision of the group. However, Michael Hartney argues that a group right must properly be vested in the 'collectivity as such' rather than in an artificial person.[16] The distinction is anything but clear. One way to understand a collectivity is precisely as that which is constituted by the rules that identify its members and determine what shall count as its actions. The alternative, it seems, is to understand the collectivity as the collection of its individual members. Why, though, should one insist that the latter is the only appropriate holder of a group right? One suspects that the objective is to render the group insufficiently determinate to be an appropriate right holder.

The strategy apparently assumes that a similar problem of indeterminacy does not arise with individuals. But just as group action is given significance and meaning through definitional rules, so too is individual action. We might just as well say that the individual is really an artificial person made up of rules unifying potentially inconsistent manifestations of will over time. Rules tell us how much an exercise of agency at a particular point in time counts for or is to be combined with an apparently contrary one at a different time in determining whether a right has been exercised or claimed. For example, what counts as an agreement to purchase a set of encyclopaedias from the door-to-door salesperson? What counts as a promise to one's neighbours to water their plants while they are on holiday? What counts as a decision to donate one's organs for transplantation? In all these cases, rules constitute certain (combinations of) actions as significant; exercise of a right cannot simply be read off from a description of natural acts. In this respect, the individual is no less artificial than a corporate personality. If it is illegitimate to resort to the artifice of rules to render group behaviour determinate, it must be equally so to use rules to render individual behaviour determinate. Unless Hartney is prepared to argue that individual rights must properly be vested in the collection of selves connected in one body that makes up the individual, I see no reason to insist that group rights must properly be vested in the collection of people that make up the group.

While it is true in one sense that recognizing the existence of another kind of individual in an account of rights does not make that account less individualistic,[17] rights accorded through recognizing only individual human beings differ significantly in content from those derived from recognition of more complex individuals. The latter will provide the kind of protection for the enjoyment of collective goods that a claim of right provides, while the former will not. This is not to say that a scheme that recognizes only individual human beings will provide no protection for collective goods, but only that protection of those goods will not be regarded as sufficient reason for imposition of duties. Such goods will thus be more vulnerable to competition from other valuable objectives. Nor is it to deny that protection of individual rights will often incidentally allow people to protect collective interests.[18]

Duties Implied by Group Rights

In exploring the duty side of the right-duty correlation, we should distinguish three possible types of duty holder. First, for the sake of a group interest, duties might be imposed on members of the same group or on non-members. Duties on non-members might target individuals or other groups. Thus the sceptic's concern is that recognition of group rights will entail imposition of morally unacceptable duties on others, whether individual members, individual non-members, or other groups. In particular, the sceptic, being inclined to individualism, wonders how group rights will affect individuals' interests, especially those that themselves ground individual rights.

Is there any reason to think that the interests of a group can never justify imposing duties (onerous or otherwise) on individuals? Since participatory goods are ultimately grounded in the well-being of human beings, as are individual goods, it cannot be objected that individuals are automatically more worthy than groups. Nor, I think, is there any reason to think that all interests of individuals are necessarily weightier than any interest of a group. One reason for general scepticism about group rights would be the worry that in case of conflict between a group and an individual right, the former would always win. If group rights were likely to conflict frequently with individual rights, recognizing the former would indeed restrict considerably the scope of the latter. One who deeply values individual rights might well be concerned at the prospect. Below, I explore one suggested claim to a group right and consider its tendency to conflict with the rights of others. Here, I want to question the assumption that group rights will always override individual ones. Again, I suspect that the fear is practically, rather than philosophically, grounded. It is born of experience with the kinds of claims sometimes made by advocates on behalf of groups. Two similarly mistaken claims on behalf of groups might be mentioned.

First, advocates sometimes seem to suggest that group rights must override individual ones, since there are more beneficiaries of the group claim than individuals whose rights stand to be infringed. Second, claims of group rights are sometimes made in support of the interests of majorities over those of minorities. Supporters of the larger group's rights may be tempted to take into account surreptitiously the size of the group in weighing the group's claim. If the weight of a group's claim increases with its membership, dominant cultural, ethnic, religious, or linguistic communities will automatically have an unfair advantage over smaller groups and individuals (who can be seen as groups of one). Both arguments improperly adopt an aggregative approach, which is out of keeping with the nature of rights. The impropriety of taking into account the respective sizes of the right holder and duty holder is highlighted if the group is treated as an artificial person. Just as the interests of a big corporation do not automatically outweigh those of a smaller one (or of an individual), a large community cannot use its size as an independent argument in balancing its rights against those of individuals or smaller groups. Once this principle is established, it is clear that group rights may not necessarily have the totalitarian implications often associated with them.

But that fear can be fully put to rest only by full, substantive accounts of the rights that groups are supposed to have. I turn now to begin that task, focusing on rights and duties regarding maintenance of language, before looking at three specific language conflicts in Canada.

Linguistic Security: Rights and Duties

The unilingual state is a thing of the past. Almost every country now consists of more than one language group. The existence of a linguistic community is a participatory good. Not only do use, maintenance, and development of a language make up a collective enterprise, but their value lies in the process of creating and recreating language rather than any end product that might be said to be useful to individuals as individuals. Further, language is intrinsically connected to culture, itself a collective good − it is the bearer of conceptual frameworks and metaphors for conducting one's life, and it is the means of expressing a community's distinctive conception of beauty and truth. Although many aspects of a culture can be separated from the language in which they are imbedded, a language is always more than a neutral means of communication. Thus to protect a group's use of its language is to help significantly to foster its culture. Indeed, this is one reason why language is so important for people. Language should be considered part of the larger good of culture, but since it is quasi-distinct, and the means of protecting it considerably easier to define, it is frequently used as an imperfect proxy in the attempt to safeguard a culture. In exploring the participatory good of the existence of a language community, its connection with culture writ large should not be forgotten.

One way of fleshing out the content of a right to this good, must be rejected from the outset. The right might be characterized as a right of the members, considered as a group, to the continued existence or survival of the group.[19] If this means that the group has a right that this state of affairs be secured, it would seem to give rise to duties on others to do whatever is necessary to sustain the existence of the language group. This right, if valid, would probably give rise to innumerable conflicts with the rights, collective and individual, of others. In certain circumstances, the right to survival could impose obligations on other individuals to stay or become members of the group, thus conflicting with personal liberty. Any new members would have to come from another language group, potentially impairing its ability to survive.

However, a group right to survival is no more plausible than the comparable individual right. A key starting point of any theory of rights is the equal moral worth of persons. Any statement of right must be consistent with others having an equal entitlement. A right to a guarantee of survival is inconsistent with others' like right. Situations are easily imaginable in which one person's survival cannot be ensured except at the expense of another's. Similarly, a group claim to a right to the survival of the language group, on this interpretation, contemplates a prima facie duty to support that group, even at the cost of the destruction of one's own. Since an account of the moral relationship between cultural groups such as language communities must embody the same principle of equality as that between individuals, a right to survival seems equally implausible here. There can be no basis for an assertion that one language group is inherently superior to another such that its vital interests should be systematically preferred to the comparable interests of another.

Linguistic Security and Duties of Non-interference

If this reasoning is persuasive, it suggests a less generous rendering of the content of the right. Elsewhere[20] I have argued (as has Leslie Green[21]) in favour of a right to linguistic security. This right must be understood against the backdrop of the normal social processes through which language use continues over time. Since language is the medium of communication, these processes are all-encompassing – so much so that it is difficult to look at them as discrete processes within one's own linguistic community. However, one can single out two key processes. First, there is socialization of children into the language. Once upon a time, this task was carried out by the child's extended family or kinship group; in modern societies, the public educational system plays a large role. Second, there is the range of contexts for use of the language, which must be sufficiently rich to sustain the complexity that contributes to future development. In a linguistically homogeneous society, these processes are invisible as processes for language preservation. They are simply the many contexts in which life is lived using language. With interaction between language groups comes the possibility of competition. In this context, especially when there are two groups of unequal power, it becomes easier to identify key spheres of language use that must be protected if the less powerful group is to have a fair chance to pursue its own good.

The right to linguistic security, then, can be understood, first, as the right to pursue normal processes of language transmission and maintenance without interference. This right would preclude any attempt to prohibit use of the language in the normal range of contexts or to prohibit the education of children of the group in the language. Given the fluidity and diffusion of language use, normally this kind of interference could be effective only if collectively organized. Although coercion of one individual by another may occur, such individual interference is unlikely to have much effect on the group as a whole. Prohibitions on use of a particular language are effective only if accomplished through law, where one group uses the power of the state to restrict the freedom of another group. A collective right to linguistic security would indeed impose duties on other groups not to use numerical superiority to prohibit use of the minority language. However, restraining groups from engaging in coercive interference with others is no more than is necessary if each is to regard the other as an equal and is hardly the sort of thing that instils fear of impending totalitarianism.

When two or more language groups share a wide range of social structures, more subtle forms of interference are possible. Whenever one community has greater power over the political institutions of the society, it may simply organize many social institutions to suit its practices exclusively. For example, it might organize the public schools system so that catchment areas are defined geographically, mixing students of different mother tongues, and then prescribe unilingual materials and hire unilingual teachers. Without directly proscribing use of the minority language in schools, this form of organization makes it close to impossible for the minority to use the public[22] education system as a locus of linguistic socialization, a use that the majority takes for granted.[23]

Similarly, the majority may organize governmental structures on the assumption that participants will speak the majority tongue. If, because of the power differential, it is more important for the minority to be able to understand what members of the other groups are saying than vice versa, incentives will be created for the minority to abandon its language without any need for its proscription. The more options are foreclosed to the minority by the majority's assumption that its language will be the medium of communication, the more corrosive the long-term impact on the integrity of the minority community. Even if each member of the minority desperately wishes to retain his or her language, the incentive structure created by the majority is invidious. For each, if she assimilates to the majority language when other group members do not, she gains the advantages of membership in the opportunities provided by the majority; if she refuses to assimilate when other members of her group do, she will be severely handicapped in her future options. Although all may prefer non-assimilation, the rational choice for each is to assimilate.

This form of coercion is not as blatant as outright prohibition by the majority of the minority language, but it nevertheless amounts to majority interference with the minority's ability to pursue the normal processes of language transmission and maintenance. Creating a unilingual school system through decisions about which institutions particular children must attend and which materials they must use and what the qualifications of their teachers shall be cannot be construed as the majority's going about its own business, with unfortunate side-effects for the minority. Without the majority's insistence on a unified organizational structure, the minority might well be capable of setting up its own system. The majority's imposition of a unified system that reflects its group interest exclusively is a denial of equality to the minority. This phenomenon is equivalent to the practice in male-dominated institutions of creating structures and standards that reflect typical male interests or attributes, which then operate to exclude women from participation. Equality requires structures that accommodate the different needs and aspirations of all members of society, whether the context is the relationship between individuals or that between groups. Again, the duties of the majority that arise out of recognition of a collective right to linguistic security are not insignificant but cannot be construed as totalitarian.

Linguistic Security and Duties of Support

Although it seems to me that the sort of public, institutional structures just analysed are among the most significant forces creating unfair pressure on minority group members to defect to the majority, they are not the only ones. Beyond the protection of negative group liberty explored above, is it plausible to include in the right to linguistic security the right to protection against non-coercive pressures, or against pressures not amounting to interference in the group's normal practices? There may be many private opportunities that are foreclosed to someone who does not speak a particular language – most significant, in the labour market. If a francophone wishes to seek employment in an industry that happens to be occupied by anglophones, or even in which there are greater job opportunities for anglophones, she would be well advised to learn English. Strictly speaking, this does not require assimilation to English; personal bilingualism is possible. However, over the course of time, particularly crossing generations, the move into another linguistic context is connected to other forces that tend towards assimilation, if not for oneself, then for one's children.[24] Does the right to linguistic security include a right to be protected from these kinds of pressures?

This right would readily give rise to potential conflicts, since it would require imposition of duties on others to either alter any state of affairs that creates pressure to defect or to take positive actions to counter that pressure. Both kinds of duties may infringe on the autonomy of the duty holder in ways against which one is entitled, prima facie, to protect oneself. We must distinguish here between two independent claims. The first would be a group claim – for example, that adequate space exist in the workplace for francophones to use their language because of its importance to the normal processes of language transmission and maintenance. The second would be an individual claim to the benefits of a particular job without having to learn English. Our main concern here is with the group claim. Even if it were valid, it would rarely, if ever, be possible to derive from it a valid individual claim to a particular job. Hence the individual claim must stand or fall as an individual claim of right. As such, it seems very implausible. But we must also distinguish a group right to certain protective behaviour by another group and by particular individuals – between claims made against individual duty holders and against another group as duty holder. This draws attention to the assignability of duties as an important precondition for when a right can be held.

Just as existence of a right presupposes an assignable right holder for whose sake the duty is imposed, so too must there be an assignable duty. One cannot claim a right if the most that one can say is that it would be a good thing if a certain state of affairs were to exist. One must be able to claim that particular others have a duty to foster that state of affairs. This situation presents difficulties for any argument for individual duties to protect others' ability to use their language. The pressure on minority members arising out of a dearth of employment opportunities in their own language is the product of myriad individual decisions that combine to produce a body of people in a particular workplace who are unilingual speakers of the majority language.

The right to use a minority language in work contexts, considered as a group right, can refer only to a level of its use sufficient top prevent impairment of the health of the language, considered as a complex social practice. But this is unlikely to require the opportunity for each minority member to speak his or her language at work all the time. (If it did, we would run into the additional difficulty that this might begin to threaten the right of the majority group to pursue its own language practices.) Supposing that it were possible to identify roughly the level of minority language use that is necessary, this would not translate to particular duties on specific individuals. From the fact that the minority language should be being used 20 per cent of the time, for example, we can derive no requirement that a particular parent encourage her children to become bilingual or that a certain employer provide a bilingual work environment. The problem is comparable to one attendant upon the claim of a right to be rescued. It is often the case that, although a particular individual stands to suffer severe harm if some action is not taken to avert it, any number of others are in a position to intervene. It seems unfair for any one person to be arbitrarily singled out as the duty holder. Thus, while not denying the threat to a vital interest, it cannot be said that the victim has a general right to be rescued.

This necessity that obligations be assignable militates against the argument that individuals can be under a duty to protect the minority from certain pressures to assimilate. What of a claim against the majority group as a whole? Insofar as individual actions are necessary building blocks in producing pressure on the minority to assimilate, any argument in favour of a right against the majority as a group must take into account the problem of the assignability of individual responsibility. If the majority can meet its alleged obligation only by imposing individual duties on particular members, a right against the group can be no more plausible than one claimed against individual members.

However, one might argue that the majority, as a group, has a duty to foster conditions that increase opportunity for the minority. For example, the minority's right to adequate scope for the use of its language might give rise to a duty on the majority to encourage bilingualism in its members and make the opportunity to achieve personal bilingualism available. This duty presupposes that the majority has at least some organizational structure that allows it to 'encourage' and 'provide opportunities.' Since the main sphere, at least in the modern world, for promotion of bilingualism is the publicly organized education system, educational bodies could be considered part of the organizational structure of the majority. From the group's duty to promote bilingualism, we would then derive a duty on school boards, as representatives of the group, to make the appropriate institutional decisions. In this way, opportunity for the minority can be expanded without individual coercion.[25]

Linguistic Security and the Duties of Members

The discussion so far has focused on behaviour by the majority that induces members of the minority to forsake their own language community and in the absence of which members would willingly stay within the fold. I have argued that the interests of the minority might well justify imposition of some duties to alter this behaviour. We should also consider the extent to which the minority might claim a right against its own members. Individual members can, of course, affect the well-being of the group. They have interests as individuals as well as as members of the group, and their individual interests may frequently conflict with their group interests in circumstances in which they judge the former to be more important. (These individual interests include the 'autonomy interest' in being able to choose one's affiliations insofar as they are amenable to choice.) Might the group have a right to restrain such behaviour? As an example, let us consider the clearest way in which an individual's behaviour can affect her group – the decision to cease partaking of the participatory good and thus cease being a member. In the area of language, it is easy to see how individual interest could lead one to such a position. One might well conclude that advancement in a particular context requiring use of the majority language outweighs one's competing interest as a member of the minority in the continued health of one's mother tongue. In such circumstances, the group's right to linguistic security conflicts with the individual member's right to autonomy. There can be no prescribed formula for dealing with such conflicts, but a few general points can be made.

First, not all rights are specifically enforceable. Thus, even if a group's claim of right against its members is valid, it does not follow that the group may properly force recalcitrant members into continued participation. We must keep in mind that, typically, group practices of the kind in question require continuous participation by members in a multitude of small ways. To enforce continued membership would be to circumscribe many aspects of an individual's life. The ongoing and detailed interference with personal liberty required can rarely, if ever, be justified.

Second, it is instructive to draw a parallel between the value of group membership and that of free expression. In both cases, we can distinguish between the abstract level and the concrete. There can be no doubt that participation in cultural or linguistic groups is one of the most important interests that human beings have, just as the ability to express oneself freely is. This can be distinguished from the importance of belonging to a particular group or of expressing a certain view. Belonging to a particular group and expressing a particular view are to be protected not because the particular group or of expression is better than some other but because only through the specific expression that group life or individual belief takes can the abstract good of community or expression be protected.

In each case, the ability to choose[26] a vision of the good life is being protected. The particular is valuable only insofar as it is chosen. The right, then, should be understood primarily as one to protection of this ability to choose. While the decision of one member of a group to leave does not show that the group's way of life is unworthy, a group practice that can be sustained only through coercion is highly questionable.

Respect for members as individuals dictates that protectors of the right first look to sources of pressure that make members reluctantly give up participation. To the extent that some communities seem disturbingly ready to coerce continued membership as the means of preserving practices, we should wonder how much this has to do with their inability to enforce the valid duties of other groups rather than to a natural tendency to ride roughshod over the conflicting claims of individual members. In the face of intransigence by another group, particularly a larger, more powerful one, it is not surprising that the minority should turn to the only people over whom it does have some control – its own members. This does not justify the infringement of individual members' right, but it does make it more understandable. It also suggests that before the majority leaps to criticism of the minority for its treatment of individual members, it should first examine whether it – the majority – is fulfilling all of its duties towards the minority.

Recent Language Conflicts

Ford v. Attorney-General of Québec[27]: *The Controversy over Bill 178*

As has been noted by Green,[28] the issue raised by Quebec's enactment of

Bill 178 involved conflict between two group rights, despite claims by the provincial government that it was a case of conflict between a collective and an individual right. Although the challenge to the legislation was litigated under the rubric of freedom of expression, which can be interpreted individualistically, it could equally effectively have been argued that Valerie Ford was representing the entire anglophone community and claiming that the restriction on the public use of English on commercial signs infringed that community's linguistic integrity. This is a more plausible reading of her claim than one that tries to trivialize it by reducing it to an idiosyncratic preference for including the letters 'w-o-o-l' on her shop sign. If Valerie Ford's claim is interpreted as a group right, the argument meets on its own terrain the Quebec government's position that the law was necessary to foster the francophone community's ability to flourish.

This sort of conflict is on a par with that between various individual rights and must be adjudicated in roughly the same way. Since no linguistic community is superior to any other, adjudication of the conflict must display equal respect for each. Such cases can best be resolved by making an assessment of which group's well-being is more seriously jeopardized and whether the infringement is minimized to the extent possible. In fact, when looked at in this light, the argument that a group right of francophone Quebecers needed protection of the sort provided by Bill 178 appears very weak. There was no evidence presented to the court that bilingual, French-English signs proposed any threat whatsoever to the francophone community's ability to flourish. (An argument to this effect could have been made with respect to English-only signs, and the court accepted that restrictions on these could be justified. Indeed, a bilingual-signs requirement would not infringe even the anglophone community's right to flourish, unless one could show that language use is so competitive that it is necessary to each group not only to have opportunities for use of its own language but also that employment of any other language must be foreclosed.) By contrast, the prohibition on English did threaten the well-being of the anglophone community, as much through symbolic devaluation of that group as through the practical impediment to commerce among unilingual anglophones. Indeed, the legislation's avowed purpose – to present the province's 'visage linquistique' as exclusively French – cannot help but convey a message that will help induce those anglophones who can to leave and those who cannot to do their best to fit the majority's mould. The long-term effect will be to weaken the anglophone community.

The Air Traffic Control Controversy

The federal government's efforts to introduce bilingualism into air traffic control in the late 1970s met with considerable resistance from English-speaking pilots and controllers. Bowing to pressure from these
sources, Ottawa froze its implementation of bilingualism, and English
remained the only permissible language for air-ground communications
at several airports in Quebec, even when both pilot and controller were
francophone. The Quebec pilots' association challenged this decision
under the federal Official Languages Act, 1969, and the Federal Court
of Appeal handed down its ruling in 1978. At the same time, a policy
introduced by Air Canada effectively requiring air crew to use English
only in communicating with each other during a flight also came under
attack, with the Quebec Court of Appeal ruling in 1982.[29] In both situations, the right of francophones to use their mother tongue on the job
was at issue. Anglophone pilots and controllers responded that extending bilingualism would jeopardize the safety of the travelling public.[30]

The actual prohibition of use of French involved in these regulations,
would clearly constitute an infringement of the right to linguistic security
if a group interest can be said to be implicated. Such a group interest is
not hard to find. It must at least be part of the normal processes of
maintenance and transmission of a language for speakers to use it whenever they are with co-linguists, even when working. Further, given that
there are so many employment contexts in which it is impossible for
minority-language members to speak their tongue because there is no
one else for them to speak to, it must prima facie be considered a violation
of the right to linguistic security to prohibit use of the language in one of
the few work environments in which it would otherwise be possible.

The rationale for prohibiting French was passenger safety. Since this is
an individualized good, the conflict here was between the minority group
and members of the public, whether members of the minority or not, as
individuals. This is a useful case to dispel any inclination to think that
group rights automatically trump individual ones, since few would argue
that if danger to safety were significant, the group right should still
prevail. This is not to say, however, that the right to safety should always
succeed. Instead, again, a balancing would have to be carried out to
determine how great the threat would be to each if the other were fully
protected. If the evidence were to demonstrate that the threat to safety is
minuscule, especially by comparison with the other risks imposed on
travellers for the sake of efficiency, an argument might be made that

protection of the French fact in this sector of the labour force is sufficiently important to justify imposition of that risk, It would also have to
be determined whether there were other ways to secure safety without
prohibiting French. This strategy would ultimately avoid the direct conflict between linguistic security and safety, but treating linguistic security
as a right compels the search for such alternatives. If there were no right
to linguistic security, these efforts could legitimately be rejected on
grounds of cost or convenience.

Use of a Minority Official Language in the Courts

Canadians have the right, in dealing with the federal courts, to 'use'
either English or French.[31] What does the right to use one's language
entail? This question was considered by the Supreme Court of Canada in
1982 in *MacDonald v. The City of Montreal.*[32] The issue was whether one is
entitled to receive a summons or charge in the official language of one's
choice. The accused's argument depended on generous interpretation
of the notion of the right to 'use' French or English, linking this with the
right to understand and be understood that arises out of the right to
natural justice. Another aspect of this issue was raised in 1986 in *Société
des Acadiens du Nouveau Brunswick et al. v. Minority Language School Board
No. 50 et al.,*[33] in which the plaintiff argued that section 19(2) of the
Charter of Rights imposed on the courts an obligation to understand a
litigant by any reasonable means. The Supreme Court of Canada decided against both plaintiffs, settling on a much narrower conception of
the right to 'use' French or English, effectively limiting it to the right to
make French or English sounds with no guarantee that one will be understood.

These cases show the importance of understanding the collective nature of the interest in language. The interest at stake here goes far
beyond any inconvenience or difficulty to the individual caused by being
required to use an unfamiliar tongue. The ability to use one's own language in important public institutions such as courts is crucial to a
community's security.[34] Absence of this right puts pressure on minority
members to assimilate both because they stand to gain as individuals and
because it publicly devalues their language and turns public agencies
into an alien force within their community. Where rejection of such
seemingly alien political authorities is an option, separatism is fostered.
Where opting out is not possible, the minority is more likely to assimilate
in order to ensure its ability to participate fully in public institutions. A

right to speak without necessarily being understood does little to alleviate this pressure. A more ineffectual 'right' can scarcely be imagined.

These cases also demonstrate the dangers of interpreting the conflicting right in these situations as an individual one. One reason offered by the court for its restrictive interpretation of the right was that a more generous interpretation would infringe the equal right of other people before the court, such as judges and court officials, to use their own language. Thus the court saw only individuals on both sides of this conflict and adopted a negative-liberty interpretation of the right to use either official language in order to avoid the inherent contradiction that would otherwise result from assertion of a positive right against a speaker of the other official language. This individual focus blinded the court to the fact that it was unnecessary to require particular individuals to speak the litigant's choice of language in order to protect the litigant's rights. If the conflict had been interpreted instead as one between the minority and the majority communities, it would have been possible to see the issue as one of the design of the court system, rather than the burdens that can justifiably be imposed on individual officials. The majority, in employing the power of the state to establish courts, is able to create a system in which litigants are matched with court officials willing to speak their language. On this construction, no equal and opposite right need necessarily be violated in asserting the right to use and be understood in one's own language.

Conclusion

I have argued for a conception of group rights that locates the right in the group rather than in its individual members but treats the group as an artificial person. I have also sketched out the normative foundation for a group right to linguistic security, paying special attention to the implications for those on whom duties must be imposed for the sake of the group's interest. Much remains to be done in working out the full conceptual analysis of group rights and in identifying the normative consequences for others, both individuals and other groups. Although political dangers are evident, I remain unpersuaded that the concept of a group right is morally noxious. I hope that in trying to outline an account of the right to linguistic security, I have gone some way towards dispelling some of the more exaggerated fears about groups as right holders and collective interests as worthy of protection.

Notes

1 Cf Mark Tushnet 'An Essay on Rights' *Texas Law Review* 62 (1983–4) 1363; Fran Olsen 'Statutory Rape: A Feminist Critique of Rights' *Texas Law Review* 63 (1984–5) 387.

2 For an excellent sample of these debates, see various articles in the recent issue of the *Canadian Journal of Law and Jurisprudence* (4 no. 2, 1991) devoted to 'Collective Rights.'

3 Joseph Raz *The Morality of Freedom* (Oxford: Clarendon Press 1986) 166.

4 Leslie Green makes a similar point, distinguishing between collective rights as rights of collective agents and rights to collective goods. Cf 'Two Views of Collective Rights' *Canadian Journal of Law and Jurisprudence* 4 (1991) 315.

5 Raz *Morality* 208.

6 Denise Réaume 'Individuals, Groups, and Rights to Public Goods' *University of Toronto Law Journal* 38 (1988) 1.

7 Ibid 7–13. These are like Raz's inherently public goods in that their publicity is not simply a product of some contingent fact, but Raz does not specify that the value of these goods lies in their public nature.

8 Leslie Green *The Authority of the State* (Oxford: Clarendon Press 1990) 206–9.

9 A more carefully nuanced statement of this interpretation of a rights claim would acknowledge that such claims are rarely absolute and indefeasible.

10 Further, it does not show that groups do not have an interest in private goods.

11 This points up the flaw in Michael Hartney's claim that my argument overlooks the contribution to individual welfare of many collective goods. It is no part of my argument to deny that individuals are affected by provision of collective goods, or even that there may be some individualizable benefits arising out of their provision that may ground some individual rights. The central point, however, is that the core right to participatory goods cannot be claimed by individuals. Cf Hartney 'Some Confusions concerning Collective Rights' *Canadian Journal of Law and Jurisprudence* 4 (1991) 299–300.

12 The distinction between universal and particular interests is notoriously slippery. Under a sufficiently abstract description, virtually any interest can be stated universally. The interest in membership in the French linguistic community may seem like a particular interest, since non-francophones may have no interest in it. But if described as the interest in participation in one's mother-tongue linguistic community, it becomes universal. It is only the statement of particular premises identifying the language community of which one is part that particularizes the universal. Thus to distinguish

meaningfully between universal and particular interests we must specify the appropriate degree of abstraction. I see no way of fixing the appropriate level of abstraction for addressing the issues at stake in determining whether there are collective rights and what they might be.

13 To interpret collective interests as interests in participatory or shared goods also avoids the difficulty encountered in the attempt to identify collective interests with interests that one has as a member of a group in distinguishing collective interests from a set of individual ones. The interests in goods that derive their value from their shared production and consumption are a subset, and a clearly delineable one, of interests that one may have by virtue of having a characteristic that is shared with at least some others.

14 Raz *Morality* 208.

15 Ibid 166.

16 Hartney 'Some Confusions' 304–7.

17 Green 'Two Views' 325–6.

18 Allan Buchanan 'Assessing the Communitarian Critique of Liberalism' *Ethics* 9 (1989) 852.

19 For further elaboration of the respective merits of these two characterizations, see my 'The Constitutional Protection of Language: Security versus Survival' in David Schneiderman ed *Language and the State: The Law and Politics of Identity* (Montreal: Yvon Blais Ltée 1991).

20 Ibid.

21 Leslie Green 'Are Language Rights Fundamental?' O*sgoode Hall Law Journal* 25 (1987) 639.

22 Private schooling is always an option, of course, but will be prohibitively expensive in many contexts.

23 While it is not necessary for one group to be larger than the other for the first to have more power, in language matters the more powerful is usually also the majority, and so I use the difference in power and the difference in size interchangeably to refer to the competing groups.

24 For example, being immersed in an anglophone context makes it more likely that one will marry an anglophone. Unless one's partner is willing and able to become bilingual, one's children will probably find it easier to affiliate with anglophone culture.

25 To continue the analogy with the feasibility of a right to rescue, this analysis parallels one in the rescuing context that says that although a right to be rescued cannot be held against any particular individual, in certain contexts of known risk a duty can be imposed on the state to provide supervision.

26 I do not mean to imply that people choose their culture in the same way in which they choose a new car, or even a political party – that is, by consider-

ing all the options and then making a decision about which is best. Many people never come into contact with a culture other than their own, except briefly, perhaps as a tourist. However, once one's culture is threatened, the choice to retain it is manifested in the effort to protect it, and this choice is worthy of as much respect as other situations of significant choice.

27 (1988), 54 *DLR* (4th) 577 (scc).

28 Green 'Two Views' 325.

29 *Association de Gens de l'Air du Québec Inc. v. Lang and Attorney-General of Canada* (1978), 22 *NR* 328 (Federal CA); *Air Canada v. Joyal* (1982), 134 *DLR* (3d) 410 (Quebec CA).

30 In both cases, the legal argument turned on whether the relevant section of the Official Languages Act created a judicially enforceable right. Deciding that it did not, the courts did not address the underlying substantive question, of more interest here, of the conflict between safety and linguistic security.

31 Constitution Act, 1867 (formerly British North America Act, 1867), section 133. This same provision extends to the courts of Quebec, and the same right exists in Manitoba by virtue of the Manitoba Act, 1879, 33 Victoria, chap. 3 (Canada), confirmed by the Constitution Act 1871, and in New Brunswick, by virtue of sections 17–19 of the Charter.

32 [1982] *CS* 998, aff'd [1986] 1 *SCR* 460. See also *Bilodeau v. Attorney General of Manitoba* [1986] 1 *SCR* 449, and *Walsh v. The City of Montreal* (1980), 55 *CCC* (2d) 299 (Quebec SC Crim. Div.).

33 [1986] 1 *SCR* 549.

34 Réaume 'Constitutional Protection.'

7

The Rights of Immigrants

JOSEPH H. CARENS

I must confess at the outset that I have some doubts both about the language of rights and about the language of groups as these might be applied to immigrants. These are doubts about how helpful such terminology is when applied to immigrants, not firm conviction that it is wrong or even inappropriate. My concerns about the discourse on rights are the familiar ones raised by criticisms of rights talk in recent years, although I do not mean to imply that I am entirely persuaded by these critiques. In any event, I am putting those to one side, noting simply that, in the moral arguments that I am advancing, nothing much hinges (as far as I can see) on whether or not they are cast in the language of rights.

My doubts about the language of groups concerns the issue of whether it makes sense to talk about immigrants as a group. For example, immigrants to a country such as Canada arrive from many places. They do not share a common language, culture, or history. They may have common interests in some respects but different ones in others. Some reach a place where they have friends and relatives; others are alone and isolated. Some find Canadian culture familiar and comfortable; others find it alien. And so on. All they really have in common is that they are newcomers to Canada. Does that make them a 'group'? They do not look like a group in the way that, say, the Inuit do. However, one can always identify a class on the basis of some criterion and call its members a group. Again, I do not think that a lot hinges on the language if one uses it with care not to imply too much.

In one sense, the group on which I am focusing is not immigrants but the people who are already in – the citizenry, the members of the political community. Their group status is represented institutionally by the state.

Their group identity or group interests are often advanced as a justification for the treatment of immigrants or potential immigrants. They make up a group whose possession of group rights seems clear (except perhaps to anarchists). But do their rights with regard to outsiders have quite the extent and scope commonly assumed and occasionally defended by political theorists such as Michael Walzer?[1] It is the claims of this group, of the political community, that I want to subject to particular scrutiny by bringing them up against the moral claims of immigrants and potential immigrants. In putting the question in this abstract form, I do not mean to prejudge the question of whether all political communities have the same moral rights and obligations with regard to immigrants.

Let me pose my questions then in the language of groups and the language of rights so as to emphasize the connections (and perhaps also the differences) between what I am saying and what is being said by the other contributors to this book. I am concerned with questions about exclusion and admission of immigrants. Do we have a right to keep people out because we have some group characteristics that the outsiders do not possess or because they have some characteristic that we do not have and do not want? The 'we' in this sentence refers not just to Canadians but to the members of any political community. If there are differences among communities in terms of the moral right to exclude, we need to say how far they go and why they are justified. Are there some criteria of exclusion that are morally objectionable or more (or less) so than others, and to what extent does the moral status of criteria of exclusion vary from one state to another? Assuming for the moment that some selection among potential immigrants is justifiable, do we have a right to select on the basis of group characteristics of the immigrants or on the basis of some group characteristics and not others? Again, this question could be cast in terms of the moral status of criteria of exclusion.

I address these questions from two quite different theoretical perspectives, which I will call idealistic moral theory and realistic moral theory.[2] The former is concerned with absolute justice – what is right and wrong, regardless of the likelihood of these standards being observed. The latter is concerned to identify moral principles that might actually guide action. Overall, I argue below that from the perspective of idealistic theory, the rights of the political community to exclude are much more limited than commonly assumed and the rights of immigrants – people who want to move from one political community to another – much greater than usually thought. From the viewpoint of realism, however, the situation is more complicated. States enjoy a great deal of latitude with regard to immigration policy, but there are some significant moral constraints on what they can do. I say more about realistic moral theory when I turn to that approach. I begin, however, with idealistic moral theory.

Idealistic Moral Theory

Many moral and political philosophers have adopted the sort of perspective that I am proposing here. For example, Aristotle asks in Book VII of *Politics* what the best regime would be – a regime without 'presuppositions' – existing under the sorts of circumstances for which one would pray to the gods.[3] More recently, John Rawls has offered what he describes as an 'ideal theory' of justice.[4] Rawls says that ideal theory deals with the question of what just social arrangements would be if we could count on everyone acting justly and did not have to overcome historically contingent obstacles to justice. That is the sort of perspective that I have in mind, although I do not want to tie it too closely to Rawls's own formulation because he explicitly limits his concern to a single, closed society and I do not want to engage here in the debate over whether that narrow focus is justified in terms of the logic of his own project.

Let us call this idealistic theoretical perspective the just-world framework of analysis. The key question then is this: in a just world, what rights would political communities have to limit immigration, and what rights would individuals have to travel freely across state borders and settle wherever they chose? In answering this question, I will draw on familiar liberal presuppositions about the moral equality of persons and the importance of human freedom, presuppositions that I will not try to defend here, although they are, of course, open to challenge.[5] Overall, my position is this. Freedom of movement is an important liberty in itself and a prerequisite for other freedoms. Thus the presumption is for free migration, and anyone who would defend restrictions faces a heavy burden of proof. Restrictions might sometimes be justified even in an ideally just world because freedom of movement is only one major human interest and it can conflict with others. In particular, restrictions on mobility might sometimes be necessary to preserve a distinct culture or way of life, and these interests might, in some circumstances, outweigh the interests of people in being able to go here they want. But such justifiable restrictions would be rare and would not bear any necessary relation to state borders. In other words, the restrictions might limit internal mobility within a state rather than or as much as movement between states.

Let me elaborate a bit. First, my starting presupposition is that people should be free to pursue their own projects and to make their own choices about how they live their lives, so long as this freedom does not interfere with the legitimate claims of other individuals to do likewise. Second, this also entails a commitment to equal opportunity. Access to social positions should be determined by an individual's actual talents and capacities, not limited on the basis of arbitrary native characteristics (such as class, race, or sex). Third, actual economic, social, and political inequalities should be kept as small as possible, partly as a means of realizing equal freedom and equal opportunity and partly as a desirable end in itself.[6]

Freedom of movement is connected closely to each of these three concerns. First, it is in itself an important freedom. It is precisely this freedom, and all that it makes possible, that is taken away by imprisonment. Second, it is essential for equality of opportunity. One has to be able to move to where the opportunities are in order to take advantage of them. Third, it helps to minimize political, social, and economic inequalities. It enables people to vote with their feet. (This does not preclude participation. It just lets people decide when and where they will participate.)

Consider the case for freedom of movement in light of the liberal critique of feudal practices that determined a person's life chances on the basis of his or her birth. Citizenship in the modern world is a lot like feudal status in the medieval world. It is assigned at birth; for the most part it is not subject to change by the individual's will and efforts; and it has a major effect on one's life chances. To be born a citizen of an affluent country such as Canada is like being born into the nobility (even though many belong to the lesser nobility). To be born a citizen of a poor country such as Bangladesh is (for most) like being born into the peasantry in the Middle Ages. In this context, limiting entry to countries such as Canada is a way of protecting a birthright privilege. Liberals objected to the way in which feudalism restricted freedom, including that of individuals to move from one place to another in search of a better life. But modern practices of citizenship and state control over borders tie people to the land of their birth almost as effectively. If the feudal practices were wrong, what justifies the modern ones? In a just world, birthright privileges would not play such a decisive role in determining one's life chances.

Some would respond by drawing a distinction between freedom of exit and freedom of entry and arguing that the two are asymmetrical.[7] The former, the right to leave one's own state, ought to be virtually absolute, precisely because restrictions resemble the objectionable feudal practices. But that does not imply a right to enter any particular place. I think that it is true that the right to leave is more fundamental in some respects than the right to enter. It would normally be a greater wrong to prevent those already living in a state from leaving voluntarily (or to expel them involuntarily) than to prevent newcomers from entering, because the interest that one has in being able to leave (or to stay, if one wants) will normally be greater than one's interest in getting into a particular place.

However, entry could be so restricted in most states that most people who wanted to leave would have no place to go. That is certainly the case in the modern world. Liberal freedoms can be empty formalities under some circumstances. We have to pay attention to the conditions (material and other) that make formal freedoms meaningful and effective. Thus a right of exit that does not carry with it some reasonable guarantee of entry would not seem adequate in a just world. However, suppose that most places were open and only a few were closed. Under those circumstances, freedom of exit would not be a purely formal right. Even if we accept this argument about the asymmetry between the right to leave and the right to enter, it does not prove that restrictions on entry are justifiable, only that restrictions on exit are worse. The burden of proof remains on those who would justify closure at the cost of human freedom.

My critique of birthright privilege does not mean that initial allocation of citizenship on the basis of birthplace, parentage, or some combination thereof is morally objectionable. Indeed, that sort of allocation is morally required because children are born into a community with ties to others that should be acknowledged. In principle, however, individuals should be free to change their membership at will. The model here is that of provincial 'citizenship' in a federal system, which is assigned on the basis of birth, but one is free to move from one province to another and to change provincial 'citizenship.'

That leads to the final point. Compare freedom of movement within the state to freedom of movement across state borders. Like every freedom involving human action, freedom of movement is not unlimited, but, because it is an important liberty, limitations have to be justified in a way that gives equal weight to the claims of all. Some restrictions on movement are easy to justify, such as traffic regulations or a right to exclude others from one's home (assuming that everyone has a home or a reasonable opportunity to obtain one). But imagine an attempt by officials in one city to keep out people from another. That sort of restriction is seen as fundamentally incompatible with a commitment to free and equal citizenship. Cities and provinces have borders, but not ones that can be used to keep people in or out against their will. Indeed, freedom of movement within the nation state is widely acknowledged as a basic human right, and states are criticized for restricting internal movement even by those who accept the conventional view of state sovereignty. People are generally free to change their membership in sub-national political communities at will.

If it is so important for people to have the right to move freely within a state, is it not equally important for them to have the right to move across state borders? Every reason why one might want to move within a state may also be a reason for moving between states. One might want a job; one might fall in love with someone from another country; one might belong to a religion that has few adherents in one's native state and many in another; one might wish to pursue cultural opportunities that are available only in another land. The radical disjuncture that treats freedom of movement within the state as a moral imperative and freedom of movement across state borders as merely a matter of political discretion makes no sense from a perspective that takes seriously the freedom and equality of all individuals.

Would restrictions on immigration ever be morally permissible in a just world? Perhaps they would if a community needed to limit entry in order to preserve its distinctive cultural structure. Will Kymlicka develops such an argument from a liberal perspective in *Liberalism, Community and Culture*, and I find the argument broadly persuasive, even though I disagree with some of it.[8] Let me highlight a few aspects of his argument that are particularly salient for my concerns here. First, restrictions on mobility are limitations on an important freedom and have to be justified by special circumstances. Kymlicka explicitly links restrictions on entry to qualification of the voting rights of short-term residents as special arrangements that might be needed to protect the cultural integrity of a community, but he notes that the burden of proof is on those who would argue for such restrictions.[9]

Second, Kymlicka advances his argument in the context of ideal theory. Although his prime example of a case where restrictions are justified is that of Native communities in North America (whose vulnerability, cultural and otherwise, is certainly a product of historical injustice), he does not make historical injustice central to his argument and introduces a hypothetical example in which a smaller cultural community could become vulnerable to a larger one in ways that justified special rights in the absence of any wrongdoing by the larger community.[10]

Third, restrictions on liberal freedoms have to be limited strictly to what is required to protect the community in a particular case. Cultural vulnerability does not give a community carte blanche to limit freedoms. Quebec, the other distinct, minority cultural community cited by Kymlicka, has managed to strengthen its cultural position without restricting inter-provincial mobility and while increasing its intake of immigrants.

Fourth, as Kymlicka presents it, the interests of the community trying to preserve its cultural structure have to be weighed against the interests of those whose rights are restricted. Limitations must ultimately be justi-fiable from the perspective of equality. They cannot be used as a means to preserve unfair advantages.[11]

Fifth, Kymlicka's argument implicitly undercuts the claims of the state to exclude. He argues that most states are plural societies and hence not cultural communities in themselves, as he defines that concept.[12]

In sum, in a just world, states would not be morally entitled to restrict movement in the way that they do today. People would normally have the right to move freely across borders in much the way that they now can within a state. The first right of immigrants – the right to become an immigrant where one wanted – would be respected.

Now, of course, this sounds wildly implausible. But I think that speaks more to the profound injustices of the world we live in than to deep flaws in the argument. There are millions of people in the Third World today who long for the freedom and economic opportunity that they could find in affluent First World countries. Many of them take great risks to come: Haitians set off in leaky boats, Salvadorans are smuggled across a border in hot, airless trucks, and Tamils pay to be set adrift off the coast of Newfoundland. If the borders were open, millions more would move. The exclusion of so many poor and desperate people seems hard to justify from a perspective that takes seriously the claims of all individuals as free and equal moral persons.

One could argue, however, that this sense that freedom of movement is an urgent moral concern is an illusion – indeed, that the whole problem of freedom of movement is essentially epiphenomenal. Other things being equal, most people would not want to leave the land where they were born and raised, a place whose language, customs, and ways of life are familiar. But other things are not equal. There are vast economic inequalities among states, and some governments deny basic liberties to their own citizens. These are the circumstances that create such a vast potential for movement across borders and that make the issue of migration seem like an urgent moral problem.

But these circumstances themselves are at least as morally objectionable as restrictions on freedom of movement.[13] In a just world, all states would respect their citizens' basic liberties, and there would not be such significant international economic inequalities. In such a world, migration would no longer be a serious moral concern, because relatively few people would want to move and those who did could and would be easily accommodated.

If someone says that states will not meet these obligations to respect rights and transfer resources, it can be replied that we gain nothing by focusing on another obligation that they are equally unlikely to fulfil. Most of the same practical and self-interested considerations that will prevent rich states from transferring significant resources to poor ones will keep them from opening their borders wide to poor immigrants. In struggling against injustice, it is a bad strategy to make admission of new immigrants to rich countries a priority: restrictions are a symptom, not a cause, of the real problems; immigration can never be a solution for more than a relatively small number, no matter how open the borders; and this focus on people who want to move from the Third World to the First may perpetuate neocolonial assumptions about the superiority of the latter. We were supposed to be considering the problem here from the perspective of an idealistic moral theory in which the problems of non-compliance would not arise. The requirements of a just world were the only ones we are to consider for the moment, and it makes no sense to ask what morally ideal immigration policies would be in the context of other policies and institutions that are far from ideal.

I think that there is a great deal to be said for this objection. International inequalities and political oppression are certainly more important moral and political problems than restrictions on migration. The sense that the latter is an urgent problem derives in large part from the size of the potential demand, and that in turn derives from international inequalities and other forms of injustice that free movement will do little to cure.

None of this really challenges the conclusion that a just world would generally permit free movement. Even if the most urgent problems that generate mass migrations today were eliminated, people would still have reasons for wanting to move across borders, just as they do for moving within states now. The right to move would be an important freedom in a just world.

The objection really reveals, I believe, the problem with using the just-world framework and the limits of an idealistic theory of morality. In assuming away the problems of historical contingency and injustice, idealistic moral theory ignores precisely those features of our world that present us with the most urgent and troubling moral problems. For example, one of the most pressing moral and political issues today in the area of immigration concerns refugees. What are our responsibilities towards them? How many should we take in, and which ones? How are our responsibilities affected (if at all) by the ways in which other countries respond to the problem? The just-world framework offers no help in thinking about these matters, because in a just world there would be no refugees, at least if refugees are people with a well-founded fear of persecution, as the conventional definition has it. The problem of responding to injustices of this sort is set aside in idealistic moral theory.

Even if we accept free movement as one of principles that would be respected in a just world, it is far from clear how that helps to guide our actions in a world that is far from just. It might suggest that restrictions on movement are morally problematic, but it does not help with priorities, tradeoffs, and strategies for change, nor does it begin to reflect the complexities and ambiguities of the moral problems that we face in the real world. Consider, for example, the debate over migration to Israel of Soviet Jews – now Russian Jews, a change that may or may not affect the moral arguments in the debate. How can that, or any other, issue in the conflict between Israel and the Palestinians be separated from historical contingencies and injustices and from well-founded fears on both sides of future injustices? Does a morally idealistic theory really help us to come to terms with this sort of problem?

Realistic Moral Theory

Because the world is so unjust and we have to live and act within it, a morally idealistic theory may provide much less help in figuring out what our moral responsibilities are and what we ought to do, individually and collectively, than an approach that starts from the alternatives that are actually before us – options that are, in one sense or another, feasible – as well as from contexts that have been shaped by historical contingencies and the unjust actions of others that we must take into account. I turn now to that sort of approach which I am calling a realistic moral theory.

This sort of moral theory is realistic in the sense that it focuses on problems that many people actually experience as involving important moral concerns or raising troubling moral issues. In other words, the first task of a realistic moral theory is to articulate widely shared moral views. These views will entail standards that we often will not meet in small ways and sometimes will not meet in large ways. But failures to meet the standards will be recognized widely as moral failures (unlike failures to meet the standards of a just world).

A realistic moral theory will start from conventional moral understandings, but it need not simply stop there. Any plausible form of moral theory entails reflective self-criticism, considering the relations among different principles that we espouse or the implications of practices that we follow and advocating changes in conventional moral understandings that seem at odds with our most fundamental commitments. But if the theory is to remain realistic, it cannot depart too far from conventional views. The changes that it urges must be feasible, at least in the sense of being up for debate in society in a way that, say, a demand for open borders is not.

Let me concede at once that this whole approach is subject to challenge as being fundamentally inadequate from the perspective of justice *simpliciter*. But that is just another way of saying that it is inadequate from the perspective of idealistic moral theory. I agree, but, as I have just tried to suggest, an idealistic moral theory has its own problems and limitations, especially when it comes to offering guidance about what to do in an imperfect world. A realistic moral theory at least starts with the world that we inhabit, including the moral world, and for that reason it may help us to figure out how we ought to act (which is not to say that it will always succeed in guiding actual behaviour).

A realistic moral theory will make use of two kind of arguments in addressing the questions that I set out at the beginning of this chapter concerning the citizenry's rights vis-à-vis immigrants. First, some arguments will be presented as part of a universalistic moral theory that sets minimum standards for all social institutions and talks about human rights and human duties as these apply to issues affecting immigrants. Such human rights claims need not be based on the supposition that these rights are based on universal, ahistorical principles. It does imply, however, that some of the things that we think of as right and wrong we regard as such for everyone, not just for members of our own community (however defined). We do not have to inquire into the content of Indonesian culture, for example, to condemn the massacre of peaceful protestors in East Timor by Indonesian soldiers or to investigate the moral views of Serbians to criticize 'ethnic cleansing' in the Balkans.

Second, the other type of argument is more internal, more tied to a particular community. It is the sort of argument that appeals to 'our' shared norms and values without supposing that they necessarily are shared or ought to be shared by other communities. Alternatively, an internalist argument of this sort could be thought to apply to all other communities that share our commitments – say, a commitment to common law traditions regarding the rule of law, without supposing that this is the only morally acceptable version of the rule of law. Whereas the first kind of argument – the universalist kind – is concerned normally only with minimum standards and is thus apt to be expressed only in the language of rights and duties or right and wrong, the second type may be put either in that language or in that of good and bad. The moral 'ought' may appeal to certain ideals of the community. It is important to see that such arguments are, or at least can be, moral arguments, not just claims about wise policy or self-interest (although those considerations could also be mixed in).

How would a realistic moral theory address the questions that I posed at the outset? First, consider admissions. The conventional moral view is that states are largely free (in a moral sense) to admit or exclude immigrants. In other words, from such a perspective, the universal moral (not just legal) right is the right of every state to control immigration in accordance with its interests and inclinations, not the right of (potential) immigrants to go where they want. So a realistic moral theory will not challenge this right of discretion head on. There are some important moral constraints on and qualifications to this general right, however. Some are clear enough even from a conventional perspective, and others can emerge from theoretical reflections that build on that viewpoint without departing too far from it.

Refugees

The most important exception to the general right of states to act as they choose with regard to immigration is that refugees have moral claims that states are not (morally) free to ignore. I begin this attempt to offer a realistic moral theory about the rights of immigrants by exploring some of the claims of refugees. Refugees have fled from their state of origin and need a place to stay, at least temporarily and perhaps permanently.

Most states formally accept the principle of non-refoulement – an obligation not to return refugees to the state from which they fled – and this is widely seen as a minimal moral standard. After that, things get murky.

For one thing, non-refoulement (unless supplemented by other principles) places the burden of receiving and caring for refugees exclusively on those states where the refugees arrive and appeal for asylum. In most cases, that means the states neighbouring the one producing the refugees. That is hardly a fair way to distribute the burden, by anyone's standard of fairness. For example, the small and poor country of Malawi has become a place of asylum for over one million refugees from the civil war in Mozambique. There may well be good reasons for refugees to stay in the area near their homeland, especially if there is some hope that they will eventually be able to return home, but it is certainly not reasonable to expect host states – often poor nations such as Malawi – to bear the financial costs of caring for the refugees. It seems far more plausible to recognize a general obligation on the part of all to share the costs of caring for refugees and to adopt some sort of cost sharing based on ability to pay.

But what should we Canadians do if we cannot reach agreement with others on a cost-sharing principle or if we reach an accord but then others do not actually pay their fair share? These are common enough experiences in practice. Should we pick up the slack (and run the risk of being regarded as suckers by the shirkers)? Should we pay our 'fair share' as determined in advance on the assumption that everyone would contribute (and leave the Malawis of the world to pick up the slack or the refugees to go hungry and without shelter)? Of course, we in North America let our fellow citizens go hungry and homeless, so it would not be surprising if we were prepared to let refugees in a far-off land suffer a similar fate. Nevertheless, one moral failure does not excuse another, and a realistic moral theory does not have to leave every practice unchallenged.

A realistic moral theory would not criticize the basic principle of state sovereignty with regard to immigration (as a more idealistic theory would), but it could and should criticize failure to provide adequate support for refugees. However, there remains the question of what to do in the face of that failure, how to identify a course of action that has some reasonable chance of being adopted. If one presses for a policy that people experience as demanding too much of them, they may respond by doing less than they would have if presented with a less ambitious proposal in the first place.

On a more positive note, it is sometimes possible to enlist particularistic moral arguments to buttress the general obligation incumbent upon all states to support refugees. For example, some political community may feel a special sense of obligation towards a particular set of refugees or towards refugees in general. These are the sorts of moral arguments that often carry great weight in practice, although they would not even appear in a purely idealistic theory.

Many refugees have some reasonable hope of returning home eventually, but many do not. They need new homes. Again, it seems to me, the obligation to provide opportunities for resettlement is, in principle, universal, but it is reasonable to look for principles of allocating responsibility for resettlement that take account of differences among societies. For example, countries such as Canada and the United States that are already taking in a significant number of immigrants ought to accept more refugees for resettlement than strict allocation on the basis of population or wealth might suggest. Again, an argument from general principles of fairness can be buttressed in the case of both these countries by appeals to their self-understanding as nations that have a tradition of generosity towards refugees. This is not to say, however, that a country can legitimately use a history of closure – of not accepting immigrants – as justification for not resettling refugees. Fair sharing of the burden entails, I believe, some responsibility for all.

Some would argue that openness to refugees is no cause for celebration, because it is extremely expensive to resettle a refugee in a Western country. The same amount of money, they argue, would do much more good for more people if spent on finding refugees new homes in the Third World. If one accepts this argument, should one conclude that a country such as Japan that provides more money and less space (in terms of resettlement opportunities) is actually following a morally superior path? That seems to follow, but I want to resist the conclusion, insisting again that some openness to refugees is essential for all.

Supporters of resettlement sometimes deny the relevance of the trade-off alleged in the paragraph above, arguing that resettlement here actually generates more support for aiding refugees abroad by given the issue a human face for those in the West. There is no intrinsic moral reason to adopt this alleged trade-off as the framework of choice, and indeed concern for refugees should lead one to resist it.

But sometimes such resistance fails. Suppose the political process works so that there is some trade-off between the two forms of assistance. It is common enough in budgetary allocations to construct trade-offs of one kind or another. The particular balancing act may always be contingent and contestable and therefore arbitrary, in the sense that some different set of trade-offs could have been used instead. But sometimes one has to make a particular sort of choice just because those with budgetary authority have framed it in this way. Does a realistic moral theory offer any guidance as to how to choose in this context? If so, it is not clear to me.

Here is another problem. Many people have criticized the definition of refugees as too narrow, because it includes only those with a 'well-founded fear of being persecuted.' Over the past several years, interpretation of who counts as a refugee has in fact been broadened under international law so that a claimant may now use evidence that a group of which she is a member has been subject to persecution in support of her claim, whereas previously she had to show unequivocally that she was personally targeted. Still, there has been strenuous resistance to the idea, advanced by some critics, that the definition of 'refugee' should be expanded to include not only victims of political persecution but also people in comparably desperate straits as a result of economic or environmental disasters. Opponents fear that such a change would open the floodgates, leading to massive increase in the number of those with defensible refugee claims. They emphasize the long tradition of distinguishing between political refugees and others seeking to migrate. Advocates of the change respond that the first argument implicitly concedes that under the present practice we are just turning our backs on those with legitimate and urgent moral claims against us and that the second argument simply ignores the merits of the claim that there is a moral equivalence between the claims of political refugees and those of economic and environmental refugees. Opponents of change reply that altering the system will undermine support for refugees in general, generate a political backlash, and ultimately lead to fewer being admitted here or helped abroad.

Can a realistic moral theory offer guidance? Those in favour of expanding the definition have the better argument in principle, in my view, but, for a realistic moral theory, I think the crucial issue would be the consequences of different definitions for the well-being of refugees. After all, what is the point of adopting a definition that leads to a political dynamic that leaves the people whom you want to help worse off? Now, whether people will respond badly or well to a change in definition and/or to an increase in number of refugees requires a contingent political judgment for which a moral theory as such, even a realistic one, offers no help. But one can see from this example that a realistic theory has to include the likelihood of moral failures, of people acting badly and not doing what they should, as a relevant variable. That is both a strength and a weakness of this approach – it may provide a better guide to action in the world as it is, but it may blur the line between right and wrong or good and bad by including as constraints on action both factors that are in themselves morally unobjectionable and factors that should be subject to moral criticism.

Another crucial problem is that there has been a tremendous increase in all of the Western countries of the number of people arriving and claiming to be refugees. In many western European nations, the vast majority of claimants are ultimately denied, but they have kept coming because there are many advantages to being in Europe while the claim is being considered, and, in many cases, those denied refugee status are, nevertheless, not sent home. In North America, too, where acceptance rates tend to be higher, especially in Canada, the number of claims has increased dramatically.

Of course, if you accept the principle of non-refoulement (and, as I noted above, everyone does and should), then you cannot send a claimant back to her country of origin until you determine whether or not she is a refugee. Even if most claims are denied, some are not. Now in every Western country, there are standard ways of assessing contested claims, namely the legal procedures used in administrative, civil, and criminal matters. These procedures are inevitably elaborate, time-consuming, and expensive, and the more so the weightier the issue at stake. One must gather all the relevant evidence, organize arguments and counter-arguments, allow for appeals, and so on. Should all this procedural panoply by employed to determine whether or not a refugee claim is valid? If so, it becomes enormously expensive. If not, you may send someone back to torture and death on the basis of procedures that your system treats as inadequate to safeguard, say, some small-scale commercial transaction.

Some point out that the amount spent on refugee determination procedures is, in some cases, significantly greater than that spent on aid to refugees abroad and provides far less human benefit per dollar. Others reply that that sort of cost-benefit analysis is not appropriate here, for the same reason that we do not reduce the costs of criminal proceedings in order to spend more on social welfare programs, and that, in any event, there is no reason to suppose that money saved on determination would actually go to refugee aid aboard.

What have countries done? The main strategy has been to adopt policies of 'humane deterrence' that make it harder for people to arrive and claim refugee status, by imposing stricter visa requirements on people coming from certain areas and then requiring airlines to enforce these restrictions through a system of punitive fines for transporting passengers without proper documentation. The basic idea is that if you can get a visa, you are not really a refugee. The unstated but inevitable corollary is that if you are a genuine refugee, you will not be able to get here. In addition, many countries have imposed stricter limits on what refugee claimants may do while their claims are being adjudicated. In some cases, this involves confinement to prison-like detention facilities. This reduces the incentive to come as a false claimant, while subjecting genuine refugees (at best) to a long, undeserved period of social isolation and deprivation as the introduction to their new home and at the moment of their having supposedly reached safety.

How would a realistic moral theory respond to these developments and to the dilemmas that they entail? I am tempted to say, 'with despair.' These are moral conundrums. There is no really satisfactory theoretical response to them. To work within the confines of realistic policy options in this area inevitably requires one to recommend courses of action that one knows are deeply problematic from the perspective of moral principle. But unless one is willing to recognize political realities and incorporate them as constraints, one cannot make a good judgment about what policy would be best from a moral point of view.

Family Reunification

Let me turn now to the question of how moral considerations might affect what states ought to do with regard to immigrants who are not refugees. As I noted above, from the perspective of a (realistic) universalistic moral theory, governments are largely free to be as open or as closed as they choose. But there is one important exception besides refugees. Every state is morally obliged to respect the principle of family unity and thus ought to admit the spouse and minor children of a current citizen or legal immigrant.

Someone might object that this stipulation does not adequately respect differences among cultures. It is certainly true that there are many different understandings of the family. Some familial relationships that are of immense importance in one culture are relatively insignificant in another. But I know of no culture in which the connections among husband, wife, and minor children are not deemed to be vital. So the issue is not whether there is a crucial human interest at stake here, but whether governments may ignore this interest in order to control immigration. At least under normal circumstances – the marriage is not a fraud, the spouse is not a threat to national security, and so on – my answer is that this is precisely the sort of case in which the concept of human rights works well. A human right is a moral claim by an individual that is so fundamental that some special justification is required to override it, not merely the normal calculation of interests. The right of spouses and minor children to live together is just this sort of moral claim. In short, even countries that do not normally permit immigration ought to permit reunification of families. A fortiori, those that do allow immigration have to give priority to spouses and minor children.

Historical Tradition

In addition to this universalistic constraint on restricting immigration, moral arguments that appeal to the history or commitments of a particular state can play a powerful role in this area. For example, people sometimes argue that it would be morally wrong for Canada to close its borders to immigrants because it would be a betrayal of an ideal of openness that has become central to the nation's collective self-understanding. Such particularistic moral arguments tend to be made in newspapers and magazines rather than in philosophical journals and are often blended with other (non-moral) arguments about the beneficial economic and demographic consequences of immigration for the existing citizenry. But in my view, this sort of appeal to a collective historical identity as the basis for moral obligation is often far more effective in motivating action than an argument based on general principles about rights and obligations.[14] It is the kind of claim that looms large in our ordinary experience of moral argument in public affairs, and it deserves more systematic attention.

A moral argument for substantial immigration based on a collective tradition of openness might carry weight in Canada or the United States, but it would have no impact, or rather the reverse effect, in countries such as Germany and Japan. There an appeal to collective tradition could be used in the name of closure, on the grounds that preservation of the shared culture and way of life of the existing population would be disrupted by substantial immigration. I am not sure whether it is appropriate to characterize such an argument for closure as moral in nature. Not every appeal to collective identity takes the form of a moral appeal. But if we take as our starting point the view that states have the moral right to control immigration, I do not see why such an appeal would be intrinsically objectionable from a moral perspective.

Admission/Exclusion

One might assume that if governments are morally entitled, from a universalistic perspective, to admit as many or as few immigrants as they wish, apart from the qualifications already noted, then they must also be morally free to select whom to admit or exclude on the basis of whatever criteria they choose, or perhaps on the basis of whatever particular commitments they have as collectivities. This freedom may reflect their legal position in international law, but I do not think that it captures their moral position, even on a highly conventional definition of morality, and certainly not on a more reflective one.

No state is morally entitled to discriminate against potential immigrants on the basis of race or religion or ethnicity. Why not? Because these sorts of discrimination are morally objectionable whenever they are part of any public policy in any regime. Again, the right not to be discriminated against on such grounds stands as a paradigm of a basic human right, one that states ought not to violate whatever their collective interests or cultural traditions.

This universalistic norm is reinforced by particularistic commitments in countries of immigration that have had discriminatory policies that they have subsequently abandoned. Australia, Canada, and the United States all had overtly discriminatory policies and practices. All now are officially committed to a policy of non-discrimination in admissions. All evoke that discriminatory past as a source of shame and celebrate the policy change as a moral advance.

Having a sense of historical experiences of discrimination can provide valuable clues to the forms that discrimination is likely to take and to the arguments that will be used to defend it. Thus one hears today from some Europeans (who formally accept the principle that one must not discriminate on the basis of religion) that limits should be placed on new entrants from Islamic countries because of the gulf between Islamic beliefs and values and those derived from the western European tradition, because Islamic fundamentalists may be disloyal and even dangerous, and so on. It is striking how much these arguments resemble the ones used against Catholic and Jewish immigrants in the nineteenth-century United States.

In sum, a state may choose not to admit immigrants at all (apart from refugees and the immediate family of current inhabitants) without violating any moral norms, but if it admits immigrants, it may not exclude on the basis of race, religion, or ethnicity.

Of course, one can argue about whether a particular practice or policy is actually discriminatory. Take the issue of the criteria of selection of new immigrants among potential applicants. If race, religion, and ethnicity may not be used as grounds for exclusion, may they be used instead as criteria for inclusion? To some, this suggestion will seem utterly sophistic. To favour X on the grounds that she has characteristic A is to disfavour Y on the grounds that she does not. Such favouring and disfavouring may be legitimate vis-à-vis some characteristics, but not with regard to race, religion, or ethnicity.

This argument may be correct at a formal level, but, at the least, it does not draw our attention to further moral judgments – moral discriminations – that we may want to make. Consider four recent or current policies with these sorts of factors.[15] (I oversimplify a bit, but I think I describe the main lines accurately.) Britain removed citizenship from holders of overseas passports and citizens of Commonwealth countries, except for those whose grandfather was born in Great Britain. Ireland grants an automatic right to citizenship to anyone with a grandparent born in Ireland, provided that the person comes to Ireland to live. Germany grants citizenship (upon application in Germany) to anyone of ethnic German descent, no matter how long since the person's ancestors lived in Germany. Israel grants automatic citizenship to any Jew who comes to live in Israel.

Of these, the British law is the most objectionable from a moral perspective, and the Irish one the least, despite their formal similarity. The British law is a thinly disguised form of racism. It was designed to preserve the citizenship rights of as many descendants of white settlers as possible, while depriving as many Asians and Africans as possible of theirs. The Irish 'grandfather' clause, by contrast, has no hidden exclusionary goal. It is merely an attempt to lure back the descendants of some of those who left. The German law is troubling for two related reasons. First, the explicit link between ethnicity and citizenship raises questions about whether those German citizens who are not ethnic Germans are really regarded as equal citizens. Second, the easy granting of citizenship to people who have never lived in Germany before, and some of whom do not even speak the language, contrasts sharply with the reluctance to grant citizenship automatically to the children of Turkish 'guest workers,' even when the children were born and brought up in Germany (and sometimes speak no other language). The Israeli 'law of return' raises questions about whether the Arab citizens of Israel whose friends and relatives do not have comparably easy access to citizenship are really regarded as equal citizens. However, the Israeli law is tied both to national security concerns and to the historic purpose of Israel as a homeland for Jews.

These examples suggest the limits of formal principles and the need for a contextually sensitive assessment of group rights that pays attention to their actual effects on the inclusion and exclusion of different groups.

What should we think about immigration policies that use linguistic and cultural compatibility as criteria of selection? In principle, I do not see why such criteria should be regarded as morally objectionable, provided that the policy is not a disguised form of racial, religious, or ethnic prejudice and that the cumulative effects of such policies by different countries do not leave out some groups altogether.

Again, the issue requires a contextual judgment about particular immigration policies. First, it might well be possible to recreate the 'White Australia' policy without ever mentioning race.[16] The policy could be couched entirely in terms of language and culture, but it would still be racist. In contrast, if Australia simply granted preference to immigrants from former British colonies, on the grounds of cultural compatibility, that would seem to be quite a different matter. Given the vast numbers of non-whites in those former colonies, it is hard to see how that could be construed as racist. (There might be other grounds for objecting to it, but I leave those aside.)

Second, Quebec's government grants great weight to the ability to speak French, relatively little to speaking English, and none at all to speaking other languages. If one accepts the goal of preserving the French language as a reasonable one for Quebec's government to adopt, as I certainly do, then I see nothing objectionable in this policy. After all, the largest number of potential francophone immigrants will come from France's former colonies in Asia and Africa, so this policy is not a disguised form of racism. However, I once had a conversation with a Quebec immigration official who told me that francophone Lebanese Christians were particularly desirable because of their cultural compatibility, in contrast to francophone Lebanese Muslims. Of course, one could not inquire about religion, he said, because that might be construed as religious discrimination, but names (such as Muhammed) often provided a clue. None of this could be said openly, he commented. I think the reason why is obvious. It was a form of religious discrimination. I do not mean that he was insincere in saying that cultural compatibility was his concern. Rather, the point is that most forms of discrimination are seen by the practitioners as issues of cultural compatibility. That is why it is such a tricky category from a moral point of view. The official's awareness that this practice could not be discussed publicly is one indication that he was conscious that it was something that many people would find morally objectionable and that might be difficult to defend – in contrast, say, to the general preference given to the ability to speak French which officials have no trouble defending openly.

Conclusion

This discussion of the way in which a realistic moral theory might address the respective moral claims of immigrants and states is by no means exhaustive but is, I hope, sufficient to give some sense of the characteristic strengths and weaknesses of this type of perspective, as against that of an idealistic moral theory.

Notes

1 See Michael Walzer *Spheres of Justice* (New York: Basic Books 1983).
2 I have explored these alternative theoretical perspectives more fully in an unpublished paper, 'Moral Realism and Moral Idealism: The Ethics of International Migration.'
3 For Aristotle, these circumstances turn out to include the existence of a large and docile slave class, but I leave aside that complexity and what it tells us about Aristotle's picture of the best regime.
4 See John Rawls *A Theory of Justice* (Cambridge, Mass.: Harvard University Press 1971).
5 Much of the discussion below of the idealistic moral perspective on immigration, though not the part on Kymlicka's work, is drawn from my essay 'Migration and Morality: A Liberal Egalitarian Perspective' in Brian Barry and Robert Goodin eds *Free Movement* (London: Harvester Wheatsheaf 1992), 25–47.
6 This sketch necessarily covers over deep disagreements among liberal theories with regard to many issues, such as the amount of inequality that is compatible with or required by the commitment to freedom; whether affirmative action for groups historically subject to discrimination is a violation of, or a means of realizing, liberal principles; and the foundations (if any) of liberal commitments.
7 See Walzer *Spheres* chap. 2. For detailed discussion of the right of exit, see Frederick Whelan 'Citizenship and the Right to Leave,' *American Political Science Review* 75 (1981) 636–53.

8 Will Kymlicka *Liberalism, Community, and Culture* (Oxford: Clarendon Press 1989).

9 Ibid 46–50.

10 Ibid 187–9.

11 Ibid 182–200.

12 Ibid 135.

13 See, for example, Charles Beitz *Political Theory and International Relations* (Princeton, NJ: Princeton University Press 1979); Brian Barry 'Humanity and Justice in Global Perspective' in J. Roland Pennock and John W. Chapman eds *Ethics, Economics, and the Law: Nomos XXIV* (New York: New York University Press 1982) 219–52; and David A.J. Richards 'International Distributive Justice' in Pennock and Chapman eds *Ethics* 275–99.

14 A moral appeal to history can be based on a negative assessment of one's collective past as well as on a positive reconstruction of it. For example, Germany has one of the most liberal laws on asylum in the world for reasons directly related to its desire to repudiate the racist past of the Third Reich. And in the current debate over reform of that law (because the nation now has many more asylum seekers than the other major European states), the law's connection to repudiation of the Nazi legacy has been a crucial symbolic and political obstacle to change. Similarly, in Canada, any discussion of tighter restrictions on refugees evokes the story of Canada's refusal to accept a shipload of Jewish refugees from Nazi Germany in the 1930s. To say that this was a shameful episode in the nation's collective history that must never be repeated is to make a powerful moral argument for caution in tightening restrictions.

15 The rest of this paragraph and all of the next one are taken from my essay 'Migration and Morality.'

16 For detailed analysis of what this sort of argument would look like, see my 'Nationalism and the Exclusion of Immigrants: Lessons from Australian Immigration Policy' in Mark Gibney ed *Open Borders? Closed Societies: The Ethical and Political Issues* (Westport, Conn.: Greenwood Press 1988) 41–60.

8

Refugees: The Right of Return

HOWARD ADELMAN

I first clarify three paradoxes concerning possession, protection, and use, which are the essential characteristics, I believe, of human rights. Four groups of Palestinians – those who fled the territory in 1948, those who fled or were absent during the Six Day War of 1967, those who left voluntarily or otherwise after 1967, and families of all the above – claim a right to return. Their claims correspond to three major theories of human rights – natural rights (refugees of 1948), contractarian (1967 and afterwards), and idealist (families). Further, analysis of the claim for a right of return shows it to be essentially a positioning of a human right, not with the traditionally noted (but essentially rhetorical) characteristics such as universality, inalienability, and inviolability, but with the paradoxes of possession, protection, and use. In that sense, the right to return is indeed a human right. The chapter argues next that the right of return is also a group right that is neither reducible to nor in conflict with individual rights. Further, and most important, it is one of three types of group rights (along with property rights and rights of asylum) that are more fundamental than individual rights in the sense of being a precondition for the latter.

The Three Paradoxes of Human Rights

Most rights are not 'natural' or 'foundational' or 'human' in the sense of being attributable to all human beings. I have a right to receive my salary once per month from the university because it is part of my employment contract. It is a right but not a human right, because it is based on the particular agreement that I made with the institution backed up by agreements made by my union rather than a right of all people as humans.

Human rights, in contrast, are said to be universal in three senses. First, all humans, as humans, possess them. Second, no one is entitled to violate them. Third, all humans as humans should be able to exercise them. Human rights are universal in possession, protection, and use. The paradoxes are related to the meanings of 'having' a right – related to three different senses of 'have' – owning, being entitled to, and being able to exercise. The verb 'have' thus has a proprietary, a recipient, and an existential sense.

Possession

Although human rights are said to be universal in ownership, there is a related paradox, which Jack Donnelly calls the 'possession paradox.' '"Having" a right is ... of most value when one does not "have" the object of the right – that is, when one is denied direct or objective enjoyment of that right.'[1] I have the greater proprietary claim the weaker my guarantor's ability to 'operationalize' my right. In contrast, my right to a salary as an employee of a bankrupt business is of least value when I do not have the object of that right – that is, my paycheque – and the duty bearer is bankrupt and there is no insurance system. In the case of rights that are other than general, human rights, the value diminishes to the degree that protections are absent and the rights cannot be exercised.

Protection

The possession paradox is, of course, only apparent; one is said to 'have' (possess) the right but not 'have' (be able to use) it because of the absence of a guarantor to ensure that one has (is entitled) it and can exercise it when it is being challenged. One values human rights most to the degree that one has been deprived of protections for rights and the ability to exercise them.

In Ronald Dworkin's famous phrase, rights 'trump' utilities.[2] Rights come prior to any other moral considerations or interests. They are entitlements that override other socially beneficial claims even if the latter foster general interests. Rights set limits for other utilities, but rights themselves are valued independent of their utility. They are not only most valued when their use is denied, but their utility is demonstrated best when they cannot be used or when they need not be used. Human rights are the very opposite of nuclear weapons as part of the doctrine of mutually assured destruction (MAD) of the nuclear-deterrent policy. Those weapons were useful only if they were never used. But if they were to be useful as a threat, each party had to believe that the other was willing to use them. Rights are most useful when duty bearers seem most reluctant to grant their use. Unlike interests or other issues of distributive justice and social policy, such as access to good health care, the value of which depends on translating them into utilities, human rights are most precious not only when they are prevented from being used but because they 'trump' other utilities and have a value independent of utility.

In the case of human rights, the duty bearer is the state. 'Traditional human rights, both civil and political and economic and social, are held primarily against one's own state.'[3] Thus they differ from other types of rights in that the party responsible for the reciprocal duties to complement those rights so that they can be exercised is the party also responsible for protecting their exercise – that is, ensuring that the duty bearer remains willing to carry out the duties. The state is also often the target of the use of those rights, as well as the ensurer that those rights can be used.

The inability and/or unwillingness of the duty bearer are not the only reasons that a rights holder may be incapable of exercising rights. Ignorance of the rights holder that s/he has those rights may be another factor. Thus the state is also given the job of educating its citizens about their rights. The duty bearer for protecting and ensuring rights is also responsible for inculcating its citizens with the conviction that they have those rights. I refer to this as the 'protection paradox' characteristic of human rights.

I 'have' the right in the sense that it is mine, but I have the right (in the sense of use) only if its ensurer, the state, 'grants' its citizens those rights. The protection paradox has an opposite formula to the possession paradox. With the former, I have the right only to the degree that its exercise is guaranteed by the state. In the latter, the weaker the state is in protecting those rights, the stronger the sense is that I have that right. The right is most valuable when the holder is denied the ability to exercise it.

Use

In addition to paradoxes of possession and protection that seem unique to human rights, there is also a use paradox. When I exercise a right to purchase a stock from my stockbroker, my right is lost with the exercise. Further, exercising the right does nothing for the rights of option holders in general or the principle of exercising options. When I vote in an election (stemming from the political human right to vote), I have exercised my right and may not exercise it again in the same election, but the general right to vote is enhanced. The exercise of human rights seems to run on anti-entropic principles. Use of them enhances their utility rather than using them up.

Human rights are like other rights in that they are claims for something, on behalf of someone, and over against some entity that has the responsibility for reciprocal action to ensure exercise of that right. In that sense, all rights are entitlements. They are not necessarily exercisable. There is no connection between having a right (in both the proprietary and entitlement senses) and the ability actually to exercise it. For example, although I may have a moral right to receive my overdue salary from the now-bankrupt firm, my legal right may be only to receive a proportion of due severance from the company's net assets, if any. Exercise of that right is a moral and sometimes legal but not necessarily an existential right. However, although human rights may be protected and guaranteed by law, the absence of such laws does not abrogate the right. The right exists morally as one basis and independent of any laws drawn up to help guarantee those rights. Thus human rights are said to exist independent of their exercise as well as of the legal means to protect that exercise. To put it another way, the possessory character of human rights exists independent of the protections afforded them and their use. But human rights, though independent of, are not separable from that protection or use.

Summary

It is this interrelated but autonomous character of possession, entitlement, and utility that leads to the apparent paradoxes. These can be summarized as follows.

Possession paradox: Human rights are valued most to the degree that one has been deprived of protections for rights and the ability to exercise them.

Protection paradox: Human rights are least useful to the degree that the duty bearer for protecting and ensuring rights fails to live up to its responsibility not only in the ensuring and protecting functions but also in inculcating in its citizens the conviction that they have those rights.

Utility paradox: Use of human rights enhances their utility rather than using them up.

Return as a Human Right

The Palestinians claim a right of return to their homeland and also claim that the right is a human right. In fact, four groups claim a right of return: those who fled the territory that became Israel during 1948, those forced to flee or who were absent from the West Bank and Gaza when the Israelis captured those areas in 1967, those expelled or deported by the Israeli Defence Force after 1967 or who went abroad and did not renew their residence permits within the allocated period, and families of those with legal residency rights, although they do not have a right of return in the strict sense, since they were not necessarily or usually residents of Palestine.

How do these four categories of Palestinians fit in the general theory of human rights and with respect to the various schools of theorists of human rights? Let me begin with the latter part of the question first. Where does the claim for a right of return fit with respect to the different schools? This may seem an odd way to proceed, since if you prove that the right to return does or does not belong to the genus human right, then its species is a secondary concern. But the approach has a rationale. There are apparent similarities between each of the rationalizations justifying return as a matter of right for different groups of refugees and one of three schools of thought on human rights – national rights (1948), contractarian (1967 and post-1967), and idealist (spouses).

The rationale for the right of return of the 1948 refugees seems most akin to the natural rights school, which holds that rights are universal because they derive from the nature of human being.[4] The rationalization of this right for 1967 and post-1967 refugees, who were expelled or not allowed to return because of their alleged breaches of administrative rules, seems directly akin to the contractarian theorists[5] who posit that human rights are constraints on conduct and the pursuit of individual interests to which all members of a society, if they are rational, agree; these include protection of persons and personal and public property and provision of necessary public services as a condition for the operation of society based on foundational principles that act as necessary and jointly sufficient conditions for any social contract whatsoever. The rationalization for the right of return of proximate family members – that is, for family reunification – seems most akin to the idealist school,[6] which holds that human rights occupy the highest rung of the ladder of moral principles and cannot be sacrificed for other moral claims, such as justice or equity, and, therefore, should be embedded in the constitution of a state so that the goal of respecting each person as a dignified human being can be guaranteed independent of who happens to be the ruler at the time.

Natural Rights and the Refugees of 1948

The right of return for Palestinians who left in 1948 was justified on the basis of the 'natural' right of every human to live and grow up on the soil on which he or she was born. Severance of the bond between the refugee and the land was seen as fundamentally damaging not only to the individual but somehow between that individual and his/her ancestors as well as among the members of the community. The right to return to the soil of one's birth was a natural right. Presumably, this characteristic of attachment to soil was true of all humans because of their character as human. This seems to be the identical rationale for human rights depicted by the natural rights school.

There is a second similarity. Israel objected to the return of the 1948 refugees on the grounds that they would pose a political, security, and demographic threat to the nascent state of Israel.[7] Israel had an absolute right to determine who could reside on the soil controlled by the state and absolute, sovereign power to determine what actions were most appropriate to secure the state and who could or could not be admitted. No outside authority, including the United Nations – in fact, especially the United Nations – was empowered to intervene in the state's sovereign power to take action in defence of its own security. Yet the refugees' proposed right of return was a constraint that the United Nations proposed for the nascent state. For natural rights theorists, natural rights perform precisely the same task – placing constraints on the activities of the state provided that activation of such rights poses no threat to national security. The issue was neither the natural rights of the refugees to return nor the right of Israel as a sovereign state to determine its own security needs, but whether the natural rights constraining the state were themselves subject to the constraint of the right of the sovereign state to determine its own security needs.

The rationalization for the right of return of the 1948 refugees and one important postulate of the natural rights school, however, do not seem to coincide. Theorists defend pursuit of the well-being and happiness of the individual as fundamental – it is both the condition of social organization and the basis for determining ultimate value. However, the natural right to return to the soil on which one had been raised was held even though holding onto that principle meant that refugees suffered for years, in light of the incompatibility between the forces pushing for return and the immovable resistance of Israel. Indeed the children suffered, too, as they languished in camps with no permanent solution directly proposed for their ultimate fate, pending a peace agreement that would decide whether they could exercise their right to return. Pursuit of the well-being and happiness of the individual did not seem to be the ultimate value on which the right of return was based.

Or is the case so clear? After all, even UN-appointed mediator Count Folke Bernadotte of Wisborg (assassinated 1948) concurred that if the refugees were not allowed to return, they should be resettled as a practical matter. Return to their own soil was envisaged as critical to their happiness, but if it could not be accomplished, he did not favour keeping them in limbo. Pursuit of individual happiness, necessary constraints on the state, and the arguable characteristic of human beings to be attached to soil were not always reconcilable in practice.

Behind the advocacy of such principles was a fundamental thesis that conflicted directly with Thomas Paine's famous exhortation: 'Lay then the axe to the root.'[8] That root was in nature. And in nature, in the attachment to soil – whether it be the granite rocks and windswept trees of my family island in Georgian Bay where I wrote the original version of this manuscript or the orange groves of the Mediterranean plain or the olive trees of the Judaean Hills – customs in forming families and communities are held together by attachments to soil. After all, Burke's *Reflections on the French Revolution* (1790) was written to defend custom built up in traditional, stable societies against the destructive tendencies of abstract reason and abstract right. There were human rights and they were natural, growing out of the natural soil of communities.

Two narratives in the construction of nationalism were deeply at odds – the Zionist vision, of redeeming the soil, returning to Jerusalem, and recovering the soul of the people, and the new narrative under construction for the national life of the Palestinian people, of recovering the soil, of the uprooted returning home, and of the Palestinian people being redeemed. As Homi Bhabha put it so well, 'The recurrent metaphor of landscape as the inscape of national identity emphasizes the quality of light, the question of social visibility, the power of the eye to *naturalize* [my emphasis] the rhetoric of national affiliation and its form of collective expression.'[9] The vision of the landscape is critical to the sense of presence of a nation, even if its space is defined only in the fulness of time. Communities, and the well-being of individuals who seem to have a natural need to belong to them, are constructs both of inherited traditions rooted in soil and of rhetorical constructs often related to uprooting from and return to that soil. The right of return of one people on the basis of natural rights doctrine was at odds with the success of return of another people and its right to defend that accomplishment. Whereas reality had been suddenly thrust into the realm of rhetorical claims for the Palestinians, rhetorical and recursive demands for return to Zion were being translated into reality, to a restoration of continuity for the Jews.

This situation, of course, suggests that natural rights are, in fact, inherently group rights. The individual claims a right of return because the right is attributed to a specific group as a whole. Each individual need not establish an attachment to the soil. This is why the right can be inherited by children who were not even born in the homeland. Exercise of the rights of the group are preconditions for the rights of the individual to pursue his or her happiness and well-being.

Contractarian Theory and the Refugees of 1967 and after

What about the rights of those who fled in 1967 and were expelled or prevented from returning on administrative grounds in the post-1967 period? Exercise of these rights presupposes three contract-related conditions: relevant international covenants, absence of coercion, and self-determination.

International Covenants

These groups' right to return was defended primarily on the basis of international humanitarian and human rights covenants to which Israel was a signatory – namely, in contractarian terms. In contractarian theory, human rights are constraints to conduct constructed by reason to produce ethical norms that restrain human behaviour to enable humans to cooperate and regulate areas of conflicting interests and prohibit coercion. Departure of the 1967 refugees, deportation of individuals on allegedly security grounds, and denial of re-entry to individuals who had not renewed their residency permits in a timely fashion all reflect the aggressive and coercive activities of the Israeli state. The implicit argument was that the Israeli government had abused the human rights of certain Palestinians because its exercise of power had exceeded norms of the international community, as embodied in international law and in agreements to which Israel was a party, such as the Convention for the Protection of Civilian Persons in Time of War, to which it adhered on 6 July 1951.

Israel defended itself not by denouncing the norms but by questioning their applicability and its own obligation to conform to their requirements. It used two arguments. First, neither the West Bank nor Gaza had a legitimate sovereign, and so the convention was inapplicable, since the territory did not belong to a recognized state.[10] Second, the territory was conquered as a result of a defensive war.[11]

Absence of Coercion

Contractarians also hold that moral constraints on coercion are a necessary (but insufficient) precondition for allowing the making and keeping of contracts. Contracts entail exchange. Protection of the right to property and provision of public goods are preconditions of exchange and necessary conditions for ensuring that contracts are kept. What could the principle of rational sufficiency have to do with the right of return of refugees in accordance with international conventions?

Article 43 of the Hague 1907 Regulations allows the occupying power to be exempted from the prohibition against deportation on the basis of 'military necessity' because the occupier assumes the responsibility for restoring and preserving order and normal community life.[12]

However, there is a corollary to this contractarian thesis. If the Palestinians are to take some responsibility for ensuring order, there must be recognition that, in order for international conventions to have effect, each side in a contract must own and control some property. Further, the moral constraints on coercion must be complemented by a system that provides public goods. In concrete terms, the Palestinians had to control their own territorial base. The basic contract had, of necessity, to be between two territorial units, with multilateral and international organizations reinforcing the agreement to ensure provision of public goods necessary and useful to both parties.

Human rights covenants might appear to support this interpretation of humanitarian law, since they require the right of return to one's own country, but Israel is not the state of which diaspora Palestinians are members. However, the formulation does not refer to one's own state. A broad reading of the provisions obligates states, irrespective of the juridical status of the returnee, to allow return if the territory to which the return is to take place is appropriately the returnee's country. However, although return does not apply only to citizens,[13] the locale of return is directly relevant, since if the intention is to return to a territory that is the recognized territory of another, sovereign state, which the returnee would refuse to pledge any loyalty to and might indeed attempt to subvert, then in this case Israel, on the basis of security, has no obligation to allow such a return. However, if the return is to a territory that may form the basis of a Palestinian state or a state in which Palestinians participated and were represented, then the obligation to allow such a return can be claimed, subject again, of course, to the security needs of the sovereign state involved.

Thus the shift in the rationale for return paralleled the change in meaning of the right of return – from that of returning to a specific piece of land and the ancestral homeland to that of returning to land controlled by one's people. The effort to ensure such control – in this case, over the West Bank and Gaza – and international efforts – to complement bilateral talks based on the principle of exchanging land for peace with multilateral negotiations on economic cooperation, water, and so on – suggest recognition of the contractarian principles of the necessary conditions for human rights protection. International covenants based on humanitarian and human rights are one thing. But if the individuals supposedly protected are not members of states, so that other nations cannot ensure their return, then the international covenants' coverage is so effectively qualified that, at least, de facto, only citizens of states have such rights. Further, the rights are unenforceable, since conditions for their effective application are absent.

Self-determination

Contractarian theory assumes that only self-determination will allow international covenants and absence of coercion to become operational. Thus the international human rights covenants also require that a people have a land base. On that land, they exercise the right to choose their own government. Without these minimal conditions, the call for the right to return of the refugees of 1967 and afterwards is but a moral cry in the wilderness, with no one to listen and respond. In sum, to carry the obligations, the call for rights requires an entity that is responsive and responsible to the bearers of the right.

Idealism and Family Members

What about the idealist principles of human rights? Can these throw light on the right of 'return' of immediate family members, even though these relatives may never have resided in the territories in question? Do the rights of family reunification trump other interests? Certainly, it is the one right to which Israel accedes fully in principle. Disputes were over the alacrity and qualifications with which these rights were implemented. The right of the immediate family to live together does seem to be the highest right and to trump any others. Further, it was on these grounds that Jews were first allowed out of the Soviet Union and permitted to enter Israel under its law of return. The sacredness of the immediate family would appear to be the sine qua non of all human rights. Finally, the togetherness of the immediate family was also seen as a utopian vision and was not mistaken for the actual reality of the world order.

That is why, in the Multilateral Working Group on Refugees that Canada 'gavels,' family reunification was one of the seven items included in the agenda at the first meeting and the only one that related directly to the rights (rather than the needs) of refugees. It was also the issue that prevented headway in the second set of talks, when the Israelis attended for the first time. The extension or outcome of this human rights vision was a common interest of both the Palestinians and the Israelis.

Return as a Human Right

Do demands for the right to return of any or all the groups and the rationales justifying those rights conform to the more general conditions of what counts as a human right? Generally, these principles are said to have the absolute, universal, inalienable, and inviolable character of such rights. But the right of return of the Palestinian refugees, certainly for those who fled in 1948, could not be considered universal, since they are the only refugees to hold such a right. The very fact that they are claimed for the descendants of such refugees, who may have never lived in Palestine, suggests that they are alienable and transferable. And the claim that they are inviolable would have to appear as great farce, if the situation were not so tragic. While all other refugee problems have been resolved sooner or later, the Palestinian issue continues to haunt the international community after more than forty years.

The right to return, however, is not akin to other rights that are not general human rights. First, it does not seem to lose value with inability to exercise it. Quite the reverse. It has become a centrepiece of mythologizing in the creation of the Palestinian nation. The further the possibility of return moves from the original situation and the likelihood of implementation, the greater its symbolic importance. Second, it is clearly not an entitlement resulting from a contract between Palestinians and the Israelis. Quite the reverse. It seems identical with human rights in that the party said to carry the burden of obligation – the Israeli government – is the same party held responsible for the abuse of those rights. Third and finally, the more it is demonstrated that the Palestinians do not have any right of return, the more they in fact seem to have it, even if the having of it seems to alter over time. In other words, insisting on having the right and suffering for over forty years in the wilderness were probably critical to the eventual ability to exercise the right, for if the Palestinians had been dispersed and absorbed into other societies, what chance would they then have to exercise any right of return at all?

Thus analysis seems to indicate that it is not the universality, inalienability, and inviolability of human rights that make them human rights, even though these are the rhetorical flags under which these rights are advanced. Rather, paradoxes of possession, protection, and use are their key characteristics. In that sense, the right to return is indeed a human right.

Return as a Group Right

What we have learned is that lurking behind claims for a right of return as a human right are three more fundamental rights – of people to have a land that they can call their own, of self-determination to select a government that can be responsible to that people for protecting those rights, and of a family to live together in the same place at the same time. The fact that all three are group rights is no accident. Further, as I now try to show, group rights are preconditions for individual rights.

What Group Rights Are Not

There are two positions concerning group rights held by individualist thinkers. First, if groups are said to possess such rights, they are not human rights. Second, if what they possess are human rights, then the group is said to possess them only in the sense that they belong to individual members. It is the latter contention to which we must now turn.

I want first to discard three views of group rights in relationship to human rights that I would not want to defend. The first is that group rights are a third generation of human rights, extending first-generation civil and political rights and second-generation social and economic rights. The principles of distributive justice are applied to the relations between and among states. The poor nations are then entitled, as a matter of right, to receive development aid from the wealthy states.[14]

The second is that group rights are a species of human rights, equivalent to the public goods of Hobbesian contractarians. In this version, all citizens as citizens are entitled to a minimum level of schooling, roads, services, and so on from the state. Provision of public goods is thus a human right. Because group rights are also foundational human rights, they 'give no guarantee of upholding such things as civil liberties and due process of law; they may lend support to the expulsion of part of the population of an established society.'[15] In other words, this definition of group rights rules out a priori protection against expulsions or rights of return.

The third version is that group rights are boundary conditions for individual rights, merely setting limits for exercise of individual rights that are otherwise unlimited unless, in the way in which they are exercised, they threaten to destroy the group of which the individual is a member. Membership in the group guarantees protection of those rights.

If group rights are not an extension, an aspect of, or a boundary condition for human rights, what are they? They have often been associated with beliefs dissociated from human rights, at least in the form of individual rights. Three such versions come to mind: participatory democratic group rights, transcendent group rights, and the rights of individuals to discover their 'true selves,' which rests on the rights of the group to probe one's inner soul as depicted in the human potential movement.[16] In all these versions, group rights trump individual rights.

For example, in the doctrine of participatory democracy, political rights could be protected only by individuals' continuous and direct involvement in the affairs of the polis, the association, or the revolutionary organization. The rights of both majorities and minorities were sacrificed on the principle that those with the biggest butts who could sit the longest and who had the greatest commitment to the issue controlled the agenda. Using one's rights all the time on all issues was a prerequisite to having such rights.[17] Since an individual had to be omnipresent, only God could properly possess rights in a participatory democracy. Hence such systems were prone to turn their leaders into gods and substitute dictatorship for democracy or, alternatively, slip into anarchy.

In transcendent group rights, whether an organization be the mafia or a body parading as a community, group rights demand obeisance to traditions. In the name of those group rights, the individual must always subordinate his or her interests and values to the overriding ones of the group. This so-called communitarian vision, which tries to build a community based on common practices and beliefs, where allegedly 'politics is not simply about protecting or enforcing individual rights but about securing the common good,'[18] is more akin to transformational identity groups, such as religious cults. An individual is, in some sense, born again, receiving a new identity through membership in the group, which provides support and nurturing. The most subtle case of such ideologies is the human potential movement, which, in the guise of healing and self-realization, effectively denies all right to private thought and feeling and makes the will dependent on the support of the group for its exercise.

I am not concerned with group rights that are subordinated to human rights as an extension, sub-species, or limiting condition, nor about those that oppose or override individual rights. The right of return is not a group right in any of the above senses. Group rights are neither a subordinate nor an antagonistic category in relationship to human and individual rights, as discussed in this chapter.

Defining Group Rights

If group rights are not any of the above, what are they, at least insofar as the concept is used here? First, they do not belong to all humans as humans. They are not universal but are given to specific groups under certain historical conditions. Nor are they even universal in applying to members of the group; only a specific sub-group has those rights. Nor is the possession of the right a condition of being a member of the group. Yet one has the right only insofar as one is defined as a member of that group. Without application of the definition, one has no such rights.

Let me give you two examples of group rights – property rights and the right of asylum. 'The Universal Declaration of Human Rights and the International Human Rights Covenants, with but one exception, include only individual rights ... That exception is the right of peoples to self determination.'[19] Further, 'two rights in the Universal Declaration that cannot be so simply derived from a conception of free, autonomous people entitled to equal concern and respect are the rights of property (Article 17) and to asylum (Article 14) ... The right to asylum can be seen as a device to assure that those who are subject to intolerable oppression by their government may find refuge in another state, so that political respect for their dignity is not completely tied to their nationality.'[20]

I have dealt briefly above with a revised version of those property rights in the form of a people's right to a territory that it controls which forms a precondition for any human rights. I do not deal further with that issue here, although it divides schools of individualist human rights theorists and is an Achilles' heel for all of them. I focus instead on asylum rights.

Right of Asylum

Rights of asylum are seen as exceptional in that they do not derive from the conception of an autonomous individual, but Donnelly sees it as a corollary of the guarantee provision of human rights. In fact, asylum rights are group rights. They accrue to members of a group and only to them, not to humans in general. Refugees may have a right to asylum if they are refugees as defined by the Geneva Convention and the country in which they claim asylum is a signatory to the convention.[21] In fact, in the original covenant, before addition of the 1967 protocol, there was a geographical and time limitation; the only people so entitled were European refugees produced by the Second World War. The Organization of African Unity grants rights to asylum on wider grounds, but it applies only within Africa. The Cartagena Declaration again has broader grounds but applies only in Central America. Environmental refugees facing death by starvation because of desertification have no right of asylum, so it is hard to see how that right can be seen as universal and as a by-product of respect for the dignity of the human being. Asylum is a contractual obligation among signatory states applying to specific groups of people if individuals within the group qualify within the terms of the definition. Unlike other human rights, for this right the legal definition of who enjoys it seems critical.

I have argued elsewhere that the right of asylum is a by-product of contractarian self-determination theory and of its implications when the whole world is divided into states and there is nowhere to go to exercise that self-determination.[22] Asylum is not provided so that an individual's dignity is not tied to his or her citizenship but to enable the individual to be a citizen somewhere so that the basic condition for protection of human rights, membership in a state, can be provided.

Right of Self-determination

Thus the most basic type of group right is that of self-determination.[23] Article 1(1) of the International Human Rights Covenant reads: 'All peoples have the right to self-determination. By virtue of the right they freely determine their political status and freely pursue their economic, social, and cultural development.' Note, first, that this right belongs to peoples, not to individuals. Second, it is classified as a *human* right. Third, it is a right whereby a people is free to determine its political status.

Donnelly sees self-determination as an exception – a group right not reducible to individual human rights – and then attempts to reduce it to individual rights. Further, he sees the right as merely the right of an individual acting as a member of a social group that is ruled by an imperial power to revolt, if necessary, against that foreign rule; the social group can then set up its own system of self-government: 'The right to self-determination, even in its collective dimensions, is essentially a right of individuals acting collectively ... Roughly it involves respecting all other human rights, and in particular rights to political participation and freedom of speech, press, assembly, and association. If these rights are fully respected, it is difficult to see how the right to self-determination could be denied.'[24]

According to Donnelly, the right of self-determination is granted to peoples and then taken away and restricted to peoples ruled by imperial powers as if only overseas rulers could act as imperial powers. Kurds in Iraq, Tamils in Sri Lanka, Basques in Spain, Québécois in Canada – none of these peoples has a right of self-determination. The Cree in Quebec, as an Aboriginal people, are granted the right to preserve their culture but not to self-determination.

Donnelly's distinctions accord neither with logical consistency nor with practice. The Cree, for example, enjoy all civil and political rights but, unlike the people of the province of Quebec as a whole, are not recognized by Donnelly as having a right to self-determination, whereas the Québécois as a whole can (and might) exercise such a right. They can vote for separation; thus far, the right of the Cree to self-determination is not recognized. And no one argues that the Montrealers from Westmount should have such a right. Only groups recognized as a people with some degree of autonomous political jurisdiction and degree of self-government have that right. That is why the government of Quebec was so wary of granting Aboriginal peoples the right to self-government to which the other provinces initially agreed and to which Quebec acceded only when fundamental restrictions were imposed.[25] It is not a right that merely aggregates the rights of individual members of a group or simply summarizes other human rights.[26] It is a group right accorded to some peoples but not others and is not reducible to individual human rights.

UN General Assembly Resolution No. 3236 (XXIX) recognizes the Palestinian right of self-determination linked to the territory of Palestine. Resolution No. 1514 (XV) begins, 'The subjection of peoples to alien subjugation, domination and exploitation constitutes a denial of fundamental human rights, is contrary to the Charter of the United Nations and is an impediment to the promotion of world peace and cooperation.' Resolution No. 2672C (XXV)(1) 'Recognizes that the people of Palestine are entitled to equal rights and self-determination.'

Self-determination, in practice, is not restricted to a founding group, as defined by an original social contract, wherein peoples, insofar as they exist, are only collections of individuals who contract together for mutual advantage. This conception is intended to prevent sub-groups, which prefer to make foundational agreements only with their own members, from seceding. For contractarians, the arrangement must be an agreement, and one made with all.[27] In effect, secession is ruled out as contrary to the social contract, though not, presumably, if rule were imposed and there were no social contract at all.

These theories, so as to define human rights as the possessions only of individuals, effectively deny the existence of peoples as real entities and restrict the right of self-determination either to imperial situations where individual rights are denied or to a foundation agreement. I argue, to the contrary, that every people has the right to self-determination as an ideal and that that right is protected best by a state that recognizes preservation of the language and culture of that specific people as central to its mandate. If a people's right of self-determination is the collective right at the core of human rights theory, then its two correlates are the rights to return and to asylum.

Group Rights as Human Rights

Together, the right of return and that of asylum are complementary arms of the central right of a people to self-determination, which requires a territorial base for its exercise. Rights to self-determination accrue to peoples, not to individuals, and are a moral ideal. To return is a natural right, inherent in membership in a people that enjoys a right of self-determination. A member of a people or of a state has the inherent right to return to that state. Rights to asylum accrue to individuals as a contractual right among states to ensure that every human has the right to be a member of some state. Lack of belonging and severance of the ties that bind are the essence of entitlements to asylum. Rights to asylum accrue to individuals who are members of a specified group found to lack the protection of a state. This finding is a political judgment, in the end, even if politicians assign responsibility for making such a decision to judicial or quasi-judicial bodies.

Rights of asylum, of return, and of self-determination are all both human and group rights. For it is only as a citizen that one has a right to return. An individual does not have a right to return as a result of a vision of what it is to be human nor by natural decree or contract. Only refugees as defined by the convention have a right to asylum. Neither return nor asylum is an individual right per se, even though individuals exercise them. But all are preconditions of there being any individual rights at all.

Thus group rights are not reducible to individual rights. They may be assigned to members of a defined group in the case of asylum or return. They are not universal, since they arise out of particular historical conditions and apply to restricted groups. Nevertheless, built into the process is a dynamic of universalizing as the effort is made to define what conditions generally allow some groups in some condition to have the right of asylum. Similarly, there are efforts to define which peoples should have the right to self-determination and a right of return.

Further, these sets of rights have something else in common with the rhetorical conditions attached to human rights, even though they are not individual rights. The duty bearer is the governing state. The state in which one files a claim of asylum has the duty of examining that claim. Some state has jurisdiction over the territory to which one seeks to return. The state from which a collectivity seeks independence has the obligation to consider the request. Rights holders may vary in nature, but the duty bearer is always a state.

If the bond uniting an individual with his/her state is broken and the person flees, he or she becomes a refugee. 'The situation of political refugees is that the normal mutual bond of trust, loyalty, protection and assistance between an individual and the government of his home country has been broken (or simply does not exist).'[28] There is an exilic bias in refugee law, whether applied to a right of return or to a right of asylum, 'a notion of disenfranchisement or breakdown of basic membership rights.'[29] There are no human rights without self-determination and creation of states responsible to and for their citizens. The right to return and the right of asylum are but corollaries of this fundamental fact.

Notes

1 Jack Donnelly *Universal Human Rights in Theory and Practice* (Ithaca, NY: Cornell University Press 1989) 11.
2 Ronald Dworkin *Taking Rights Seriously* (Cambridge, Mass.: Harvard University Press 1977) 90. See also Dworkin 'Rights as Trumps' in J. Waldron ed *Theories of Rights* (Oxford: Oxford University Press 1985) 153–67.
3 Donnelly *Universal Human Rights* 146.
4 'By *natural* or *human rights*, I mean right that each person has by virtue of some characteristic which he possesses as a human being, and not by virtue of considerations of utility or contractual arrangements.' Eric Mack 'Individualism, Rights, and the Open Society' in Tibor R. Machan ed *The Libertarian Reader* (Totawa, NJ: Rowman and Littlefield 1982) 3, reprinted from Tibor R. Machan ed *The Libertarian Alternative* (Chicago: Nelson-Hall 1974).
5 Cf David Gauthier *Morals by Agreement* (Oxford: Oxford University Press 1986).
6 The idealist school would include philosophers such as Jack Donnelly, Ronald Dworkin, and John Rawls.
7 Israel was not the only state in the region in which the security and sovereignty of the state were threatened by Palestinians' determination to exercise the right of return. So too were Jordan, Lebanon, and even Syria. As Michael Hudson phrased it in *Arab Politics: The Search for Legitimacy* (New Haven, Conn.: Yale University Press 1977) 296: 'The emergence of a coherent, authoritative Palestinian movement was also seen increasingly as a challenge to the sovereignty of the main host Arab countries – Jordan, Lebanon, and Syria. Were these Palestinians to be considered just as guests in these countries, enjoying certain privileges conferred by the host governments? Or were they brother Arabs, equal in status yet possessed of the special right to organize themselves to recover their homeland? Were the host governments, by virtue of their commitments to the Palestinian cause, obligated merely to provide minimum facilities for refugees or to support the Palestinian movement for national liberation, even if this meant giving up sovereignty to a limited extent and suffering Israeli reprisals?' In each case, the principles of security and sovereignty won out over support for Arab brethren.

8 Cf Thomas Paine *The Rights of Man* (1791–2), which was a direct attack on Edmund Burke's *Reflections on the Revolution in France* (1790).

9 Homi K. Bhabha 'DissemiNation' in *Nation and Narration* (London: Routledge 1990) 295.

10 Rex Zedalis, in 'The Right to Return: A Closer Look' (*Georgetown Immigration Law Journal* 6 no. 3 (October 1992) 499–517, argues quite persuasively that article 49 of the Civilians Protection Convention of 1949 does not require the territory to have been formerly in the possession of a legitimate sovereign whereas article 43 of the 1907 Hague Regulations did. Zedalis cites H. Levie *The Code of International Armed Conflict* (1985) as supporting this interpretation.

11 These two defences were first enunciated by Yehuda Blum in 'The Missing Reversioner: Reflections on the Status of Judea and Samaria' *Israel Law Review* 3 (1968) 279–301 and criticized because neither 'legitimate sovereign' nor 'defensive conquest' is a concept of the supporting documents or the convention itself.

12 Zedalis 'Right' 502.

13 Ibid 505–6.

14 Cf Philip Alston 'Prevention versus Cure as a Human Rights Strategy' in *Development, Human Rights and the Rule of Law* (Elmsford, NY: Pergamon Press 1981) 31–120, 'International Trade as an Instrument of Positive Human Rights Policy' *Human Rights Quarterly* (4 May 1982) 155–83, and 'Making Space for New Human Rights: The Case of the Right to Development' *Harvard Human Rights Yearbook I* (Spring 1988) 3–40; see also Paul Brietzke 'Consorting with the Chameleon, or Realizing the Rights to Development' *California Western International Law Journal* 15 (Summer) 560–606.

15 David Braybrooke 'Gauthier's Foundations for Ethics under the Test of Application' in Peter Vallentyne ed *Contractarianism and Rational Choice: Essays on David Gauthier's Morals by Agreement* (Cambridge: Cambridge University Press 1991) 57.

16 George Kateb's 'Democratic Individuality and the Meaning of Rights' in Nancy L. Rosenblum ed *Liberalism and the Moral Life* (Cambridge, Mass.: Harvard University Press 1989), 183–206, a vigorous defence of individualism, includes in somewhat different language not only these three alleged group rights, which he considers anti-individualistic, but also communitarian beliefs which, if my argument is persuasive, I believe to be an erroneous addition. Communitarian rights are the necessary preconditions for individual rights.

17 Cf my article 'Rochdale College: Power and Performance' (publication pending) for a case study that offers a critique of participatory democracy.

18 Chandran Kukathas *Hayek and Modern Liberalism* (Oxford: Clarendon Press 1990) 217. Cf. Alisdair MacIntyre *After Virtue: A Study of Moral Theory* (London 1981); Michael Sandel *Liberalism and the Limits of Justice* (Cambridge 1982) and 'Morality and the Liberal Ideal' *New Republic* (7 May 1984) 15–17; and Michael Walzer *Spheres of Justice: A Defence of Pluralism and Equality* (Oxford 1983), who all defend communitarian theories, but ones that respect individual rights and where the common good does not readily translate into the pursuit of evil in common.

19 Donnelly *Universal Human Rights* 20.

20 Ibid 25.

21 Donnelly observes (ibid 25–12) that article 14 of the Universal Declaration includes a right to asylum, which is a restricted right not applicable to all humans. Donnelly interprets this as an assurance that those intolerably oppressed may find refuge in another state so that respect for their human dignity is not tied to their country of citizenship. But only those outside their country of origin have a right to asylum; those with cannot run to a foreign embassy and claim such a right, Further, individuals need not have been abused at all. They need have only had a well-founded fear that they might be persecuted because they were members of a social group. The restrictions on place and conditions (wider in some ways and narrower in others) do not suggest that the right of asylum is merely a corollary to reinforce the principle of respect for individual dignity.

22 Howard Adelman 'Obligations and Refugees' in Anna Bramwell ed *Refugees in the Age of Total War* (London: Unwin Hyman 1988).

23 I have argued elsewhere that, in fact, the right of asylum is a by-product of contractarian self-determination theory and its implications when the whole world is divided into states and there is nowhere to go to exercise that self-determination. Asylum is not provided so that an individual's dignity is not tied to his or her citizenship but to enable the individual to be a citizen somewhere so that the basic condition, membership in a state, for protection of human rights can be provided. Cf Howard Adelman 'Refuge or Asylum: A Philosophical Perspective' *Journal of Refugee Studies* 1 no. 1 (1988) 7–19.

24 Donnelly *Universal Human Rights* 149.

25 The Aboriginal peoples, though, rejected the compromise. 'One area that caused First Nations grave concern [in the debate over the Charlottetown Accord in 1992] was the restriction on self-government to the effect that these provisions were not to be construed as creating new land rights. The provision was added at the request of the premier of Quebec, who believed self-government in Quebec would not "sell" because Quebeckers are nervous about the status of the Cree and Inuit territories in northern Quebec;

specifically, Quebec did not want to act to bolster Aboriginal territorial claims. While this might not be a profound restriction from a crafty legal viewpoint, because it recognizes existing land rights that are arguably extensive, politically it was hard for Aboriginal leaders to endorse. For Aboriginal peoples who are stuck on undersized reserves, have no land base, or are without access to their traditional territories, the notion of a provision explicitly stating there would be no new land rights was enough for an immediate rejection of the package.' Mary Ellen Turpel 'Aboriginal Peoples' Struggle for Fundamental Political Change' in Kenneth McRoberts and Patrick Monahan eds *The Charlottetown Accord, the Referendum, and the Future of Canada* (Toronto: University of Toronto Press 1993) 126.

26 In *Universal Human Rights,* for example, Donnelly discusses Aboriginal rights, as well as the rights of Kurds, Tamils, French Canadians in Quebec, and Basques, only to deny them to involve a right to self-determination and redefine them as a right to autonomy to protect their culture. Respect for individual rights and tolerance he views as strategies to prevent self-determination, but the theory also delegitimizes the effort.

27 Cf David Gauthier 'The Social Contract: Individual Decision or Collective Bargain?' in C.A. Hooker, Jim Leach, and Edward McLennen eds *Foundations and Applications of Decision Theory* 11 (Dordrecht, Holland: D. Reidel 1978) 47–67. See also Gregory S. Kavka *Hobbesian Moral and Political Theory* (Princeton, NJ: Princeton University Press 1986), where the secession problem is specifically addressed.

28 Atle Grahl Madsen *The Status of Refugees in International Law* (Leyden 1966) 79.

29 James C. Hathaway *The Law of Refugee Status* (Toronto 1991) 135.

9

Human Rights, Peoples, and the Right to Self-determination

JAMES A. GRAFF

The collapse of the Soviet Union has unleashed nationalist and irredentist political forces demanding and seizing territory in which to create new, ethnically defined nation states. The process involves secession, double-secession, partition, 'ethnic cleansing,' war, terror, and atrocities. Various peoples are claiming their rights to self-determination with blood and rhetoric. Making good on those claims is one way in which minorities become majorities, 'resolve' their grievances, and achieve those nationalist aspirations that had been denied them as subject peoples. Just how a right to self-determination is to be justified is not a purely academic question in the present context of renewed, often virulent and conflicting nationalisms. The arguments offered for or against statehood will reflect a range of political and moral attitudes that can serve as motives for political action.

By recognizing a right to self-determination, one accepts that a collectivity has the right either to establish or to maintain a sovereign state within some defined territory or to choose some other mode of governance. If a people has such a right, justice requires that its exercise not be blocked. Since everyone is subject to some government, each people is in fact subject to some government or governments, no matter how one may choose to identify a people.

A people can be conceived either as a body of citizens – for example, the Canadian People – or as an ethnoculturally identified collectivity, such as the Inuit. To speak sensibly about a collectivity of the second kind having a right to self-determination requires that its numbers be sufficiently numerous and diverse to operate and populate a sovereign state. Although one can imagine such a people being so isolated and scattered that it neither has any governmental structure(s) of its own nor is aware of the government(s) in whose territory(ies) it resides, none exists. No such ethnoculturally defined people is now (if it ever was) ignorant of the governmental arrangements to which it is subject. Each must therefore be construed as content with those arrangements, indifferent to them, or opposed to them. If it is content or indifferent, the people can be said to consent to those arrangements: if it opposed, the arrangements would be against its will. It is not possible for a people neither to consent to the system to which it is subject nor to be subject to those arrangements against its will. There is no middle ground now, although one could *imagine* one. These considerations have a curious implication for those who hold that each people has a right to self-determination – either that right has been exercised or its exercise is effectively being blocked by the operations of the state or states to which it is subject. Each people must be viewed as having a government of its own, as consenting, either as a totality or in diaspora form, to the government or governments to which it is subject, or as subject to governmental arrangements to which it does not consent and which, therefore, effectively block its exercising its right to self-determination. If each people has that right, justice would now require its exercise if that has not already taken place.

I think that most of those who subscribe to the conception of a people and its right to self-determination would hold that a people has a right to alter the arrangements by which it is governed if it 'chooses' to do so and that therefore the 'exercise' of its right to self-determination at some point in its history does not bind it for ever to the political arrangement to which it once consented. In view of the realities of power and the brutal history of ethnocultural nationalism, the image of the kind of fragmented and reframenting world *dis*order that an ideology of ethnocultural peoplehood would count as the price of justice should, by itself, cast doubt on the moral and political wisdom of that ideology.

How one views the right to self-determination will depend ultimately on how one understands the relations between the rights of collectivities and the rights of the individuals who comprise them. If one believes that the moral rights of collectivities must be justified by appealing to the rights of individuals and to what their well-being requires, one will, I believe, have to reject the claim that each ethnoculturally defined people has a right to self-determination. I argue below that the concept of each such group's having such a right is incompatible with an ethic that espouses, as its guiding principle, respect for the equal worth and dignity of individuals and that requires respect for those of their rights that elaborate or are grounded on that ideal. It seems to me that the concept of the equal right of peoples to self-determination must give way to the equal rights of individuals to certain freedoms and to certain socially providable elements of their well-being. This appears to me to be true whether one interprets 'a people' as referring to a citizen body or to some ethnically, culturally, or ethnoculturally defined collectivity.

The Right to Self-determination

Some talk about rights of collectivities is elliptical for talk about the rights of the individuals who comprise those collectivities. The right of women to equal pay for equal work, for example, is not conceptually distinct from the right of each woman to be paid the same wage as any man who does the same job. The rights of Chinese Canadians not to be discriminated against in employment, education, and so on are the rights of individual Chinese Canadians not to be subjected to discrimination on the basis of their ethnicity, cultural heritage, or original nationality if they happen to be Canadian citizens by naturalization or by birth. However, the right of a people to self-determination is not equivalent to the rights of the individuals who make up that people. There are some rights ascribed to collectivities that are not equivalent to the rights of the individuals who comprise them. This does not mean, however, that the justification for ascribing those rights to collectivities cannot be found in the rights ascribed to those individuals and to the goods, services, and modes of treatment required for their well-being.

Accepting a right to self-determination for some collectivity is accepting the moral legitimacy of a sovereign state controlled by members of that collectivity within a defined territory. It is recognizing the moral legitimacy of that state's exercising sovereign jurisdiction within that territory. Furthermore, it is acknowledging the moral legitimacy of citizenship for members of that collectivity within that territory and therefore of their bearing the rights and obligations of citizenship within such a state. If the collectivity is dispersed, its right to self-determination may imply special rights for some of its members to immigrate to that state and be granted citizenship there. A right to self-determination for a scattered people may imply the moral legitimacy of carving up existing states to establish a unified or geographically fragmented territory for that people's state. It also implies condemning as morally wrong the use of force or other coercive measures to prevent that collectivity's political leadership from establishing a sovereign state on its behalf in the relevant territory(ies). Also, other governments or foreign guerrilla organizations may not use force, coercion, or subversion to dismantle that state, alter its borders, or transfer its population. Outside military intervention may, however, assist a popularly endorsed leadership of that collectivity in establishing a sovereign state in 'its' territory, and that leadership may use force against an existing government or controlling power to establish or re-establish a sovereign state for that collectivity within that territory.

A People and Its State

A people cannot exercise its right to self-determination (or any other right, for that matter) unless it has a leadership whose political activities could count as that people's establishing its state. It is not clear to me whether a people can be said to 'choose' the political arrangements under which it lives in the absence of some voting procedure or political activities by its leaders, but perhaps it can. Perhaps acceptance of governmental arrangements by some 'critical mass' (a plurality, bare majority, or overwhelming majority) suffices to count as that people's 'choosing' to live under those arrangements. What is clear is that claims to self-determination have to be taken seriously when they are advanced by political leaders on behalf of some 'people' when they and their claims have the support of a politically critical mass of individuals who identify with that 'people,' are prepared to make sacrifices on 'its' behalf, and are ready to resist existing authorities to achieve 'its' independence. That proportion need not constitute even a plurality of those who qualify as members of the 'people' concerned, or even of those who identify themselves as members of that 'people.' Political leaders may have to create the 'people' on whose behalf they claim a right to self-determination. They may have to invent an ethnic or cultural identity, as took place in a number of European colonies in Black Africa. They may have to elevate an existing mode of self-identification, of self-definition by which individuals mark off 'us' from 'them,' to a primary self-identification so as to form a collectivity to whose welfare many or most of its members are committed. In Rousseau's terms, nationalist leaders may have to create a general will, or elevate a general will of an existing ethnoculturally defined group into the General Will for as many of its members as their movement and the success of their political aspirations require. Humanity is divided into politically significant peoples, but which modes of division have yielded and may yet yield such bodies is an accident of the history of states, of political ideology, and of geography, trade, and migration.

A World of Sovereign States

The conception of a right to self-determination has moral legitimacy only within the framework of a world political order of sovereign states. If such an order comes to be morally indefensible, then the right would no longer be a morally acceptable guiding conception for political organization. The ideal world order envisioned in the UN Charter is one in which sovereign states, using their own human and natural resources, or cooperating with others, would establish democratic societies within their borders, upholding and promoting human rights and refraining from aggression and subversion against their neighbours. It seems to me that this vision is an illusion, given the gross inequalities of power, wealth, and technological, human, and natural resources available to the industrialized countries of the world and the dominance and dynamics of realpolitik. National self-interest and various kinds of nationalisms, on the one hand, and the prevalence of rule by entrenched elites whose power requires systematic repression, on the other hand, are structural elements of the world order of sovereign states. Sustaining those inequalities of wealth and power requires use of coopted local elites in poor, resource-rich countries to suppress efforts to redistribute domestic wealth and power. The repression that marks many Third World regimes involves massive violations of parts or all of the full range of human rights. Furthermore, there are bound to be acts of aggression and subversion aimed at redressing regional inequalities or at enhancing some state's control over valuable resources. The dynamic of a world order of sovereign states will probably continue to ensure that the basic human rights of millions in the Third World will continue to be violated.

The principle of non-interference in the internal affairs of sovereign states is central to the conception of sovereignty. Its general observance is essential to the present world order. Observing that principle, however, leaves brutal regimes free to kill, torture, imprison without charge, and brutalize their opponents *en masse.* Although there have been interventions, even UN-sanctioned ones, that had the effect of preventing genocide or of improving the human rights situation in some states, they have been selective and have always been coincident with the interests of the intervening powers – for example, the UN-authorized, primarily US intervention to protect the Kurds in Iraq from genocide after the conclusion of the Gulf War of 1991, when it suited US interests to contain Iraqi dictator Saddam Hussein. Only a few years earlier, the United States was massively aiding his war effort against Iran while he was actively pursuing a genocidal war against the same Kurdish community. When no power's interests have been served by intervention, even to stop genocide within the context of a civil war, as in Bosnia, the most atrocious violations of human rights have been allowed to continue. Resolutions of the UN Security Council condemning gross violations will continue to be proposed selectively, passed selectively, and enforced selectively because the dynamic ethos of sovereign states is one or other form of realpolitik. Pursuit of economic, military, strategic, or other interests first and foremost will continue to exclude or override concerns for human rights when addressing the latter conflicts with or does not promote great powers' interests.

Only a world order that transcends the sovereign state system, or so it appears to me, could begin to realize the moral ideal of the equal worth and dignity of persons. That ideal is affirmed in the UN Charter and articulated more fully in the Universal Declaration of Human Rights and in other major instruments of international human rights law. The present world order, dominated by a single superpower, leaves the power free to launch interventions to protect human rights when its other major interests are served and to immunize itself and its clients against interventions when it or they grossly violate basic human rights. It is questionable whether there would be impartial and conscientious UN-legitimated enforcement of the basic human rights provision of the UN Charter and Universal Declaration even were, say, a united Europe to replace the United States as the dominant world power. The problem of enforcement is structural, related intimately to the system of sovereign states and to the gross inequalities of wealth and power that that system functions to preserve. So long as the world body remains a creature of that system, it will be incapable of fulfilling its human rights mandate. If people are ever to be treated as equal in worth and dignity, and the full range of their most important human rights honoured, the right to self-determination must ultimately give way to a wide range of democratic political and legal rights for the sake of even more fundamental human rights.

The existing world order is, however, one of sovereign states, and thus some geographically or ethnoculturally defined and self-defining 'peoples' must have their own sovereign states if their individual members are to enjoy the rights to which an ethos of equal worth and equal dignity entitles them. Bosnia, East Timor, and the Israeli-occupied Palestinian territories come to mind as examples. There are, and probably will be, many others, as violent sectarian and ethnically based nationalist struggles make statehood the only politically feasible alternative to indefinite ethnic repression, guerrilla warfare, state terror, ethnic cleaning, and genocide.

The resurgence of ethnocultural nationalisms, dressed up as many are by the rhetoric of ethnically exclusivist democracy, is now proliferating sovereign states in the Balkans and the former Soviet Union. Some of those states have been established self-defensively, and others, aggressively, inspired by the ideology of an ethnoculturally based right to self-determination. The ghettoized world envisioned by advocates of that right for each such people is racist in character. In practice, and, I argue, theoretically, such an ideology must countenance favouring one ethnocultural community over others within the same territory and, therefore, favouring promotion of the well-being of individuals based on ethnicity/culture. Whatever the democratic overlay or veneer of commitment to human rights, such an ideology is fundamentally inconsistent with observance of human rights.

Ethnic States v. Human Rights

Sovereign states that happen to be controlled by a numerically dominant ethnocultural group, but that are not characterized by an overt ideology presenting the state as the state of and for that group, have not had histories of tolerance or openness to minorities. Sovereign states controlled by an ethnocultural minority also have had histories of intolerance and discrimination against other ethnocultural minorities or majorities. The dismal records of inter-ethnic strife, of racism, and of religious and other forms of cultural intolerance demonstrate the dangers avowedly posed by ethnoculturally based sovereign states for realization of egalitarian and humanistic values. The problems encountered by those who advocate human rights and respect for the equal worth and dignity of all citizens without regard to race, colour, ethnic or national origins, religious convictions, or cultural heritage continue to be major even in countries such as Canada, whose federal government and most of whose provincial governments have officially espoused multiculturalism, respect for human rights, and the ideal of equality. Those problems are compounded, however, when the state's official ideology presents the state itself as the state of (and for) a particular ethnocultural community. Contemporary examples have included Israel,[1] expansionist Serbia, apartheid-based South Africa, and most of the newly independent, ethnoculturally based states of the former Soviet Union.

Talk about Peoples

Personifying the 'People'

The nineteenth-century ideal of a sovereign state as the political expression of a single, ethnoculturally defined people gathered within its historical territory should by now have been discredited by the horrors wrought in this century by adherence to that ideal. Far from being discredited, that ideal continues to be passionately embraced, functioning as a unifying and dynamic political force justifying separatism, secession, conquest, expansion, colonization, oppression, and, again in this century, genocide. That ideal presents a people's right to self-determination as the right of each ethnocultural group capable of statehood to a sovereign state of its own within 'its' historical territory. If that territory is divided into several sovereign states, the ideology pushes towards unification, as in Germany and Italy in the last century. If it is divided among several sovereign states, it pushes towards separation of territories from those states and unification under nationalist leadership (the present situation of Kurds, Macedonians, and Armenians). If it is occupied by another ethnoculturally defined people or shared with it, the ideology may support colonization, conquest, expulsion, or indefinite domination over what by force had become a permanent minority. Israel and the regions of Croatia and Bosnia-Herzegovina seized by Serb militias exemplify this last scenario.

It is tempting, perhaps unavoidable, to talk and think about collectivities, organized or not, as if they were individuals. There are at least three reasons for this temptation. First, we have to think and talk about what governments and other organized collectivities decide and do and about their rights and obligations, their histories, and their futures in order to make sense of our social realities. Second, we need to think in terms of structures and roles within those structures that a succession of individuals fills and because of which a host of decisions we know nothing about made by individuals whom we do not and cannot know count as the decisions and actions of collectivities. Third, even if we knew what decisions and actions certain individuals took, we could not understand them as the decisions and actions of a collectivity unless we understood them within the context of roles and structures. To make sense of our social world, we must think in terms of institutions and therefore of entities that can remain the same for generations, change over time, or even move from place to place from one generation to the next. We have to think in terms of entities that, like individuals, can have a spatio-temporal history but, unlike them, are collectivities of successive generations of individuals. However, we tend to forget how dissimilar to individuals these collectivities are, generalizing too often about the values, the 'character,' and even the 'minds' of ethnically and politically defined peoples. It is all too easy to shift from this mode of thinking to more blatantly racist modes of thinking by which the generalizations, even if 'true enough,' become the stereotypes by which all members of an ethnocultural group are understood, and in terms of which hostile, discriminatory, or even genocidal policies are justified. I suspect that this tendency to think and talk about peoples as if they were individuals is not only embedded in the rhetoric of a people's right to self-determination, but is also central to it.

Individuals are natural units: organized collectivities are constructed 'units.' Ethnoculturally defined peoples are, I believe, groupings whose 'unity' can be made to appear or disappear depending on which 'ties that bind' one may wish to emphasize for political, anthropological, sociological, or historical purposes. The conception of a given ethnoculturally defined people replete with its rights and obligations is a politically and emotionally powerful fiction – but it is a fiction and nothing more. Fictitious entities have no rights, although it may sometimes be convenient as short hand, or important for the entities that do have rights, to speak as if they did.

'Our' Homeland

The relationship between an ethnoculturally defined people and 'its' territory illustrates the point. 'Its territory' can be understood as the geographical region within which generations of its members have resided and in which many of its members currently reside. In the ideology of a people and its right to self-determination, however, 'its' territory is understood on the model of individually owned property. 'Our homeland' is analogized to 'my home': who lives in it is up to me, and whether that person shares in the management of 'my' home is also up to me. If I leave my home, I can return to it and evict anyone who has moved in without my permission. If I have been forcibly evicted by armed thugs, I have the right to reclaim it and expel its present inhabitants or permit them to stay on my terms. If I need to add on to my home on my land in order to accommodate my family, I have the right to do so and to evict those who may have 'squatted' there. The analogy between 'my home' and the land on which it sits and 'our homeland' breaks down when it comes to 'building additions.' Were there unclaimed, unoccupied, habitable territory up for grabs, then the first to colonize it might be thought of as legitimately 'building an addition' to 'their' territory by expanding into it. Since there is no such territory, and was not even in the days of European colonization of the Americas and of what became South Africa, 'adding to our homeland' must come at the expense of some other peoples or states. 'Adding' then requires armed force to seize and hold the 'additions.'

'Evicting squatters' from 'our homeland' also requires force, confiscating individually owned property or forcing others out of territory that they had traditionally inhabited and used. In practice, 'evicting squatters from our homeland' requires the dismal routine of terror and atrocities that are endemic to inter-ethnic armed conflicts over territory. 'Claiming our homeland for ourselves' and 'reclaiming our homeland' mean in practice dispossessing, massively displacing, terrorizing, and subjugating others. The process of 'transferring ownership' to individuals of the appropriate ethnicity under the laws of their newly established state – 're-claiming' what is rightfully theirs or taking what is theirs by 'manifest destiny' or 'divine donation' – is invariably brutal. It also involves theft on a grand scale. In 'evicting squatters' from our homeland, 'we' must seize their lands, their homes, their shops, and whatever they could not take with them as 'our' troops 'escorted' or drove them across our frontiers or simply butchered them. These processes of claiming or reclaiming 'our homeland for ourselves' involve massive and gross violations of the most fundamental human rights of others. They involve treating the well-being of the 'squatters' as inferior in weight to that of the members of the favoured community and therefore regarding their rights to security of person and possession and so on as overridden by 'our' rights to 'our' homeland. 'Evicting squatters' leaves no room for respecting the equal worth and dignity of persons and their equal rights to well-being without distinction of ethnicity, culture, faith, and so on. Analogizing a people and its homeland to an individual and his/her home can be a way of glossing brutal, ethnoculturally discriminatory practices: it can thereby become a rhetorical device to 'legitimate' them. Thus even if the ideology of a people and its territory is not overtly racist or inegalitarian on grounds of ethnicity, culture, or religion, it must be viewed as implicitly racist or racist in character if it countenances 'reclaiming' or 'claiming' our homeland for 'our people' by forcibly removing 'squatters.'

Forcibly restoring communal and personal property, as recognized by the laws of some ancien régime, to forcibly dispossessed individuals or organizations, their heirs, or their successors is a different matter, although the scale of restoration may constitute 'reclaiming our homeland.' It is different because of two principles – that individuals and organized collectivities wrongfully deprived of their property have a right to its restoration or, if they agree, to fair compensation for its loss, and that other persons and organized collectivities should not be permitted to gain from wrongful acquisitions. Even in these cases, with the passage of time and passing of title in good faith, evicting present owners without compensation would seem unfair, just as it would be unfair not to arrange for some form of fair compensation for the original owners or their heirs if eviction and dispossession of the present holders of the property would be unfair to them and their families. There is a sense in which it is legitimate, from a human rights perspective, for individuals of one ethnocultural group literally to reclaim their property and, thereby, secure for that people 'its' territory without massive theft and without engaging in de facto racist or racist-like practices in doing so. That sense of 'a people's reclaiming its territory' treats the land in question as the collection of parcels of property owned by individuals or organized groups of individuals who happen to belong to the collectivity in question. This conception does not treat a territorial expanse as, somehow, the possession of the group as a multi-generational entity. On that conception, present members are entitled to take possession of properties to which neither they as individuals nor their actual forbears (for all anyone can tell) ever had legal title and from which they were forcibly expelled. The conception of the territory of a people as the collection of parcels of property to which members of a particular ethnocultural group have legal title does not offer a shred of justification for seizing, in the name of 'claiming' or 'reclaiming' a 'homeland,' properties to which individuals of other ethnicities are legally entitled. The ideology of a people and 'its' homeland does not require such measures in dealing with 'squatters,' but it legitimates them.

Privileged Access

A sovereign state of and for a given ethnocultural people does require discriminatory practices against others within its territory because the state must favour 'its' special people. A sovereign state can arrogate to itself the powers to exclude people from citizenship on the basis of ethnicity, race, faith, gender, and so on, to establish a de jure or de facto status of second-class citizenship on any of those bases, to expel ethnocultural communities, or to incorporate them as equals. When a given sovereign state views itself as the state of and for a particular ethnocultural community, minorities (or majorities of the 'wrong' ethnicity) cannot consistently be treated as equal in rights to the favoured group. Discrimination on the basis of ethnicity is implicitly legitimated and required by the ideology. What 'state of and for' means must be explained in terms of privileged access, based on ethnocultural identity, to power, opportunities, and those protections, goods, and services that the state offers. The role of the state must be understood as, first and foremost, preserving and protecting a particular community and doing what it can to ensure that it flourishes. This means, at the least, favouring that community when allocating limited resources and favouring its members over others in the mechanisms by which political and economic power is made accessible. It requires discriminating on the basis of ethnicity in education, employment, and the political process itself. The only alternative is to ensure an ethnoculturally 'pure' population through ethnic discrimination in immigration policy. The ideology is incompatible therefore with an ideal requiring us to treat persons as equal in worth and dignity, and therefore in rights, without regard to ethnicity, national origins, cultural heritage, faith, or gender. It is therefore inconsistent with a human rights ethic. Since there are no 'ethnoculturally pure' states, practice of such an ideology guarantees systemic violations of human rights.

Although one can imagine a situation in which the conception of the interests of the favoured group supports an egalitarian approach to others residing within 'its' territory, the rights of the latter in theory must be viewed as dependent upon the interests of the favoured 'people.' As I said above, however 'egalitarian' a society may be with respect to members of the favoured ethnicity, the ideology of ethnocultural peoplehood will ensure discrimination in practice. Discrimination will always advantage the favoured group in important ways, and its members, like people generally, can be expected to pursue advantages, especially when they view them as their birthright. Nationalist leaders in states dominated by ethnoculturally based nationalism are bound to play on the ethnocentric and xenophobic attitudes that help to strengthen nationalist loyalties.

There can be a broad spectrum of discriminatory practices, ranging from inequity in employment, education, housing, health services, sentencing, and so on to pogroms, state terror, expulsions, and ethnocide. The 'ideal' of an ethnoculturally defined sovereign state can be neither implemented nor sustained without systematic violations of human rights. No wonder, then, that apologists for such an 'ideal' often launch attacks on human rights theory or practice. Political philosophy, after all, ultimately reflects moral and political agendas.

Conflicting Claims

From the ideological perspective of ethnocentric nationalism, when political leaders lay claim to the same territory on behalf of two peoples – for example, the Jewish people and the Palestinian people – the ideology demands denial of the peoplehood of one, rejection of the contested territory as 'homeland' to one of the peoples, insistence on the unworthiness of one people to have a sovereign state of its own, partition based on 'equally valid' claims, or an appeal to paradox. All these ploys have been used in Zionist and Palestinian political rhetoric. From this ideological perspective, if one of the claims to a particular territory is specious, then that people has no right to that territory or to statehood within it and should vacate or submit to sovereign control by its rival 'people.' Power-sharing in a bi-national state is not an option for an ideology that insists that each 'people' must have its own state whose role is to enable it to flourish.

'Who owns this house – you or we?' If you own it, we should get out or pay the rent that you want if you will let us stay.

Suppose, as I believe, that the claims put forward by supporters of a Jewish right to Palestine are specious – would that be sufficient justification for establishing a Palestinian state in all of Palestine which is the ethnocultural counterpart of Israel as a state of and for the Jewish people? It would if one accepted the ideology of a people, its state, and its homeland. I do not believe that from an egalitarian, human rights point of view one could at this point consistently accept such a position. Its implementation would require the kind of force that not only will never be available to those who may endorse it but that, if it were available, would involve yet another human tragedy of massive proportions. Furthermore, the envisioned state would be the mirror-image of the present Israeli one – it would be for the Palestinians, and the Jewish population would be subjected to discrimination, oppression, and perhaps expulsion. It too would be a state imposed against the will of a significant segment of the population within the territory that it would control, which means that coercion and violence would be needed not only to impose it but also to sustain it. If the consequences of implementing a policy dictated by a set of supposedly morally acceptable principles would in fact be wrong, then some of those principles must be wrong. If one takes in a serious way human suffering to be an evil, one cannot accept the implications of an ideology of peoplehood that would legitimate oppression, intimidation, or outright expulsion of people from their homes, businesses, towns, and cities, all in the name of 'reclaiming a people's land.'[2] However, settlers on illegitimately seized land have no right to their holdings. Some faits accomplis are politically and morally reversible – others are not.

Suppose that one could somehow justify an equal right of two peoples to the same territory. Some observers adopt this stance as a requirement of a genuinely 'balanced' attitude towards the Israeli-Palestinian conflict. Such a position requires that one urge a special kind of bi-national state, partition, or a 'tragic paradox' to be resolved ultimately by power. A bi-national state structured consistently with an ideal of ethnocultural sovereignty would seem to require some mode of separation of jurisdictions along ethnic lines, as well as segregation of neighbourhoods or separation into 'autonomous,' ethnically defined regions or quarters.

Integration of neighbourhoods, schools, and businesses, with equal opportunities for members of both ethnicites, would both threaten the 'ethnic integrity' of each community and could, over time, yield a distinctive ethnocultural mix, defeating the rationale for ascribing rights to self-determination and to a homeland to each 'people.' 'Separate and equal' must characterize the nature of such a bi-national state. Experience has amply demonstrated that separate cannot be 'equal,' because legally supported separate ethnic enclaves or jurisdictions require entrenched discrimination on the basis of ethnicity for the sake of preserving ghettoization. Both the practice and the theory of 'separate but equal' ideologies guarantee racist-style discrimination because they require racist-type attitudes to be sustained. 'Separate but equal' and 'different but equal' are ideologically and practically distinct conceptions. The latter requires integration and pushes towards minimizing ghettoization.

Partition of territory into separate sovereign states for each contending ethnicity may appear as another 'viable option' by which 'equally strong claims' to the same territory could be accommodated. Partition in practice appears viable when a significantly powerful political leadership of at least one community is unwilling to share power with the leadership of other communities within a single state structure. Partition almost invariably requires 'transfers' of some people from one territory into another. The transfers can be 'voluntary,' meaning that outright terror and force are not used, or forced – they are rarely truly voluntary. 'Ethnic cleansing' practised by Serbian militias in Croatia and Bosnia-Herzegovina to empty territory of non-Serbs and permit Serbs to take over the property of others, like the 'transfer' of Palestinians from more than 70 per cent of what had been Palestine, is an example of 'partition' at work.

In most instances, partition involves dispossession, displacement, impoverishment, destruction, deaths, injuries, atrocities, and large-scale theft. The ideology of ethnic sovereignties can and sometimes does provide a 'moral' rationale for the ugly realities of partition. I am not arguing that partition cannot be justified as a lesser evil when the alternatives are ethnic oppression, outright warfare, or 'ethnic cleansing,' nor do I wish to argue that a 'separate but equal' model of bi-nationalism could never be justified in view of practicable options all of which may be worse. Rather, I want to emphasize that partition of a territory into ethnically based sovereign states should not be viewed as satisfying the demands of justice understood from an egalitarian, human rights perspective. It may be the political option that, in the circumstances, best accommodates those demands. Given political realities, partition may be the least unjust political solution to an already unpleasant situation. Indeed, partition into separate, ethnically based states does not arise as a realistic option unless inter-ethnic strife has become very bitter.

The resort to 'paradox' is either literally nonsense or a rhetorical device aimed at sanctioning whatever outcome one of the contending parties can force on the other. It means shifting from a conception of a people with a right to territory that excludes the right of any others to that territory (a demand right) to the conception of a people with a right to a territory that does not exclude the competing right of other peoples to the same territory (a liberty right). To treat these rights as liberty rights is to conceive the conflict as one in which each competing claimant is morally free to do what it can to seize and hold that territory for itself. Someone who adopts this position may insist on certain moral constraints on the methods used to seize or hold the disputed territory. For example, genocide and terror may be ruled out. However, the more closely the constraints on permissible tactics approximate the demands of a human rights ethic, the more vacuous the claim that each competing people has a liberty right to seize or hold the same territory. The whole point of the view that the rights to territory and self-determination are liberty rights is to legitimate the use of force and hence the massive violation of a host of rights of individuals of the competing ethnicity in seizing a territory for one's own people.

Rousseau on the Rights of a People

The shift from demand rights to liberties pushes towards a Rousseauean view of a people and its right to establish its own sovereign state – to be 'free.' For Rousseau, our people's right to be free does not exclude the right of some other 'people' to be 'free' in the same territory if it can wrest its freedom from us. For Rousseau, the 'rights' in question are liberties, not demand rights. By this view, too, a territory that 'belongs' to a people is the territory that it controls – no more, no less.

Rousseau's position, stripped of its penchant for city-states, holds some attractions for those who support rights to self-determination and statehood for a collectivity whose membership is ethnically and culturally heterogeneous. A collectivity identified, say, by religious conviction and/or the faith of ancestors may comprise a variety of ethnic, linguistic, and cultural communities. It may lack the levels of ethnocultural homogeneity demanded by the standard nineteenth-century model of a people entitled to its sovereign state. According to Rousseau's theory, a collectivity could be a 'people' even if it were not ethnoculturally homogeneous – what is central to peoplehood is the loyalty of its members to the collectivity, however defined. From such a perspective, if enough individuals identify themselves with the collectivity defined, say, by religious affiliation, identify themselves in terms of their membership in it, and are prepared to support the right sorts of political claims and to make the right kinds of personal sacrifices to implement those claims on its behalf, then that collectivity would be a 'people.' In short, from such a perspective, if a 'critical mass' of individuals views itself as belonging to a people with a right to self-determination, and if it is prepared to do what is required to implement that right, then the collectivity is a 'people,' whether or not the collectivity itself is ethnoculturally homogeneous.

Rousseau's position is also attractive to those who need to rationalize some ethnoculturally defined group's colonizing or seizing by force territories long inhabited by others. The attractiveness of the approach for some people stems from its rejection of human rights and its insistence that moral obligations and moral rights hold only within communities bound together by loyalty to the community, by mutual acknowledgment of the rights of and obligations to its members, and, therefore, by some consensus on values. From this perspective, the only individuals who could be viewed as equal in worth and dignity are members of one's own 'people,' because they are the only ones who really have rights that one should respect and the only ones to whom one really owes obligations.

Also from this perspective, a growing consensus among its members favouring an overarching human rights ethic would threaten the integrity and very existence of the 'people' in question.

By Rousseau's view, any collection of individuals could in principle be transformed into a people provided that its members share some ties that bind – kinship, language, religion, customs, broadly similar moral values, perhaps even race. The conception of the American people can broaden to include Blacks and Hispanics, people of southern Mediterranean stock, Jews as well as Christians of all varieties, even, but not yet fully accepted, Muslims, Hindus, Confucians, and practitioners of the Shinto religion. A multi-ethnic, multicultural people is possible, however problematic, on such a conception of peoplehood. This conception is inconsistent with the demand for an ethnoculturally based sovereign state. It also opens up other ways of conceiving those politically significant collectivities whose members view themselves and are viewed as belonging to a 'people,' albeit multi-ethnic and multicultural. The concept of such a people with a right to its own sovereign state requires an understanding of the proper function of a state as serving the interests of the people(s) who constitute its citizen body without regard to ethnicity or cultural heritage.

Politically Significant Peoples

'The American people' and 'the Canadian people' refer to collectivities defined by citizenship, not by ethnicity, faith, or cultural heritage. 'The Muslim nation' refers to a set of faith communities of disparate ethnicities and cultures, as diverse as the faith communities referred to by 'Catholics.' The ties that bind there are emotionally powerful aspects of culture that constitute a common faith encompassing a host of disparate religious and cultural perspectives. 'The American people' and 'the Canadian people' refer to politically significant collectivities; 'the Muslim nation' refers to a collectivity that some Muslim religious/political leaders are seeking to make into a politically significant collectivity.

Such a collectivity possesses leaders with significant constituencies who conceive the group as having interests that reflect the aspirations, shared values, or worldviews of its members. It has a politically critical mass of members that identifies with it and is loyal to it. Individuals identify themselves as distinct from others and are willing to make or to suffer sacrifices, support political action, and endorse the leadership required for effective political action. Such activity can range from special legislation to special constitutional arrangements, from power-sharing to domination, and from territorial 'adjustments' to ethnic or religious 'cleansing.'

Ethnocultural groups may or may not be politically significant collectivities. The latter may or may not be ethnoculturally defined and may or may not count as 'peoples' – a socio-economic class may qualify. The 'peoples' with respect to whom claims to self-determination must be taken seriously, however, include those ethnocultural collectivities that are politically significant. Those collectivities cut across class lines, generations, and gender. They may be more culturally than ethnically defined, and their common ethnicity understood in terms of kinship may be more mythical than real. The notions of a distinct ethnicity and of a distinct culture are vague, indeed elastic. The line between communities defined principally by kinship and those defined by faith may be blurred by religious or traditional prohibitions against interfaith marriages, for example. How 'ethnically' or culturally distinct are Serbs, Croats, and Bosnian Muslims, after all? What is brutally significant is not so much the 'objective' criteria of identification of distinct 'peoples' but their status as politically significant collectivities violently pressing or resisting claims to exclusivist control over territory inhabited by others for generations.

Peoples and Self-determination

Whose Right?

Talk about the American, Canadian, Belgian, Kenyan, or Swiss 'people' expresses a conception of a citizen body as a politically significant collectivity, of a 'people' defined by citizenship. From a political point of view, such a collectivity must have ties that bind a critical mass of its members to each other and to the collectivity as such. Kinship, ethnicity, race, language, culture, religion, citizenship, even geography can, among other shared real or mythically based features, be ties that bind. In a world still plagued by racism, ethnocentrism, xenophobia, tribalism, clan rivalries, and inter-ethnic strife, ethnoculturally identified and self-identifying collectivities remain politically significant and, in some regions, are the most powerful ones when it comes to drawing or redrawing borders. Since the moral costs of denying statehood to some of those groups may be unacceptable, one can speak of them as having a 'right to self-determination.' In context, this formula can be used to emphasize that no other available political option to sovereignty or self-governance would be morally acceptable. The formula is always used to stress that the final disposition of the governance of those collectivities should be left up to them and, therefore, to their political leadership, not imposed by force or maintained primarily through intimidation and cooptation.

Whether to acknowledge some collectivity's right to self-determination becomes a practical issue when that group is politically significant and its leaders press for powersharing, self-governance, or statehood on its behalf. This typically happens against a background of real grievances involving domination by other such collectivities; systematic discrimination or worse, directed against the members of the collectivity; and systemic frustration of the aspirations of its members for themselves, their families, and the people as a whole. From a human rights perspective, self-determination becomes an issue wherever there is domination by one ethnoculturally defined, politically significant collectivity over other ethnoculturally defined communities that either are, or could become, politically significant and where power-sharing as a mechanism for ending systemic discrimination is not a viable option. From the same perspective, however, any political arrangement involving domination by one such community over another must be opposed no matter how ardently supported by the political leadership of that community and its constituents.

From the moral perspective embodied in international conventions on human rights, it is difficult to justify preventing self-determination for politically significant collectivities whose leadership, with wide popular support, and access to the required human and other resources, is pressing for statehood but not for 'transfers,' subjugation, or discrimination against minorities within the borders of their proposed state. Denying that right means, in such contexts, maintaining a governmental structure against the will of a significant number of people bent on statehood and capable of it. Holding on to power in those circumstances requires repression, with its predictable, morally unacceptable consequences for fundamental personal and political rights. A sovereign Quebec respecting the rights of minorities, for example, would be morally preferable to a Quebec under indefinite anglophone-Canadian military occupation. A sovereign Quebec whose leaders pursue a policy of 'francizing' Quebec by intimidating and overtly discriminating against anglophone and Aboriginal minorities, expropriating their properties for francophone use only, and entrenching discriminatory practices would be morally unacceptable from a human rights perspective. Blocking its establishment by force or subversion probably would be morally preferable to letting 'the will of the people' prevail.

The UN Charter, among other relevant documents of international law, leaves open the interpretation of what counts as a people entitled to self-determination. Citizen bodies, such as the Canadian people, are said to enjoy such a right. That right of a citizen body to self-determination would be violated by such acts as foreign conquest, foreign-orchestrated subversion, or de facto foreign control over its government. One seems to be underscoring the impermissibility of such foreign interventions by ascribing a right to self-determination to the citizen body of an existing sovereign state. More generally, one is emphasizing the rights of citizens to share in determining both their own constitutional arrangements and the leadership by which they are governed, through some mechanisms by which their informed, uncoerced preferences become politically effective. These rights express a commitment to principles of democratic political organization implicit in liberal conceptions of popular sovereignty, which can be formulated by talk about a people's right to self-determination. The conception of a people's right to self-determination presupposes popular sovereignty. The core of that notion is the view that the moral legitimacy of government is rooted in an uncoerced consensus of those subject to it.

Popular Sovereignty and Human Rights

According to one conception of popular sovereignty, if and only if citizens 'freely chose' such an option would there be moral legitimacy in their leadership's surrendering sovereignty in forming a broader political union or agreeing to a partition of their state. By a weaker interpretation, moral legitimacy for such changes would require consensus among citizens. The absence of consensus on constitutional issues means, in effect, that constitutional changes must be imposed from above. Since governments that rule without such consensus usually must employ repressive measures violating a wide range of human rights, one can usually justify insisting on popular consensus as a requirement for morally acceptable constitutional arrangements. From a human rights perspective, however, moral legitimacy must be conferred on those feasible constitutional arrangements and political practices that best accommodate practical respect for the equal worth and dignity of persons. Only certain types of democratic institutions and practices meet that requirement. They are those that protect the wide range of individual freedoms partially definitive of contemporary conceptions of democracy, protect the 'rights' of certain kinds of identity-forming, cherished communities, and actively promote the material and psychological well-being of all those subject to their jurisdiction.

There are four broad components of respect for the worth and dignity of persons: ensuring immunities against a broad range of physical and psychological violence; ensuring immunities from interference over a broad range of choices; and both ensuring opportunities and making available goods and services integral to their well-being. Equal treatment is notoriously more difficult to characterize fully. Respecting the equal dignity and worth of persons rules out advantaging some and disadvantaging others on the basis of familial, clan, or tribal origins, ethnicity, race, faith, cultural heritage, gender, sexual orientation, or age past maturity. The central conception of equality, I believe, is that it is as important to promote and protect the freedoms and other aspects of the well-being of any person as it is to promote and protect those of any other and that the measure of its importance is expressed best in the language of rights. Respecting the equal worth and dignity of people requires that political institutions and practices give weight to certain communities within which individuals are always situated and whose preservation and flourishing are normally integral to their well-being. I have in mind those communities with which they identify, in terms of which they identify themselves, which help to shape their individual personalities, whose histories are part of their history, and whose future is normally theirs and, usually, one of their major concerns. Those special communities are families, clans, tribes, ethnocultural collectives, faith communities, and a host of others, some more and some less central to the identities and well-being of their members. It is not possible to respect the equal worth and dignity of persons while undermining, denigrating, or discriminating against their cherished communities. Non-discrimination is indeed essential to respecting their equal dignity and worth, but it is not sufficient. Within broad limitations set by the moral ideal of respect for the equal human rights and the equal importance of the well-being of individuals, equal respect for those identity-forming, cherished communities whose preservation and flourishing are also elements of their members' well-being is required as well. The ideal of the rights of individuals to respect for their equal worth and dignity is a starting point from which . to argue the equal rights of those communities to be respected as communities and to flourish within parameters set by that ideal. Political institutions that entrench the privileges of one ethnocultural or faith community by systematically discriminating against individual members of subordinated ethnicities or faith communities clearly violate the human rights of those individuals. Political institutions that enforce legal prohibitions against such discriminatory practices while countenancing a disadvantaged status for some of those special communities also fail to meet the requirements imposed by that ideal. Which kinds of those special communities are most important within a particular political jurisdiction is an accident of history. In some regions, they may be a certain subset of families, clans, tribes, ethnically-cum-culturally identified or more culturally than ethnically defined faith communities, and more culturally than ethnically or religiously defined collectivities; in other regions, they may comprise quite a different subset of those kinds of communities.

Conflicting Claims

From a human rights viewpoint, neither a people's right to self-determination nor a conception of popular sovereignty, however the vague notion of a 'people' is to be sensibly interpreted, can be a first principle by which political institutions and practices should be assessed. This point can be illustrated dramatically in examples of conflicts between the leadership of a people defined as a citizen body and the leadership of an ethnoculturally defined segment of that people, with each party appealing to its own brand of nationalism and each laying claim to a right of self-determination.

The issues raised by separatism in Quebec could be couched in terms of such apparently conflicting claims of the Canadian people and of the Quebec people to self-determination and sovereignty within the same territory. The example illustrates a theoretical and sometimes practical problem with the notions of peoplehood: significant numbers of individuals may belong to two or more 'peoples' with claims to sovereignty over the same territory. This difficulty can arise either when the conception of a people is interpreted in terms of citizenship or when it is interpreted ethnoculturally. When the claims of a people defined in terms of citizenship conflict with the claims of a people defined ethnoculturally, which claim, one may ask, is stronger? Which claim should be supported? Which 'people,' for those who take peoplehood seriously as itself a basis for a right to self-determination, is 'real'? Both questions miss one of the central issues in dealing with both peoplehood and conflicting claims – whether, in resolving the political dispute, it would be morally acceptable for either party to use force or subversion either to effect or to block secession.

If the answer is 'no,' one need not worry about which 'people' is the 'real' one or which has the stronger claim to sovereignty over territory. From a human rights perspective, there is a clear presumption against use of force and subversion in such contexts. The situation would be different in Quebec were the province under military occupation or subjected to anglophone colonization and political domination.

A standard set of objections to the view that each people, understood as an objectively identifiable ethnocultural group, has a right to self-determination depends on the fact that sociologists, anthropologists, and historians can non-arbitrarily use different, more or less finely tuned criteria for identifying such collectivities. One can non-arbitrarily identify sub-groups and sub-sub-groups within most of the collectivities reasonably identified as ethnocultural. Thus there is no non-arbitrary way of settling on which collectivities do and which do not constitute a people with a right to self-determination and on which of an indefinitely large and mutually incompatible possible division of the world into more or less ethnoculturally 'pure' sovereign states would be morally legitimate. People of mixed ancestry may have to choose whether 'their group' is, for example, Italian, Sicilian, German, Swabian, English, Cockney, Jewish, or Anglican. Focusing on self-identification with some politically significant collectivity may offer a way out of this morass, but the community with which individuals of mixed backgrounds and ancestries may identify could be multi-ethnic and multicultural. With the exception of those who are stateless or living under military occupation, most members of every ethnoculturally defined group are citizens of some state, very few if any of which are 'ethnoculturally pure.' Should individuals identify with their citizen body or with some politically significant, ethnoculturally defined collectivity to which they also belong? Insisting on the right of every ethnoculturally defined and self-defining collectivity to self-determination would seem to posit ethnicity over citizenship as the basis of politically significant loyalties, without being able to provide a non-arbitrarily selected set of criteria for individuating the relevant ethnocultural communities that should be politically significant, or are entitled to be so. Without such a commitment, supported by non-arbitrarily selected criteria for individuating the sorts of ethnocultural collectivities to bear the relevant political rights, it is difficult to understand how an ideology of ethnocultural peoplehood and self-determination could be rationalized.

It would be bizarre to resolve these conceptual and practical difficulties by holding that any politically significant ethnocultural community whose leadership, with at least majority support within the collectivity, claims a right to self-determination thereby has such a right. Claiming a right is not the same thing as having it; some further justification is needed, especially when the stakes – political control over territory and those who inhabit it – are so high. Serbian nationalists, like the Nazis before them, lead a politically significant ethnocultural community claiming the right to statehood within 'its' ancestral territories. Both Serb nationalists and Nazis should have been stopped by sanctions and/or force of arms when they first moved to 'exercise' those 'rights' in Croatia and Bosnia-Herzegovina and in Czechoslovakia and Austria, respectively.

Ethnocultural Nationalism

In view of the dismal history of ethnocultural nationalism, and its recent resurgence in some of its most virulent manifestations in the Balkans and elsewhere, the image of a world in which most individuals identify with their ethnicity, claiming and implementing that ethnicity's 'right to self-determination,' is both a theoretical and a practical nightmare. Whatever the theoretical difficulties of individuating a people with recourse to citizenship, those difficulties have not prevented political and intellectual leaders from forging or sustaining politically significant, ethnoculturally defined 'peoples.' This process has often been a defensive response to ethnically based discrimination, oppression, or worse. How others identify one's ethnicity and treat one because of that label can itself result in self-identification primarily with that ethnicity rather than with a citizen body or other ethnicity to which one also belongs. One's ethnicity can be thrust upon one. Politically significant, ethnically or religiously defined peoples can be created by other such 'peoples,' too many of whose members are bent on domination. However real the ties that bind and the interlocking sets of special communities, cultures, and sub-cultures that help make us who we are, a people remains a conceptual artifice, constructed by selecting some of those underlying realities while ignoring others. Which broadly described aspects of these underlying social and cultural realities, and which more narrowly specifiable aspects of them, can be drawn upon to construct a people as a politically significant collectivity depends in part on available forms of political organization and available ideologies. The French people could no more have existed as such a collectivity in the twelfth century, given the parochial cultures and feudal structures of Europe then, than could liberal democratic institutions in the cultures of antiquity. There is no point in looking for the right way of demarcating peoples independent of citizenship in order to locate the real bearers of a right to self-determination that a political leadership would be entitled to press. However, the plight of ethnoculturally identifiable communities may provide good moral reasons for construing a politically significant collectivity using a conception of a 'people' that embraces the kinds of cherished communities needed for effective political action leading to statehood. For example, many view the Zionist movement as a morally legitimate response to the pogroms and persecutions targeting eastern European Jewish communities under the tsars.

The Rhetoric of Peoplehood

Some of the rhetoric employed to talk about an ethnoculturally defined people, like that used to discuss a citizenship-defined people, must be understood as metaphor designed to serve ideological or political objectives. The language of collective merit and collective guilt, for example, serves those purposes. Collective merit bolsters loyalty, self-identification with one's 'people,' and self-esteem as a member of that 'people.' It is also used to secure political support for establishing and maintaining strategic alliances and economic links with foreign states. The rhetoric of collective merit and collective accomplishment plays an important role in building and sustaining all sorts of communities and organizations. When the Toronto Blue Jays win the World Series, 'we' (Torontonians, Ontarians, Canadians) win; because Canadians captured Vimy Ridge over 70 years ago, we, as Canadians, can be proud. These accomplishments form part of our individual consciousness of our own identities and become, by a fiction, part of our own histories as Canadians. The language of collective merit is often used to forge the ties that bind – so is the language of collective guilt by identifying 'the enemy' and inculcating a sense of having been personally wronged by what 'they' did generations ago. Such languages are helpful in underscoring present responsibilities to the descendants of the victims of past injustices wrought by some of our biological or 'communal' forbears. They can serve to motivate us to avoid similar wrongdoing. Conceptions of collective guilt are also useful devices for justifying ethnocultural domination, punitive attacks on civilian populations, and a host of other evils serving the strategic or other power interests of states. However useful, and however powerful its grip on the emotions, this manner of thinking and talking is conceptually skewed and, especially with regard to collective punishment justified by collective guilt, morally reprehensible.

Applying conceptions of collective responsibility to a multi-generational collectivity such as a 'people' requires treating that collectivity as if it were a clearly identifiable, single spatiotemporal agent, which these abstractions clearly are not. In its extreme form, this way of talking and thinking has been employed to legitimate racism, segregation, colonialism, apartheid, conquest, repression, pogroms, and genocide. Referring to a people as an entity not only permits talk about a people doing something, such as killing Christ, that 'it' may properly be made to regret later, scores of generations later, but allows us to talk about 'it' as moving, being scattered, and returning. 'It' can be said to 'return' when some of 'its' members colonize and seize by force a territory that others of 'its' members had ruled thousands of years earlier. 'Returning' can be applied to individuals who had never set foot in the territory to which they are said to 'return.' If the people is identified by faith and not by actual lineage, individuals can be said to 'return' to a territory in which neither they nor their biological ancestors ever resided, displacing and subjugating its inhabitants in order to 'reclaim' that people's homeland. This mode of talk legitimates any form of irredentism that one may wish to advocate for one's cherished 'people,' provided, of course, that one has selected one's 'people' using criteria that enable 'it' to lay the appropriate territorial claims. For example, one could press claims to all of the Levant, including the Holy Land and most of North Africa, in the name of Greek Orthodox people, insisting on a 'return' to territory that was the homeland for people of that faith community during centuries of Byzantine rule. The example is absurd, of course, but the example of mainly Slavic-speaking Macedonia in the former Yugoslavia to which Greek nationalists lay claim is not, because it must be taken seriously for political, not conceptual reasons.

Talking about collectivities as if they were individuals and then applying the conceptions appropriate to individuals to them may be politically useful and linguistically convenient. It is obfuscating, however, when it involves systematic ambiguity and vagueness of reference. That ambiguity and vagueness of reference permit the grossest of wrongs to be rationalized as somehow morally justified. Statements that 'the Croats deserve to be severely punished for what they did to us Serbs fifty years ago' have been used to whip up the ethnic hatred that has spawned 'retaliatory' Serbian massacres of totally innocent Croats.

Ethnocultural Identity v. Citizenship

From a human rights perspective, if any form of nationalism could be morally acceptable, it would have to define the 'people' who constitute the 'nation' by reference to citizenship, not ethnicity, faith, or ethnocultural identity. It would have to incorporate respect for human rights and for those special, identify-forming, cherished communities whose preservation and flourishing are intimately tied to the well-being of their members, within its defining image of the national ethos. Certain forms of Canadian nationalism come close to meeting these requirements. Even so, nationalism and the nation state system emancipated from their roots in the ideology of ethnocultural peoplehood may not measure up to the moral demands of a consistent and coherent human rights ethic.

The world is now witnessing a repetition of the Palestinian catastrophe in what used to be Yugoslavia. Once again, the major Western powers are unwilling to intervene militarily to put an end to a process of clearing the land of one or more peoples for the benefit of another. Once again, they refuse to guarantee the partitions that they apparently wanted to impose. As the Serbs consolidate their holdings and Bosnian Muslims regroup in refugee communities, will Europe be the scene of seemingly endless reciprocal terror and low-intensity warfare? Will the dispossessed rightly insist that their confiscated homes and stolen properties be restored, their families reunited, and their communities re-established in the territory that they and generations of their forbears inhabited? Probably.

Some people really do have a right to return, and, as in the cases of the Bosnian Muslims and the Palestinians, they are sufficiently numerous that it makes sense to talk about a 'people's' returning to its homeland. Their descendants, too, will have special rights to restitution and compensation. In both cases, ethnoculturally based statehood within Bosnia-Herzegovina and Palestine, respectively, seems the political option that best accommodates their human rights and the resulting rights of their respective communities to be preserved and to flourish 'back home.'

I have discussed the right to self-determination as it bears on two types of nationalism distinguished by alternate conceptions of a people – based on ethnocultural identity or on citizenship – and therefore of 'the nation' that is entitled to its state. I have argued that the ethnocultural conception of peoplehood, with its accompanying political and territorial rights, is implicitly flawed, both conceptually and morally. It is flawed conceptually because there is no non-arbitrary way of selecting from among a range of equally legitimate criteria for individuating ethnocultural communities those that do and those that do not individuate the proper bearers of the political and territorial rights claimed for such 'peoples.' This difficulty is further compounded, and sometimes disguised, when we talk and think about ethnocultural and other collectivities as if they were multi-generational individuals, which they are not. That mode of talking and thinking too often 'legitimates' gross injustices. I have also argued that the political ideology of ethnocultural peoplehood is racist both theoretically and as practised and is therefore incompatible with observance of human rights. I have also argued that a commitment to the equal worth and dignity of persons requires in some contexts supporting creation of new, ethnoculturally based sovereign states or self-governing entities. At the same time, a human rights ethic requires us to support efforts to establish effective supra-national mechanisms to protect, at the least, those human rights that are essential to the welfare of individual human beings. The ideal of the equal worth and dignity of persons, pregnant with rights, points the way towards a decent world order which ethnocultural nationalisms have so abysmally failed to achieve.

Notes

1 Some may contest this example, but the conception of a Jewish state as a homeland for, and state of, the Jewish people is that of an ethnoculturally based sovereign state whose function is to protect and promote, first and foremost, the interests of that people. Several factors – the law of return granting citizenship to Jews from whatever country who immigrate to Israel, the Seven Star program of increased Jewish settlement in areas still heavily populated by Palestinian Arabs who hold Israeli passports, and a complex set of laws that legalizes expropriation of Arab-owned lands for Jewish-only settlement and use, which has extended Jewish ownership from roughly 6 per cent of the territory that is now Israel in 1948 to roughly 92 per cent, reducing Arab Palestinian ownership from about 93 per cent to approximately 7 per cent – clearly show that the state authorities and those who support them view the state as the agent of its Jewish citizens and act accordingly.

2 For documentation on the ways in which the Palestinian majority in what became Israel was transformed into a minority, over 300 of its villages were eradicated, and its homes, furnishings, personal possessions, shops, businesses, and lands were handed over to Jews or to Jewish organizations, see

Michael Palumbo *The Palestinian Catastrophe* (London: Faber & Faber 1987) especially chaps. 3–5, 8, and 10. See also Simha Flappan *The Birth of Israel: Myths and Realities* (New York: Pantheon Books 1987), especially 'Myth Three,' and Benny Morris *The Birth of the Palestinian Refugee Problem, 1947–1949* (Cambridge: Cambridge University Press 1987), especially chaps. 2–4, 6, and 8. Destruction of the villages of Beit Nuba, Imwas, and Yalu and expulsion of their inhabitants in June 1967 and forced eviction of residents of the Old City of Jerusalem in the same year to reconstruct the Jewish Quarter and establish the plaza by the Wailing Wall are other examples of the reality of 'reclaiming territory.' Israeli government expropriation of more than 60 per cent of the occupied West Bank, including Arab East Jerusalem, and of more than 30 per cent of occupied Gaza, and establishment of over 140 Jewish-only settlements in those territories, all in violation of the Fourth Geneva Convention, serve as other instances of 'reclaiming' territory for one people at the expense of another. For documentation, see, among other sources, Raja Shehadeh *Occupier's Law* (Washington, DC: Institute for Palestine Studies 1985) and the series of studies published under the supervision of Meron Benvenisti by the West Bank Data Base Project in Jerusalem and distributed by the Jerusalem Post, PO Box 81, Jerusalem 9100, Israel.

Index

Contributors

Judith Baker   Department of Philosophy, Glendon College, York University

Will Kymlicka   Department of Philosophy, University of Ottawa

Melissa S. Williams   Department of Political Science, University of Toronto

Sherene Razack   Ontario Institute for Studies in Education

Wayne J. Norman   Department of Philosophy, University of Ottawa

Leslie Green   Department of Philosophy, York University

Denise G. Réaume   Faculty of Law, University of Toronto

Joseph H. Carens   Department of Political Science, University of Toronto

Howard Adelman   Centre for Refugee Studies, York University

James A. Graff   Department of Philosophy, Victoria College, University of Toronto